Independent and Free

Independent and Free

Scottish Politics and the Origins of the
Scottish National Party
1918 – 1945

RICHARD J. FINLAY

JOHN DONALD PUBLISHERS LTD
EDINBURGH

ISBN 0 85976 399 4

British Library Cataloguing in Publication Data
A catalogue record for this book is available from the British Library.

Typeset by IMH (Cartrif), Loanhead, Scotland
Printed and bound in Great Britain by J. W. Arrowsmith Ltd., Bristol

Preface

The main purpose of this book is to trace and examine the origins and development of Scottish nationalism primarily as a political movement. The wider role of cultural nationalism, although important in itself, has not been considered here. In essence, the main concern is to explain the process which led to the creation of the modern Scottish National Party. It starts with the circumstances which forced those interested in obtaining self-government to look for alternative means of attaining their goal; namely, the setting up of their own political party. The predecessors of the SNP are examined, as is the evolution of nationalist strategy and identity. The main thread of the story follows those who argued that the SNP could only achieve its goal by contesting elections and advocating distinct economic and social policies. Both of these issues, which by no means commanded universal support, were of crucial importance in establishing a unique nationalist political ethos which has lasted up until today. Much of the text is devoted to reviewing the internal disputes over strategy and policy that were fought in order to create a nationalist orthodoxy.

Glasgow, 1994   R.J.F.

Acknowledgements

Firstly I would like to thank Dr William Ferguson and Mr John Simpson for their unstinting help, advice and encouragement with this project. They have saved me from many errors and helped me to illuminate some of the darkest corners of the history of the SNP. I owe a considerable debt of gratitude to Dr John Bannerman who freely gave of his time, knowledge and expertise on this subject. Professor Michael Lynch was a tower of support and has been a constant source of encouragement and advice. Their C in C at the Department of Scottish History, University of Edinburgh, Mrs Doris Williamson, saved me, on more than one occasion, from the perils of modern technology. To them all I am eternally grateful. The Department of History, University of Stirling, deserves a special note of thanks. Professor George Peden and his team gave a lot of encouragement and support to a young (or maybe not so young) academic at the start of his career. In particular, I have benefited from the boundless knowledge of Dr Iain Hutchison who has given freely and generously of his time and advice on many aspects of modern Scottish political history.

Dr Dauvit Broon, Dr Irene Maver and Dr John Durkan from the Department of Scottish History, University of Glasgow, have helped me with their discussions on this subject. Dr James Mitchell of the Department of Government, University of Strathclyde, has freely contributed advice, ideas and information, and has contributed greatly to my understanding of modern Scottish nationalism and politics.

Professor Tom Devine and Professor James McMillan and my colleagues at the Department of History, University of Strathclyde, have been unstinting in their support and advice. They have made me very welcome and I have benefited from their constant and stimulating discussions on all aspects of Scottish history.

Others on the roll call are: Graham and Fiona Wynn, Duncan and Greta Stewart, Mrs Brenda Kemp, Iain Paterson, Catriona MacDonald, David Forsyth, the late Tom Finlayson. My family, Jack and Edd have put up with my meanderings in the past with a remarkable degree of fortitude. My mother, Eleanor, Colin, Kate, John, Seonaid and family, have all helped in their own ways. Dr Robert McIntyre helped to start me off with this project; it has been a privilege to know him and I have benefited from his experience and wisdom.

Finally, my greatest debt, and most enduring one, is to my closest friend, Evan Stewart, who has for a great many years now been a constant source of inspiration and strength. He, May and my Godson, Alistair, have always made me welcome in their home and Ev has sharpened up my intellectual abilities over many long hours of discussion. Without this, the book would have been undoubtedly poorer.

Contents

Abbreviations

CP Communist Party

GUSNA Glasgow University Scottish Nationalist Association

NPS National Party of Scotland

SHR *Scottish Historical Review*

SHRA Scottish Home Rule Association

SI *Scots Independent*

SNC Scottish National Convention

SNL Scots National League

SNM Scottish National Movement

SNP Scottish National Party

CHAPTER ONE

The Scottish Home Rule Association and Scottish Politics 1918-1928

Prior to the outbreak of war in 1914, the Liberal Party had been the principal, but not exclusive, champion of Scottish Home Rule. This was not the result of a deep-seated political conviction, but was mainly a consequence of the pressure brought to bear on the leadership by party activists and organisations such as the Young Scots Society. Also, it was believed that by advocating Scottish Home Rule, Irish Home Rule would become more palatable to the electorate.[1] However, by the end of the war in 1918, the resultant social, economic and political changes induced by the exigencies of the wartime situation, effectively sealed the fate of the Liberal Party's hegemony in Scotland.[2] At the General Election of 1918, the Liberals only managed to return eight members without Lloyd George's coupon, while Labour made an electoral breakthrough which eventually culminated in them being able to eclipse the former as the main party of opposition at the subsequent election of 1922.[3] It was against this background of political turmoil and change, that the decision was taken to reform the prewar Scottish Home Rule Association in September, 1918.[4]

The principal architect behind the postwar founding of the SHRA was Roland Eugene Muirhead, who was a fairly well-off businessman and owner of the Gryffe Tannery Company of Bridge of Weir.[5] Before the war, he had been an active member of the Young Scots Society, and had campaigned vigorously within the Liberal Party for a firm commitment to enacting Home Rule legislation. However, having become disillusioned with the failure to pass the requisite self-government Bill in 1914, Muirhead left the Liberals and instead joined the Independent Labour Party in 1918.[6] In any case, he had always been more in sympathy with the socialist principles of the ILP, which suited his radical and republican tendencies, and in 1906 he played an important part in helping Tom Johnston set up the socialist weekly newspaper; *Forward*[7]. Muirhead was essential in the re-establishing of the Association, as it was he who provided the necessary finance and the organisational abilities required to get the organisation off the ground.

At the time of the 'Khaki Election' in 1918, the SHRA was not sufficiently organised to make any impact on the outcome of events, and, in any case, the issue of Scottish self-government was likely to be overshadowed by events in Ireland, where demands for Home Rule had ended in bloodshed, military occupation and ultimately, civil war. Many members of the SHRA were afraid that unwelcome comparisons might have been made by their opponents, especially elements within the Scottish Tory Party.[8] It was only by May, 1919, that the Association felt confident enough to hold its first public meeting, at which the broad aims of the organisation were outlined:

> ... whilst the objective of the meeting was political; it was nonparty. They were out to band together people of all different political faiths, so that the widely spread feeling in favour of Scottish self-government might be focused and an effective demand made for the re-establishment of a Scottish Parliament in Scotland to deal with Scottish affairs and administration.[9]

It was believed that the SHRA would be non-political in the sense that it would appeal to, and receive support from, a wide spectrum of Scottish society. Muirhead argued that the issue of Home Rule was of such importance that it would transcend normal party politics, and act as a unifying force which would bind together people who held disparate political beliefs into a common cause.[10]

However, the reality of the situation was quite different, as can be seen from the initial composition of the hierarchy of the SHRA, which was predominantly made up from Labour Party interests. Although the Labour leadership discouraged any of its members from joining an organisation over which they had no official control,[11] it was largely ignored, and it was from the labour movement that the Association received most support. At an official level, the STUC was represented by its Secretary, Robert Allan, while the Scottish Miners' Federation's Secretary, Robert Smilie and the Scottish Farmservants' Union's Secretary, Joseph Duncan, also played an important part in forming the SHRA. Other prominent Labour Party officials who were involved at the inception of the Association, were Thomas Johnston, the Rev. James Barr, William Gallacher, who was President of the Scottish Co-operative Society, and Catriona Cameron, a member of the Highland Land League.[12] Muirhead saw fit to invite only two Liberals, neither of whom could be said in any way to occupy an important role in the running of their party.[13] Perhaps this was a reflection of the low esteem in which the former champions of Home Rule were now held. Also, in an attempt to make the Association genuinely cross-party, Muirhead was able to attract a solitary Conservative, although he was soon to leave in any case.[14] The party political composition of the early SHRA mirrored the wider changes which had taken place in postwar Scotland, in which the Home Rule mantle fell firmly into the hands of the Labour Party.

The role of the Association, as envisaged by Muirhead, was that it would act as a pressure group which would endeavour to keep the Home Rule question to the forefront of Scottish politics. It was decided that attention ought to be focused on Parliamentarians, as they were considered to be especially lax when it came to promoting and defending Scottish interests. The failure of Scottish MPs to support the second reading of the remnants of the prewar Home Rule Bill in 1919 was cited as evidence to justify the existence of the SHRA:[15]

> This meeting of Scottish citizens views with alarm the evidence of indifference and neglect shown by the elected representatives of the people, especially the Scottish members in absenting themselves from the House of Commons when the Scottish Home Rule Bill came up for a second reading...[16]

However, at a time when it was not envisaged that the Labour Party would soon be in a position to form a government, the Association was not content to leave the matter in the hands of Westminster. Aside from propaganda and demonstrations, it was proposed that a National Convention ought to be set up to add non-parliamentary weight to the case for self-government:

> ...this meeting... reaffirms its conviction that instead of depending on the present parliamentary machinery to obtain self-government, the Scottish people should call together a National Convention in order to consider what steps should be taken to the early establishment of a parliament in Scotland.[17]

The idea of calling a Convention was Muirhead's, because although he believed that a majority of Scottish MPs might advocate and support Home Rule, as was the case in the past, Westminster had proved to be an untrustworthy institution when it came to meeting such demands.[18] He believed that the existence of a Convention, which represented popular Scottish opinion, would act as the necessary focal point to bring sufficient pressure to bear on Parliament for the passing of self-government legislation.[19] However, it would take several years for such an organisation to come into effect, mainly because there were other more accessible avenues for the Association to follow, such as securing Home Rule pledges from candidates at election times. Also, after the General Election in 1922, the Labour Party appeared to be able to win power, and with this prospect came the belief that the party which had had a long-standing commitment to self-government, would enact the necessary legislation.

The popular definition of Home Rule within the SHRA was that it was something akin to Dominion status, but with Scotland still playing a full part in the running of the British Empire. Indeed, many believed that Scottish self-government was part of the process in the evolution of the British Commonwealth of Nations ideal. Home Rulers took inspiration from the greater freedom allowed to the Dominion nations and argued that Scotland should take her place among the other countries which would, it was thought, make up an Imperial Federation. Developments in the British Empire were a major influence on the ideas which formed the postwar Home Rule movement:[20]

> So far as the whole population is concerned, the British Empire is a Home Rule Empire. The great white dominions enjoy self- government in such large measure as to make them rather sister than daughter nations, and yet they are all loyal members of the Empire. They are even separately represented on the Assembly of the League of Nations, and they determine their own foreign policy... Home Rule is the Empire's bond of union.[21]

By emphasising the self-government case within the context of the Imperial ethos, there was no question of separatism, as the President of the SHRA, William Gallacher, told an audience in September, 1919:

> We are not a separatist party. We merely wish for Scottish self-government, leaving the Imperial Parliament to deal with the higher questions of Imperial policy.[22]

Instead of advocating Home Rule, first and foremost, as the right to national self-determination, members of the Association tended to base their claims on the fact that Westminster was over-worked and therefore unable to give the necessary time and attention to Scottish affairs.[23] Also, it was claimed that the Imperial Parliament was not as efficient as it might otherwise be on account of having to deal with trifling Scottish issues, which were best left to the Scots to sort out for themselves. This case was put forward by Duncan Graham, the Labour MP for Hamilton, when addressing a SHRA meeting in July, 1920:

> It seems clear to us that some such method will have to be adopted to relieve the pressure of business in the Imperial Parliament, as it is quite obvious that it cannot meet the demands made on it ... What we want is Home Rule, and what we mean by that expression is that we should have the right and the power to make our laws at home, and not merely administer laws that are made for us in another country.[24]

Home Rule, it was claimed, would benefit the government of the United Kingdom and the running of the British Empire, by introducing a more efficient and manageable form of administration.

One of the first tasks facing the Association was the need to define in precise terms what was meant by Home Rule and also, what would be the implications of such a policy. This was necessary in order to provide the political credence to their claims that self-government would result in beneficial gains for the Scottish people. From the outset, the SHRA stressed that Home Rule would not mean a lessening of commitment to the British Empire. Also, the extent of self-government was strictly limited to domestic Scottish affairs only. In general terms, the objectives of the Association were:

1. The creation of a National Scottish Parliament, to sit in Scotland and pass laws on all matters affecting Scotland, and Scotland only.
2. The creation of a National Scottish Executive or Ministry, to control the administration of Scottish affairs, subject to the Scottish Parliament alone.[25]

Within the SHRA there was a broad consensus that the Crown and Succession, foreign and colonial policy, army, navy and airforce, together with currency, weights and measures, should remain under the jurisdiction of the Imperial Parliament at Westminster.[26] While, on the other hand, the devolved Scottish government was expected to take control of the following:

(a) the Judicature and Executive, (b) a Scottish National Treasury, into which all taxes levied in Scotland ought to be paid and which should arrange from time to time with the Imperial Treasury, the payments to be made for Imperial purposes, (c) Land tenure in town and country, (d) education, (e) agriculture, fisheries and mines, (f) Labour, including national insurance against sickness and unemployment, (g) Local Government and health services, (h) Board of Trade and transport.[27]

Also, it was envisaged that Scotland would take part in the Imperial Conferences and would be represented at the Assembly of the League of Nations.[28] However, with regard to defence and foreign policy, it was expected that the two nations would jointly supervise the one set of machinery and pursue the same set of objectives.[29] There was no question of having a separate set of armed forces and it was also unlikely that there would be an independent Scottish diplomatic service. Having defined the parameters of its objectives, the Association had then to convince politicians and people alike that they were worth endorsing.

By June, 1919, the SHRA had about 700 individual members, and more importantly, over 100 organisations had affiliated membership and pledged support to the cause.[30] A period of steady growth ensued, and by July, 1920, the Association launched its own monthly bulletin, *Scottish Home Rule*, and its membership had risen to 1,150 individuals

member of the Government, it would be appropriate that I should take part in the meeting.'[44] The Liberal Party, on the other hand, was in a state of irreversible decline, and few protagonists of the self-government cause thought that there was any realistic chance of them recovering to an extent that would enable a return to government, especially after the formal split in 1920.[45] Also, as the Labour dominance of the Association became more pronounced, Tories and Liberals shied away from the organisation, believing it to be nothing more than a front for socialist activities.[46] The ending of the Irish troubles in 1922, which had constantly overshadowed the issue, together with the emergence of Labour as the largest parliamentary party in Scotland, pushed the self-government question on to new territory. Labour could finally lay claim to be heirs of the Home Rule tradition.

During the war, the Scottish Labour movement had become increasingly nationalistic, largely in response to the attempts by the British party and the TUC to curb their independence and bring them under greater centralised control.[47] Although the Scottish section had been in favour of devolution before the war,[48] Home Rule was given greater prominence in the period following 1918. Government control during the war was criticized as being inefficient and too far removed from the problems faced by the Scottish people. The trouble was, as far as they were concerned, a severe lack of knowledge about Scottish affairs, and this point was stressed by the STUC in their annual report of 1918:

> If any reconstruction is to take place in Scotland after the war, then we should not be humbugged by writing and sending deputations to people in London who know absolutely nothing of our wants. A Parliament should be set up in Scotland, thus saving time and expense and giving the people of Scotland a fair opportunity of working out their salvation.[49]

A further factor in making Labour more committed to the self-government cause was the defection of a substantial number of prominent Home Rulers from the Liberal Party, many of whom were to play an important role in the SHRA.[50] Scottish Trade Unionists were especially keen on the devolutionist principle as a method to stave off the TUC's centralising influences, which would mean a loss of local power and freedom of action.[51] It was no coincidence that the Association's first President, William Gallacher, made strenuous efforts to maintain the independence of the Scottish Co-operative Societies in the face of determined attempts to integrate it more thoroughly into the British organisation.[52] In 1919, a draft bill in the annual report of the Labour Party's Scottish Council illustrates the depth of feeling concerning nationalist grievances:

Whereas, Scotland, though temporarily deprived, without the consent of her people, and by corrupt means in 1707, of the exercise of her right to self-determination, is at present, as anciently, entitled to legislate for the governance of her national affairs in a Parliament of her own.[53]

However, it has to be pointed out that although there was a passionate feeling for the need to implement some form of devolution by members of the Labour movement in 1918, there was no corresponding political commitment in the form of detailed policy studies or any other such forms of elaboration. Also, there appears to have been little in the way of internal debate and discussions of the ramifications of adopting a policy of self-government.[54] Home Rule was simply one of the many issues which went into the melting pot that was part of the process of the formation of a coherent Labour Party philosophy and strategy. It was only by the middle of the 1920s that there emerged a reasoned assessment of the significance of devolution.[55] Until that time, Home Rule was taken on board as part and parcel of the Scottish radical tradition and although the idea received support, it did not necessarily command a serious political commitment.[56]

One of the main reasons why self-government was popular within the Scottish Labour Party was that it appealed to popular nationalist sentiment and, in the absence of properly defined policies, it could be used as a panacea for a whole range of social, political and economic problems. Also, it acted as a unifying force, bringing disparate elements, such as the Rev. James Barr and James Maxton, together in common cause. The use of nationalist rhetoric was a speciality with Labour politicians when addressing large audiences who, probably because of the simplicity of the Home Rule idea, responded enthusiastically to the demands for a redress of Scottish grievances.[57] Many Clydesiders blamed their lack of progress in attaining social legislation on the fact that Westminster was slow and cumbersome, and bound down by English traditions. According to George Buchanan, what had taken seven months to complete in Parliament could have been done in seven hours in Scotland.[58] What is striking about these home Rule arguments is their simplicity and naivety, which was in itself an indication of a lack of seriousness.

However, as the Labour Party was the only major political organisation which had given a commitment to Home Rule, and, more importantly, was soon likely to be in a position of government, it was not unnatural to find its members playing an important role in the running of the SHRA. The party, and especially the STUC, brought thousands of indirect members and potential recruits to the Association, as well as providing a large platform for their propaganda efforts. By the end of 1928, there were over 300 organisations affiliated to the SHRA, of which most were a result of the unions' connections.[59] Within the General Council of the Association, the power of policy making was in the hands of the union leaders, especially the STUC's Secretary, Robert Allan, and its President, Peter Webster.[60] Given the fact that the Labour movement had such a large influence in the running of the SHRA, it comes as no surprise to find that the organisation's direction and strategy were shaped to suit their political masters' ends.

By the Summer of 1924, the Labour grip on the Association was absolute, and blatant attempts were made to eschew all other political elements. According to one former Liberal, there was now not even a pretence that the SHRA was a cross-party organisation:

> Mr. Maxton then spoke and the meeting rapidly dissolved into a Labour Party meeting. He indulged to a great extent in what was pure and simply propaganda from the point of view of the Labour Party and against that of other parties.[61]

The same writer lambasted the Labour Party for refusing to co-operate with Scottish MPs from other parties in order to present a united front when representing Scottish interests at Westminster. He concluded bitterly that 'The SHRA is an adjunct solely of the Labour Party'.[62] Writing in April, 1924, Roland Muirhead was also showing signs of unease at the apparent hi-jacking of his organisation by the Labour Party:

> Speaking personally I often differ with decisions that are come to but as an individual having had my opportunity of putting my case before others, I have simply to accept the majority decision.[63]

He was also concerned by the fact that the bellicose attitude to people from other parties was driving away potential Liberal and Tory support, and had effectively scuttled his original idea of making Home Rule an issue of cross-party co-operation.[64] However, there was little that Muirhead or other activists could do as, by virtue of their holdings of large affiliated membership, the Unions would always hold a controlling interest in the leadership of the Association.[65] In any case, in early 1924, with the advent of a minority Labour Government, such misgivings were only of a minor nature. This was especially the case as the MP for Gorbals, George Buchanan, had obtained through the private member's ballot a chance to put a Home Rule bill on the statute book. With the prospect of attaining their objective in sight, few Association members believed that the Labour hold on the organisation was a disadvantage.

However, the speed with which events happened took everyone by surprise, and it also highlighted the latent divisions which existed within the Home Rule camp. As soon as the news reached the Association, several activists took it upon themselves to prepare a draft bill and this was done without the authority or knowledge of the Labour Party.[66] It was proposed that once a Scottish Parliament had been set up, there would be a withdrawal of Scottish MPs from Westminster. Those areas of joint interest between the two nations would then come under the authority of a reconstituted Imperial Parliament.[67] However, although many members of the Labour Party accepted this long-term vision of Home Rule, they would not, at this stage, countenance any Scottish withdrawal from Parliament, as this would seriously weaken their position, given the disproportionate number of socialist MPs who were elected north of the border.[68] The sponsors of the Bill were also against pulling out of Westminster. According to George Buchanan:

> The majority of Liberal and Labour Scottish members would like to retain a connection with the English House of Commons, thinking that this connection would be valuable as a means of co-ordinating industrial legislation in the two countries, and another reason for keeping a Scottish contingent at Westminster is that, both in the past and recently, Scotland has been the stronghold of Radicalism, so that every democratic movement that has an English wing realises that it must have people from the north of the Tweed to give it inspiration and outlook.[69]

By way of a compromise, the subject was kept in abeyance, with most Home Rulers being thankful that the issue would be debated in Parliament. Instead, efforts were concentrated on drumming up popular support to add weight to the self-government claims.

The Association organised a rally at St Andrew's Hall, Glasgow in April, to demonstrate for Buchanan's Bill, and by all accounts, the meeting attracted a large and responsive audience.[70] David Kirkwood and James Maxton were the two principal speakers, who delighted the crowd with anti-English and anti-establishment jibes.[71] The SHRA was confident of success, and it was claimed that 'the demonstration marks an epoch on the road to Scottish self-government'.[72] The Association also initiated a campaign to enlist the support of all those MPs who were even only mildly in favour of Home Rule.[73] However, such preparation was all in vain as the debate, which took place on the 9th of May, only lasted for several hours and ended in a shambolic uproar. Things got off to a bad start when the Scottish Secretary, William Adamson, opened the proceedings with cautious approval for the Bill, although it was obvious that he was not enthusiastic.[74] The debate was, for the most part, orderly, until the Speaker refused to allow a vote because a Tory back-bencher had not been allowed to speak. This caused an uproar of the type that the Clydesiders were rapidly becoming famous (or infamous) for, and they accused the Speaker of having taken sides. The net result of all this was that the Bill would not be considered again that session.[75]

This failure led many activists to question the sincerity of the Prime Minister, Ramsay MacDonald, and his commitment to the Home Rule cause. In many ways, his support was taken for granted as he had been the Secretary of the London branch of the SHRA in the prewar years.[76] However, his apparent lack of zeal in promoting Buchanan's Bill tended to suggest to many members of the SHRA that he was no longer as avid a Home Ruler as they had thought. Indeed, as early as March 1923, there were some questioning eyebrows raised about MacDonald:

> It fills one with dismay to find the leader of the Labour Party, a Scotsman, elected to the leadership chiefly by Scottish votes, I presume - talking...of a system of devolution which would give Scotland, Wales and England an 'opportunity of exercising individuality in local affairs and at the same time enable the Government to work out more freely the general principles of national policy'. Will this wishy washy stuff satisfy the Scottish members? Surely not![77]

Such suspicions were reinforced by his failure to get the issue moving again, especially as it was promised that another day would be set aside in order to pursue the debate. However, in June, MacDonald informed Buchanan that the second debate would not take place, although it was hoped to set up an all-party select committee to discuss and consider the question. Even this limited action fell through. MacDonald, according to one contemporary source: 'regretted to find that the Conservative Party was not prepared to concur in this course, and it could not be carried out. As to the future, he declines to give any pledge'.[78]

He lowered his reputation further by refusing to meet members of the SHRA when he visited Glasgow to receive the freedom of the city.[79] As far as R.E. Muirhead was concerned, the failure to pass a measure of self-government by the first Labour administration was the responsibility of MacDonald:

> I see from today's *Glasgow Herald* (19th June, 1925) that you [MacDonald] still take an interest in Scottish life. Why the Government of which you were head last year failed to support the Home Rule Bill, I cannot explain...I must candidly admit that the failure of your Government to make any serious attempt to pass a Scottish Home Rule Bill caused your stock as a Scotsman to fall heavily in my estimation.[80]

Further evidence that MacDonald's interest in devolution was not serious can be gleaned from the correspondence between himself and Muirhead. In January, 1924, when MacDonald had newly taken up the position of Prime Minister, Muirhead wrote to him suggesting that a National Convention ought to be set up to hammer out proposals and details for a Home Rule bill. The Premier's response was lukewarm and it was emphasised that the SHRA could not expect his personal involvement in initiating the process:

> I am afraid at the present moment it is impossible for me with all the burdens of straightening out matters, to go into details about Scottish Home Rule. I am covered up under suggestions from my friends about everything that ranges from the most important matters to the most insignificant. You will all have to keep me out for a while until I make the general arrangements, and then I will come in and tackle details. In any event, the man who would have to handle the matter, first of all at any rate, would be the head of the responsible department.[81]

Also, the same lack of commitment was in evidence when the Scottish Parliamentary Party tried to get MacDonald to set up a select committee, even without the Tories. MacDonald was reluctant to push the issue and stated that any future bill would have to meet the objections of several of his ministers who were hostile to it in its present form.[82] On 21 July 1924, the MPs Tom Johnston, Neil McLean and Duncan Graham had a meeting with the Prime Minister, who it transpired was unsympathetic to their Home Rule claims.[83] At this stage in his career, MacDonald had no enthusiasm for the self-government cause as he was too busy with foreign affairs and other domestic problems which were, he believed, of greater importance than an issue which had already proved to be divisive. In any case, he believed that the best remedy for Scottish grievances was the action taken by a Labour Government in Westminster and not a separate Edinburgh Parliament.[84] The net effect of the failure of Buchanan's Bill was that it led to a lack of confidence in the abilities of the Labour Party by SHRA activists. Also, it speeded up a process of reassessments of the issue by many prominent Labour politicians, who would never support the cause again with the same degree of enthusiasm (see below).

In response to this setback a Scottish National Convention was set up in November, 1924, by the Association. An indication of the declining support for Home Rule among the Parliamentary Labour Party was the fact that only seven of their MPs turned up to offer support, which was a significant decrease on previous Home Rule activities.[85] It was decided to form a Parliamentary Committee to press for, and draw up,

some form of self-government bill. However, by April, 1925, little
progress had been made:

> Great difficulty has been experienced in getting representatives from the
> three Scots Parliamentary groups. The Labour group had appointed the
> Rev. James Barr and Mr. Neil McLean as their representatives. The Liberals
> had not yet appointed representatives but it was hoped that they would do
> so soon. The Unionists do not propose to appoint representatives. As
> soon as the Liberal representatives are appointed, the Committee will get
> to work.[86]

The Liberal and Labour Parties were both hostile to the idea of setting
up an unofficial committee, and there was little agreement on the method
to be used to forward the campaign in Parliament. Worse still was the
fact that the Labour representatives on the Committee could not claim
that they would receive the endorsement of their own party for any
proposals that were put forward. James Barr spelled out the position in
June, 1926:

> The Parliamentary Committee of the Scottish Labour Members feel that
> three points must be kept in view:
> 1. The committee of Scottish Labour Members cannot commit the Labour
> Party as a whole [The British Labour Party], to any decision they may
> come to on this Draft Bill.
> 2. The question of the retention of Scottish Members of Parliament comes
> into existence; it is considered essential by several of the committee.
> 3. Scotland's place and influence in Imperial affairs must be secured in
> any scheme of Self Government which is agreed to.[87]

Members of the Association were faced with coming to terms with the
fact that they were being left out of the framing of any future Home
Rule bills. Also, it was quite apparent that any measure of self-
government which was to receive Labour support would have to take
account of wider party interests. Bluntly, the SHRA was told to mind
its own business:

> The Sub-committee of the Scottish Labour Group think it right to point
> out that...a future Labour Government will exercise its own judgement as
> to the lines on which it will frame a bill for the granting of Self Government
> to Scotland.[88]

The Labour Party's exclusive approach to Home Rule was in evidence
in May, 1927, when Barr's private member's bill was put forward without
any attempt to secure cross-party support. However, by this time,
divisions in the SHRA had become more obvious and more entrenched.

After the failure of Buchanan's Bill in 1924, a number of dissenting
voices were heard within the Association, who increasingly vented their

frustration at the Labour Party. It was argued that by relying on Westminster and especially the existing political apparatus, the SHRA was totally at the mercy of party interests, and it could do little that was effective on its own. In October, 1925, suggestions were mooted within the Association that the time was ripe for the formation of a national party.[89] In December, 1925, Muirhead's brother, Robert, put forward the argument for the creation of a nationalist party on the grounds that the British political organisations were not interested in Scottish affairs, and that the only way to overcome this obstacle was to put into Parliament a body of MPs whose first and foremost commitment was to obtaining Home Rule.[90] Those members of the SHRA whose loyalty lay with the Labour Party dismissed the idea as impractical. David N. MacKay stated that it was better to wait until the Labour Party came back to power. He also hit upon the crux of the problem now facing the Association when he made the statement that he was a socialist first and a nationalist second.[91] This sentiment was not shared by a large section of activists, many of whom believed that socialism would best be served by a Parliament in Scotland as a principal priority. Robert Muirhead expressed the rising tide of frustration within this group when he wrote in May, 1926:

> The SHRA has now been in existence for seven years, and Scotland is still ruled from London. It is time to take stock of our progress, with a view to finding out whether further activity on the lines on which we have been and are now working is well directed and likely to secure Scottish self government at the earliest possible date, and whether some change of policy or method is not required.[92]

He wanted to abandon the passive approach of the Association, and instead advocated that in future all prospective candidates for Parliament should be vetted 'for a mandate to put Home Rule first when they got to Westminster...then a Scots National Party would be in being'. Robert Muirhead rounded off his argument by concluding that 'the demand for Home Rule must be made more insistent and more passionate. This means that the SHRA must revise its programme and adopt a more effective policy than it has hitherto used'.[93]

Implicit in Robert Muirhead's statement was a criticism of the Labour Party members who lacked commitment and kowtowed to the demands of their London headquarters. In August, 1926, he made an open attack on Labour's credibility as a party of Home Rule:

> The British Labour Party as a whole has, so far as we are aware, never committed itself to support our cause - certainly at the last General Election Scottish Home Rule found no place in its manifesto nor did the late Labour

Government show any eagerness to get the question brought to a decision...
The fact is that the most effective way to get the Labour Party or any other
party to take up Home Rule in earnest, is to show it votes will be lost if
neglected... Until Scotland takes the trouble to have its claim for self
government vowed in a more unmistakable manner than has hitherto been
done, there is small hope that any of the British political parties will do
anything effective for Scottish Home Rule.[94]

Roland Muirhead had likewise come to the same conclusion about the
efficacy of complete reliance on the Labour Party and in a private letter
of June, 1925, he wrote:

I take the view that if party candidates in Scotland will not put the question
of a National Parliament in Scotland first on their programme that we
should put forward independent candidates as soon as resources permit.[95]

After the collapse of the 1924 Home Rule Bill, there were increasing
calls for some new form of activity in order to circumvent the
stranglehold of the Labour Party's British interests. Some members of
the SHRA advocated a national party on the lines of the Irish model,
while some merely wanted to get a more emphatic commitment from
existing MPs.[96] Although Muirhead and others had as yet little idea as
to what form a national party would take, it was becoming clear that
this was the most attractive option available to break out of the impasse
in which the Home Rule movement now found itself. Accordingly,
there was an increase in co-operation between the Association activists
and other nationalist organisations, and among the many things which
were discussed, the formation of an independent national party featured
predominantly.[97]

At first, Robert Muirhead wanted to form an electoral pact with the
Labour Party, and contest constituencies on the Home Rule ticket,
which perhaps a socialist on his own would not win. The inspiration
for this mode of thought was the activities of Edwin Scrymgeour, the
Prohibitionist MP for Dundee, who seemed to have been tolerated by
the Labour Party:

I think there are quite a number of constituencies where a good candidate,
in earnest about Home Rule, and otherwise acceptable to the electors,
would have a good chance.[98]

Robert Muirhead wanted to prove that Home Rule was a vote winning
issue, and that if the Labour Party stepped up its commitment, their
electoral standing would rise correspondingly. In many ways, the idea
of putting up independent candidates was only a tactic designed to put
pressure on the existing political establishment to take the self-

government issue more seriously. (see chapter Three) However, given the divisions which now existed within the SHRA, the opportunity to reach some form of compromise was rapidly diminishing.

One of the principal reasons why the split within the ranks of the Association became increasingly bitter was the dominance of the Trade Union block vote. All attempts by the activist wing of the SHRA to initiate any sort of change in strategy found their efforts blocked by the overwhelming power of the STUC's affiliated membership. The majority of the activists, most of whom were also members of the ILP, were the real workers who made the Association exist as a functioning organisation. They were responsible for raising finance, arranging speaking tours, and distributing propaganda and literature. It was this section which was the most vocal wing of the SHRA, and it was they who took part in the debates on policy and strategy. Their frustration at having their efforts to make the Association a more dynamic force in Scottish politics continually vetoed by Trade Union leaders, who relied on a passive membership which took no part in the running of the organisation, was very great indeed.[99] By the middle of the 1920s, these two groups moved further apart, while elsewhere, there existed a general mood of despondency about the chances of achieving self-government. Contrast Wheatley's statement on arriving in London in 1922, that 'there is no greater issue that arouses more interest in Scotland than that of Home Rule',[100] with that of William Wright MP, writing to Muirhead in 1925:

> I am renewing my annual subscription to the SHRA with some reluctance. Not because of the amount subscribed, but one feels the golden moments are passing and little progress is being made. I feel had we met with Self-government in Scotland in 1923, we should have accomplished ten times as much work.'[101]

Throughout this period, attitudes hardened and members of the SHRA were forced to choose between conflicting priorities. Former Home Rule supporters openly began to display signs of hostility towards those who would not accept that there were more important political objectives. Calls for cross-party co-operation were dismissed outright by Maxton:

> I cannot see myself combining with any Scottish Members either Liberal or Unionist ...I am not going to say to the Tories, 'Combine with me in handicapping the Labour Government in order that we get Scottish Home Rule.'[102]

Also, other members of the Association made it quite clear that they would not support any change in tactics which would impinge on their loyalty to the Labour Party. As one person put it:

He was a Labour man first and a Nationalist afterwards. If the choice lay between a Tory Nationalist Parliament in Edinburgh and a Socialist Parliament in Westminster, he would prefer the latter.'[103]

In any case, by this time prominent Labour politicians had reasoned out their attitude towards Home Rule and had also made a judgement on its significance. Their findings and conclusions would, at the end of the day, prove unacceptable to many SHRA activists.

As was mentioned earlier, the heady days of Home Rule euphoria took place at a time when the Labour movement was still in the process of defining a coherent political philosophy, and the self-government cause was not subject to any form of analysis. Indeed, in 1922, the Rev. James Barr stated that Home Rule was necessary primarily for the protection of the Scottish Church's national identity, land abuse, and the need for a stronger Temperance Act, all of which could not be deemed of great importance in the mid-1920s.[104] By this time, the leading theorists of the Scottish Labour Party, such as Wheatley and Johnston, had concluded that it was impossible to separate the Scottish economy from the rest of the United Kingdom.[105] It was believed that any form of self-government which was unable to control the economic forces which governed national life would be ineffective and doomed to failure.[106] More and more, the idea became accepted that the British economy was a complete unit, and consequently it was decided that it was only from Westminster that the necessary powers required to rectify the excesses of the capitalist system could be obtained. Much of this thought was induced as a result of the prevailing economic climate and the widespread social problems which followed in its wake. Although Home Rule sounded fine in theory, it was deemed to be largely irrelevant to the bread and butter issues of the day, and, accordingly, it was to those matters such as housing, unemployment and poverty, that Labour MPs turned their attention. What was wanted was immediate action, which, it was believed, could be attained from Westminster, and these problems were to be tackled first by any future Labour government. The theoretical nature of devolving sufficient powers to a Scottish Parliament, in order to deal with these issues, was believed to be an unnecessary distraction when the solution was already at hand.[107] It was thought that the only role for self-government would be in an administrative capacity, and as an issue of importance, this did not rank too highly.

Also, of crucial significance in the decline of the Labour movement's commitment towards Home Rule was the attitude of the STUC. At a time of rising unemployment and deflationary government policies, most

Scottish Trade Union leaders accepted the principle of safety in numbers, and in an effort to secure better protection, they became more firmly enmeshed within the TUC.[108] Smaller and separate Scottish unions, it was believed, would make easier targets for employers who were set upon reducing wages and manpower.[109] Also, this tendency towards greater integration was further reinforced by the psychological effects of the failure of the General Strike, which put the Trade Union movement, as a whole, on the defensive.[110] Another factor which diminished the devolution commitment, were the reforms of the Labour Party's organisation, initiated in the mid 1920s by Arthur Henderson. The purpose of these changes was to bring greater central control and discipline, while also removing any traces of sectarianism.[111] The idea of Home Rule was unlikely to find much sympathy in a party which was committed to establishing a greater uniformity and removing ethnic and geographical differences. In any case, few people believed that the self-government cause was a political issue which commanded popular support. Attendances at the SHRA rallies during the period after 1925 declined steadily as people became more concerned with the bread and butter politics of the day.[112] By the time of the introduction of the Rev. James Barr's private member's bill in 1927, which was in itself a fortuitous accident, few members of the Labour movement believed that the effort of introducing Home Rule was worthwhile. As the author of 'The Better Government of Scotland Bill' and its sponsor, Tom Johnston, were later to admit, the attempt was half-hearted, especially as there was a clause calling for the withdrawal of Scottish MPs from Westminster.[113]

In contrast to such lukewarmness, the activists in the SHRA believed that this was the most thoroughly prepared of all Home Rule Bills yet submitted.[114] However, several were warning that if it proved to be a failure 'a more assertive policy is called for'.[115] On 7 May 1927, the Bill was debated for only 45 minutes, after which the Speaker refused to allow a vote in view of the short period of discussion and, consequently, it was dropped.[116] The *Scotsman*'s comment was typical of the Scottish press at the time: 'an absurd project by a negligible number of excessively narrow and unthinkingly sentimental patriots.'[117] However, as far as the Home Rule activists were concerned, it was the last straw, and it stiffened their resolve to find an alternative policy. Within the SHRA, one body came increasingly to the forefront in the call for independent political action. 'The Scottish National Party Group' announced its existence in October, 1927, and one of its members explained the reasons behind its foundation:

This group was formed to press for the formation of a Scottish National Party – and when funds permit to fight every seat, both for Parliament and municipal contests... It would be too much, perhaps to expect it to be passed by a majority at the present time, but at the same time I think most of the delegates and those who attend the National Convention realise that something drastic is called for or will be necessary sooner or later.[118]

Meanwhile, the Scottish National Convention was also suffering from the reverberations of the failure of Barr's Bill. At a meeting of the Committee of the Convention on 29 May, 1927, the activist anger at the present policy, spilled over into outright condemnation of the Labour Party. An apologist for the Party suggested that the best solution to the problem would be to persuade the Labour headquarters to officially take on Home Rule and table a resolution in the House of Commons.[119] This option was greeted with derision by the activist wing, which pointed out that the Labour Party, as far as they were concerned, had failed twice already, and that there was little point in continued reliance on this method.[120] Antagonism between both groups became very bitter, with the bulk of criticism going against the Labour Party:

I certainly agree that the Parliamentary method is now absolutely out of date... The Labour Party...when it was in office, it did nothing and I am going to tell you straight that the Labour MPs, with especial reference to Glasgow, have revived instructions to do nothing to imperil the future prospects of the Party holding office at Westminster.[121]

The activists had come to the conclusion that Home Rule was being sacrificed for party interests, and more importantly, many now believed that the Labour Party was hostile to their intentions. The leader of the nationalist organisation, the Scottish National Movement, Lewis Spence, continued the attack:

It is common knowledge to every press man in the House of Commons that Mr. Ramsay MacDonald almost went down on bended knees to the Scottish Labour Members, and asked them not to back, not this last bill, but its predecessor.[122]

Upon what information such accusations were based is not known. However, they are a striking example of the depth of feeling and the suspicion which was now abounding within the ranks of the activist wing of the SHRA. The section of the Association which rejected Labour involvement turned its attention to formulating alternative strategies and policies. Although suggestions were made to operate through local government and to petition for the setting up of a Royal Commission, the area of greatest interest centred on the question of setting up an independent political party. It was decided that such an organisation would be formed on the following basis, 'that any member of Parliament representing it would undertake to put the question of Home Rule for Scotland in the first place, and give it precedence to all other Parliamentary questions that should arise'.[123] The Labour loyalists were horrified at such a proposal, and the suggestion that James Barr should leave the Labour Party and join the new organisation, was treated with more or less disbelief. According to the trade unionist, George Mather:

> To cut himself [Barr] adrift from the party he had done a great deal to make, and that almost entirely has made him the personality that he is in a parliamentary sense, would be, in my judgement, to ask Mr. Barr to descend from the position of being an influential and serious politician, and turn him quite definitely into a freak or a crank.[124]

In many ways, Mather's attitude typified the belief held by the majority of the Scottish Labour movement that those who so vehemently advocated Home Rule were nothing more than an isolated section of opinion on the fringe of Scottish politics, and as such they could not be taken seriously.

At the meetings of the Convention which took place in November and December, 1927, the arguments continued in an atmosphere of complete intransigence. Robert Muirhead put forward the case that the Convention ought to turn its attention to considering how best to create a National Party, which was, of course, blocked by the union vote.[125] Undeterred, the Nationalists continued the attack, and in December the outline of the proposed party was clearly taking shape:

> The Nationalist Party is a political party to represent the idea of a Scotland that it should have its own Government... I wish to put before the members a fact which I did not find in the 'Forward' that seventeen English Members voted against Mr. Johnston and Mr. James Barr in the House of Commons. Those English Labour members went out of their way to support the English Tories against a motion which was favourable to Home Rule for Scotland. These seventeen included seven members of the late Labour Cabinet. It seems therefore, that there is no hope in leaving this matter over until you have a Labour Government...There is no sign whatever that the Tories or Liberals or the Labour Party are thinking of making Home Rule an issue in Scotland. Therefore, we must make it an issue ourselves. We can only do this by creating a party to be called the Scottish National Party, which shall put up candidates at elections for this one question and this alone.'[126]

The Labour loyalists naturally opposed such a move, as it meant a direct challenge to the authority of their party. However, it was perhaps an indication of their loss of the moral high ground that none of their

MPs took part in the debate. They all, quite bluntly, stated that they had more important business to attend to, which was fuel to the nationalist claims that they no longer took Home Rule seriously.[127] The loyalists were under increasing pressure to vindicate the Association's present course of action, and judging by the dwindling attendances at SHRA meetings,[128] it appeared that few could be bothered with facing up to the challenge. Many, such as David Kirkwood, believed that the Association was nothing more than a working-class ancillary organisation of the Labour Party:

> The English many a time thought they could buy Scottish independence. They had bought the aristocracy, even the middle classes. But the good thing about the Home Rule Movement today was that it was composed of the working class, and the working class has never been bought.[129]

It was taken for granted that the SHRA would follow the aims and objectives of the Labour movement, and the ultimate goal was socialism, which they all had a duty to strive for.[130] It was also assumed that those activists, the majority of whom belonged to the ILP, would observe Labour Party discipline. The Labour loyalists in the Association were unable to comprehend the motives which compelled the activist wing to promote the cause of Home Rule at the expense of socialism. Indeed, it was this lack of comprehension which led J.L. Kinloch to accuse those who wanted to form a Scottish National Party of 'being more interested in destroying socialism than getting Home Rule'.[131] He also believed that the formation of an independent political party, which would challenge Labour in the electoral arena, was tantamount to a declaration of war against the socialist movement.[132]

Things came to a head in January, 1928, when R.E. Muirhead announced his intention to stand as an independent Home Rule candidate for the West Renfrewshire constituency. His attempts to receive endorsement from the SHRA were blocked, and although there was no official Labour candidate at that moment, no time was lost in appointing Captain Wedgewood Benn; significantly a man with a strong devolutionist record.[133] As a result of this, Muirhead announced that he would resign as Secretary of the Scottish National Convention, although he was persuaded to stay on a little longer while attempts were made to dissuade him from his present course of action. However, the damage had already been done. In April, 1928, he expressed his dissatisfaction with the current state of affairs in an article for the *Scots Independent*, monthly organ of the nationalist organisation, the Scots National League. The first point he made was that Home Rule could not be attained through the medium of British political parties because they had no genuine interest in the issue. Also, he blamed the latent hostility of English MPs as a salient factor in thwarting previous attempts to pass self-government legislation:

> It transpires that the English Labour members take a very similar view about Scottish Home Rule to what the English Liberals did when Gladstone was in power many years ago... It is well known that among Scottish Labour members the English Labour members are not at all anxious to give Scotland Self Government...It did not find a place in any of the three manifestoes issued by the three Parliamentary parties at the 1924 General Election. To me, personally, this was the death knell of my reasonable hope of the Labour Party, or any other mainly English party, passing a Scottish self government measure of its own accord.[134]

Muirhead explained how he interpreted contemporary events in the Home Rule movement, and as far as he was concerned, the cause could only be forwarded by independent political action:

> Lately there has been a marked increase in the number of those who have come to realise the hopelessness of expecting any effective steps to be taken by one or other of the present London controlled parties. Although there are still a large number of earnest Scotsmen and women, potential nationalists, who fail to perceive the futility of continuing to expect a national Parliament through the initiative of the present parliamentary parties, there is a very evident and large increase in the number of thorough going Scottish Nationalists who realise the need for an independent Scots National Party to ginger things up at Westminster and force to the foreground the demand for self-government.'[135]

He rounded off his argument by concluding that the only way in which the self-government cause would make a serious impact on Scottish political life, was for nationalists to make a full scale assault on the electoral battlefield:

> Nationalist candidates to contest many of the Scottish constituencies at the coming general election. If Scotsmen and women awaken to their own interests, there is no reason why the Scots National Party should not put forward a candidate in each of the constituencies in Scotland.[136]

By calling for the unification of all nationalists, both within the SHRA and from other nationalist organisations, in order to form a new party which would challenge the Labour Party for electoral support, Muirhead made any reconciliation between the two factions in the Association impossible.

Labour loyalists were furious, although still reluctant to accept the fact that Muirhead was intent on breaking up the SHRA. Peter Webster threatened to withdraw STUC affiliation, but Muirhead had called his bluff.[137] At the annual meeting of the Association, which took place a few days after the founding of the National Party of Scotland in April, 1928, Muirhead announced that he had joined the new organisation and urged those who were likewise disillusioned with the Labour Party's commitment to Home Rule, to follow suit.[138] His action had effectively ostracised himself from the Labour movement, and within a short time the new party was categorised as 'communist or other party which is not eligible for members to affiliate to or become members of'.[139] When Muirhead left the SHRA, he took with him his financial support, and his call to join the NPS decimated grass root membership and activities. Throughout the rest of the year, the Association faded away with more and more branches closing down until the annual meeting of April, 1929, when it was decided that the organisation should dissolve itself.[140] The short postwar history of the SHRA had, if nothing else, forced nationalists and Home Rulers to come to the conclusion that they would have to take control of their own political destiny in order to achieve their ambitions.

NOTES

1. I.G.C. Hutchison, *A Political History of Scotland 1832-1924* (Edinburgh 1986), pp 171-173, pp 241-243.

2. Hutchison, op.cit. pp 277-328. Iain McLean, *The Legend of Red Clydeside* (Edinburgh 1983). Joseph Melling, *Rent Strikes: Peoples' Struggle for Housing in West Scotland 1890-1916* (Edinburgh 1983). C.Harvie, *No Gods and Precious Few Heroes* (London 1981) pp 28-34. W.Ferguson, *Scotland 1689 to the Present* (Edinburgh 1978) pp 352-364.

3. Hutchison, op.cit. pp 277-321.

4. The pre-war SHRA was founded in 1886 and collapsed after the outbreak of hostilities in 1914. H.J. Hanham, *Scottish Nationalism* (London 1969), pp 64-91. The history of the post-war founding of the Association is to be found in the pamphlet, *Self-Determination for Scotland* (Glasgow, 1919), Muirhead Mss. Mitchell Library, Glasgow.

5. Muirhead's biography can be found in the *Scots Independent*, April 1928, pp 81-83. Thomas Johnston, *Memories* (London, 1952) pp 231-233. Helen H. Corr in William Knox (ed.) *Scottish Labour Leaders 1918-1939* (Edinburgh 1984) pp 217-221.

6. *Scots Independent*, April, 1928, p 82.

7. Helen H. Corr op.cit. Graham Walker, Thomas Johnston (Manchester 1988) p 3.

8. T. Gallagher, *Glasgow the Uneasy Peace* (Manchester 1987) pp 134-177.

9. *Self-Determination for Scotland* p. 3.

10. Ibid

11. Labour Party Scottish Executive memo, January, 1919, Muirhead Mss. Mitchell Library, Glasgow.

12. *Scottish Home Rule*, July, 1920, p 3-4.

13. They were; Robert Hay who had been President of the Young Scots Society and Mrs. J.M. Crosthwaile, *Self-Determination for Scotland* pp 1-2.

14. H.S. Keith, a future Tory provost of Hamilton, *Self-Determination for Scotland.*
15. H.J. Hanham, op.cit. pp 98-107.
16. *Self-Determination for Scotland,* p 5.
17. Ibid
18. *Scottish Home Rule,* August, 1920.
19. Ibid.
20. *Home Rule for Scotland: The Case in 90 Points, with a foreward by the Rev. James Barr, B.D.* (Glasgow 1922), p 2, pp 9-10.
21. Ibid.
22. *Self-Determiniation for Scotland,* 3.
23. *Home Rule for Scotland: The Case in 90 Points,* pp 9-10.
24. *Scottish Home Rule,* July, 1920, p 2.
25. *Home Rule for Scotland: The Case in 90 Points,* p 1.
26. *Scottish Home Rule,* January, 1921.
27. Ibid.
28. *Home Rule for Scotland: The Case in 90 Points,* p 1.
29. Ibid.
30. *Scottish Home Rule,* August, 1920.
31. Ibid.
32. *Scottish Home Rule,* September, 1920, pp 4-8.
33. Ibid.
34. *Liberty,* February, 1920, p 22.
35. For example, in Leith, the Liberal candidate was more in favour of Home Rule than his Labour opponent, although the local SHRA was run mainly by the ILP. As a result of party interests, the most favourable candidate did not receive full endorsement from the Association.
36. Hutchison, op.cit. pp 309-328.
37. *Scottish Home Rule,* April, 1922, p 37.
38. Ibid.
39. *Scottish Home Rule,* July, 1922, p 3.
40. *Scottish Home Rule,* June, 1925, p 106.
41. *Scottish Home Rule,* December, 1922, p 33.
42. Hutchison, op.cit.
43. *The Campaign Guide: National Unionist Association,* (1922) pp 916-930.
44. Robert Munro to R.E. Muirhead, 11th January, 1922. Muirhead Mss. Mitchell Library.
45. Hutchison, op.cit. p 310.
46. Duke of Montrose to R.E. Muirhead, 17th April, 1921. Muirhead Mss. Mitchell Library, Glasgow.
47. Michael Keating and David Bleiman, *Labour and Scottish Nationalism* (London 1979) pp 59-101.
48. Christopher Harvie, 'Before the Breakthrough 1888-1922' in Donnachie, Harvie, Wood (eds) *Forward: Labour Politics in Scotland 1888-1988* (Edinburgh 1989).
49. STUC Annual Report, 1918.

50. Among those were the Rev. James Barr, R.E. Muirhead, J.L. Kinloch and Rosslyn Mitchell. See the biographical entries in W. Knox (ed), *Scottish Labour Leaders.*

51. Keating and Bleiman, op.cit. pp 57-77.

52. *Scottish Review*, Summer, 1918, pp 109-110. Keating and Bleiman op.cit. pp 59-79

53. Annual Report of the Scottish Council of the Labour Party. Muirhead Mss. Mitchell Library, Glasgow.

54. Keating and Bleiman, op.cit.

55. Ian S. Wood, 'Labour in Scotland in the 1920s', in Donnachie, Harvie, Wood (eds), op cit.

56. McLean, op.cit. p 209.

57. Based on the texts of speeches published regularly in *Scottish Home Rule.*

58. George Buchanan speaking in Paisley, January,1927. *Scottish Home Rule*, February, 1927.

59. *Scottish Home Rule*, February, 1928.

60. Keating and Bleiman, op.cit. pp 103-107

61. Tom Gibson's memorandum on the SHRA, June, 1924. Gibson Mss. Acc 6058, Box l, NLS

62. op.cit.

63. R.E. Muirhead to Tom Gibson, 17th April, 1924, Gibson Mss. Acc 6058, Box l, NLS.

64. ibid. 18th June. Muirhead stated that Maxton was driving even moderate Labour people away.

65. Records of the Scottish National Convention, 30th October, 1925. Muirhead Mss. Acc 3721, Box 81, NLS p 56.

66. *Scottish Home Rule*, April, 1924.

67. ibid.

68. Hutchison, op.cit. p 277.

69. *Scottish Home Rule*, April, 1924. p 89-90.

70. *Scottish Home Rule*, April, 1924. pp 74-75.

71. Ibid.

72. Ibid.

73. Ibid.

74. *Glasgow Herald*, 10th May, 1924.

75. *Scottish Home Rule*, June, 1924.

76. David Marquand, *Ramsay MacDonald* (London 1977)

77. *Scottish Home Rule*, March, 1923. p 59.

78. *Scottish Home Rule*, June, 1924. p 105.

79. *Scottish Home Rule*, May, 1925. pp 99.

80. R.E. Muirhead to Ramsay MacDonald, 19th June, 1925. Muirhead Mss. Acc 3721, Box 4, NLS.

81. MacDonald to Muirhead, 11th January, 1924. Also MacDonald consistently refused to attend any SHRA meetings. Muirhead Mss. NLS.

82. *Glasgow Herald*, 7th July, 1924.

83. *Scotsman*, 22nd July, 1924.

84. *Daily Record*, 9th January, 1929.
85. Scottish National Convention records, November, 1924. Muirhead Mss. NLS.
86. *Scottish Home Rule*, May 1925. p 99.
87. *Scottish Home Rule*, July, 1926. p 8.
88. *Scottish Home Rule*, August, 1926. p 19.
88. *Scottish Home Rule*, October, 1925. p 19.
90. *Scottish Home Rule*, December, 1925. p 53.
91. *Scottish Home Rule*, December, 1925. p 54.
92. *Scottish Home Rule*, May, 1926.
93. Ibid.
94. *Scottish Home Rule*, August, 1926. p 17.
95. Roland Muirhead to Tom Gibson, June, 1925. Gibson Mss. Acc 6058, Box 1, NLS.
96. Evidence taken from the monthly reports of meetings and debates in *Scottish Home Rule*.
97. In particular, there was increasing correspondence on this issue between Muirhead and Gibson. See the respective Mss. collections.
98. *Scottish Home Rule*, October, 1926. p 32.
99. The Minutes of the meetings of the Scottish National Convention. Muirhead Mss. Acc 3721, Box 81, NLS. Also reports published monthly in *Scottish Home Rule*.
100. Quoted in W. Knox, 'The Red Clydesiders and the Scottish Political Tradition' in Terry Brotherston (ed) *Covenant, Charter and Party: Traditions of Revolt and Protest in Modern Scottish History* (Aberdeen 1989).
101. *Scottish Home Rule*, December, 1925.
102. *Scottish Home Rule*, July, 1924. p 7.
103. *Scottish Home Rule*, December, 1925. p 53.
104. *Scottish Home Rule: The case in 90 points.*
105) David Howell, *A Lost Left: Three Studies in Socialism and Nationalism* (Manchester 1986) pp 229-265. Graham Walker. op.cit. pp 59-91.
106. Ibid. Also, T. Johnston, op.cit. pp 66. W. Knox, op.cit. pp 100-101
107. 'There is vital need for emphasis upon the prior attention that should be paid to our industrial economy and there is no instance in the world's history of a people who have achieved economic power being denied political power.' Thomas Johnston, *Memories*, pp 66. Also, MacDonald stated that the United Kingdom could not be broken up as an economic unit. *Daily Record*, 9th January, 1929.
108. Keating and Bleiman, op.cit. pp 98-101
109. Ibid.
110. See Keating and Bleiman op.cit. pp 79-101. See also Barbara W. Robertson 'The Scottish Farm Servant and his Union: From Encapsulation to Integration' in Ian MacDougall (ed.), *Essays in Scottish Labour History* (Edinburgh 1978) which unfortunately gives only minimum of detail on the incorporation of the Union into the Transport and General Workers Union in 1932. See also I MacDougall 'Some Aspects of the 1926 General Strike in Scotland' in MacDougall (ed.) op.cit.
111. F.M. Leventhal *Arthur Henderson* (Manchester 1989),

112. *Scottish Home Rule*, Reports of monthly meetings.

113. Johnston, op.cit.

114. *Scottish Home Rule*, November, 1927.

115. *Scottish Home Rule*, April, 1927. pp 83.

116. *Scotsman*, 8th May, 1927.

117. Ibid.

118. A.L. Henry (Secretary of the Scottish National Party group) to Tom Gibson, 13th May, 1927. Gibson Mss. Acc 6058, Box 1, NLS.

119. Scottish National Convention records, May, 1927. Muirhead Mss. Acc 3721, Box 81, NLS.

120. op.cit. p 20

121. op.cit. p 23.

122. Ibid.

123. *Scottish Home Rule*, October, 1926.

124. Scottish National Convention records, 27th June, 1927. p 11. Muirhead Mss. NLS.

124. In April, 1926, the Labour group refused to hold an extra general meeting to discuss the proposal to found a National Party. They refused to adjourn the discussion in November 1927 along with disputing the right to put forwarde such a motion. An illustration of Labour strength in the general council can be drawn from the following facts: on 23rd of April, 1927, Nationalist motion rejected by an 'overwhelming' majority; May 28th, 1927, by 49 votes to 8, June 11th, 1927, by 18 votes to 8; and on December 10th, 1927, 57 votes to 34.

126. Scottish National Convention records, November, 1927. Muirhead Mss. Acc 3721, Box 81, NLS.

127. Ibid.

128. According to Scottish National Convention minutes only a handful of Labour activists remained to battle it out with the nationalists. Only on certain occasions did high ranking Trade Unionists like Peter Webster turn up.

129. *Scottish Home Rule*, September, 1924. p 8.

130. This was constantly emphasised in the debates of the Scottish National Convention.

131. *Scottish Home Rule*, December, 1927. p 175.

132. Ibid.

133. Wedgewood-Benn, formerly Liberal MP left to join the Labour Party. He was the most active Liberal in the Home Rule movement after 1918.

134. *Scots Independent*, April, 1928. p 81-83.

135. Ibid.

136. Ibid.

137. Scottish National Convention report, February, 1928. Muirhead Mss. Acc 3721. Box 82, NLS.

138. *Scottish Home Rule*, May, 1928. p 239.

139. Rev. James Barr to R.E. Muirhead, June, 1928. Muirhead Mss. Acc 3721, Box 3, NLS.

140. Keating and Bleiman, op.cit. p 106.

CHAPTER TWO

The Scots National League 1920 – 1928

In many respects the Scots National League was the most important of all the inter-war nationalist groups, especially with regard to the future development of Scottish nationalist philosophy. Much of the mainstream thinking of the postwar Scottish National Party has its roots in ideas originally expounded by the League. From a hazy beginning, in which the principal idea was a form of 'Celtic Romanticism', members of the SNL gradually built up a credible political organisation and were to the forefront in developing nationalist strategy and objectives designed to meet the challenges posed by the contemporary social, economic and political problems faced by Scotland in the inter war years. Much of the relevance of the SNL's thinking to modern Scottish nationalism is accountable by the fact that many similar problems such as unemployment, de-industrialisation, housing, state welfare, the Scottish Assembly, or lack of it, etc., have continued up until the present. After 1924, the SNL was the first nationalist group to formulate and implement a policy of separation and independence from the main British political parties, arguing that the existence of English majorities in these groups would militate against Scottish interests. Unlike their contemporary and previous nationalist associations, which relied on the established political parties to represent their interests, the League advocated the creation of a new Scottish party which was to be set up solely for the purpose of obtaining Scottish self-government. This new party was to run candidates at local and general elections and its loyalty was to be first and foremost to the principle of Scottish Home Rule. Indeed, the Scots National League was the first nationalist organisation to run a candidate at an election, albeit an unsuccessful one at local government level. In 1926, the League set up the nationalist newspaper, the *Scots Independent*, which is still on sale today. The *S.I.* acted as a valuable mouthpiece for the propagation of detailed social, economic and political policies, which in turn, gave the League more credibility among nationalists in other organisations. The fact that many other nationalists had come round to the SNL's way of thinking was borne out in 1928 with the creation of the National Party of Scotland, whose *raison d'être* was the League's dictum that political independence for Scotland could only be achieved by a party set up specifically for that purpose.

The Scots National League was formed sometime during the year of 1920.[1] There is no official founding date of the organisation because most of the original members had known each other, and their mutually held political ideas, for a considerable amount of time during their association with the Highland Land League and various Gaelic cultural organisations. Initially, the League was built up around a group of Scottish nationalists, most of whom lived in London, who wished to set up an organisation which would give further emphasis to their political and cultural ideas. Most of the London exiles were Gaelic speakers who had a passionate interest in all things Celtic. Of primary significance in the decision to form the SNL was the need to frame an organisation which would be able to act as the successor to the once influential Highland Land League. Most members of the London SNL had been, at one time or another, members of the Highland Land League, which had seen its heyday in the second half of the ninteenth century under the leadership of John Murdoch and was now in a state of continual decline, being constantly disbanded and reformed.[2] It was hoped that the new organisation would provide the necessary impetus required for a Gaelic political and cultural revival in Scotland, which was something the Highland Land League had not really attempted to do. Another important stimulus in the creation of the SNL was the situation in Ireland after the Easter Rising in 1916, which witnessed an organised suppression of Irish Gaelic culture by the British Government. Members of the League had a great affection and admiration for the Irish and their nationalist aspirations, and regarded them as being part of the great Celtic family of peoples. It was argued that, given the similarities between Irish and Scottish Celtic culture, Gaelic might also receive the same treatment of out-and-out suppression. Many believed this was probable and considered that it was necessary to set up an organisation which would promote and protect Gaelic culture. This, in turn, led to the creation of the Scots National League.

Perhaps the most valuable insight available to the historian as to the thinking that underlay the formation of the League can be obtained by a brief examination of the careers of the two principal leaders of the organisation: William Gillies and Stuart R. Erskine of Mar. William Gillies (Liam Mac Gille Losa) was born in Galloway, but was to spend most of his adult life in London.[3] The son of a merchant in the City of London, Gillies as a young man taught himself Gaelic and, at the age of seventeen, befriended John Murdoch, the editor of the *Highlander*, while working as a propagandist for the Highland Land League. In the late 19th and early 20th centuries, Gillies was impressed by the rise of the Sinn Fein movement and Irish nationalism in general, and it was his hope that a similar phenomenon would appear in Scotland. With this objective in mind, he launched the Comunn nan Albanach in 1912, which however, soon passed into oblivion without achieving any success. Gillies was an important contributor to the Gaelic cultural movement and was the Secretary of the Gaelic Society in the years from 1904 to 1905. However, he left this organisation after the rejection of his motion that the Society's objective should be the extension of Gaelic as a living tongue and its recognition by all as the national language of Scotland. He helped form the London Gaelic Choir and frequently gave sermons in the London Gaelic Church. He also wrote five plays in his adopted language, which were produced on the stage in London between 1904 and 1908. He contributed some material to Erskine of Mar's periodicals; *Guth na Bliadhna* and *Alba*. Like many who had joined the Highland Land League, Gillies was inclined towards the left of the political spectrum, declaring himself to be a committed socialist. He was a consistent supporter of Sinn Fein and an original member — the first Scot so honoured — of the Gaelic League in London, where he met and formed a close friendship with Art O'Brien, who was later to become the head of the Irish Self Determination League in Great Britain. In 1916, he openly supported the Easter Rising in Dublin and was dismayed at the lack of support it received from both Scottish socialists and Gaelic enthusiasts alike. However, in spite of this, Gillies worked tirelessly as a propagandist for the Irish cause and it was during this time that he came into increasing contact with Erskine of Mar; both men finding that they had much common political and cultural ground between them.

Ruaraidh Erskine of Mar (Ruaraidh Arascain is Mharr), the second son of the fifth Lord Erskine, was born in Brighton in 1869.[4] He was a fluent Gaelic speaker and writer, having learnt it as a child from his Lewisian nanny. Arguably Erskine, because of the proliferation of his Gaelic periodicals and his untiring work as a propagandist, was to do more than any other individual to implant Gaelic national ideals in Scotland in the first quarter of the twentieth century. In 1901, he was the Scottish delegate at the pan-Celtic congress held in Dublin where he met and was influenced by many Irish nationalists. In 1903 Erskine founded the influential periodic *Guth na Bliadhna*, which acted as a platform for his pro-Gaelic, pan-Celtic ideas. Erskine was motivated by a belief that the growth of Irish nationalism would be reciprocated by a similar movement in Scotland because of, he argued, the underlying 'racial cohesiveness' of the two nations. This was part of his idea that, at some point in the future, there would eventually be a Celtic federation comprising of Scotland, Ireland, Wales, the Isle of Man, Cornwall, Brittany and any other Celtic regions which could be unearthed. However, before any of this could be done it was necessary, he argued, to re-Celticize Scotland and this would entail making the Gaelic language and culture dominant over the whole of the country. At this juncture it is important to stress the fact that Erskine believed that at one time in the dim and distant past, all of Scotland had been Gaelic, although the evidence upon which this thesis was based received little elaboration.[5]

Like Gillies, in 1916 he supported the Easter Rising believing it to be a 'racial obligation' to his Celtic brothers in Ireland. At the end of the First World War, Erskine led an attempt to have Scotland represented at the Paris Peace Conference. The 'Petition National de l'Ecosse pour obtenir sa Representation au Congress de la Paix' had the support of many Scottish politicians including Tom Johnston, David Kirkwood, John Maclean, Neil Maclean, James Maxton, Edwin Scrymegeour and Emanuel Shinwell among others.[6] Although in prewar times he denounced socialism as a 'predatory creed',[7] Erskine, by the end of the war, had moved to a more left wing stance. He was impressed by the Bolshevik Revolution, which he claimed was a popular rising against oppression. This, he believed, had great implications for Scotland as a guide to future political action. Erskine displayed a remarkable degree of ideological agility in incorporating left wing revolutionary tendencies into his own political philosophy. This hybrid creation called 'celtic communism' was based on the way the clan system was supposed to have operated in the dim and mystic past. It is hard to tell if this was what Erskine genuinely believed, or whether it was a sop to his only potential ally at the time who had considerable popular appeal, the Clydeside revolutionary, John Maclean. Both men had certain features in common. They shared an anti-British, anti-militarist outlook and had both supported James Connolly's action in Ireland, although Maclean was the slower of the two in coming round to this opinion. Both men were in agreement that the English labour movement was more reactionary than its counterpart in Scotland.[8] However, perhaps the most important reason for their cooperation was the fact that Maclean was becoming more and more isolated from the mainstream of Scottish Labour's political thought and desperately needed allies. His advocacy of the nationalist question within the context of socialism, á la Connolly, brought him opposition from both the moderate and extreme sections of the Scottish socialist movement.[9] Maclean's postwar objective was 'the definite forming of a communist party composed of all the left wing elements in Scotland', which would have non-affiliation to the Labour Party as one of its philosophical tenets.[10] Although much of this idea was, in the end, undermined by William Gallacher,[11] it is fairly safe to assume that Maclean's contact with Erskine was a result of his plan to create a unified Scottish left wing movement. In any case, the net result was that both men worked well together and cooperated in an attempt to stop Clydeside workers shipping Government arms to Ireland. Erskine wrote articles on 'celtic communism' for Maclean's newspaper *Vanguard*, which revealed just how shallow his 'socialism' was. He believed that some form of communism was an intrinsic value of the Celtic peoples and was, in many cases, primarily attributable to racial qualities and characteristics.[12] Erskine's socialism was not based on economic factors, or marxist historical determinism, which he had little time for, but rather on romantic images of the Gaelic past. This was in direct contrast to the rigid materialist conceptions which underlay Maclean's thinking. However, it was from the background of prewar cultural nationalism that Erskine and Gillies founded the Scots National League.

As already stated, most of the initial League members lived in London and, for an organisation dedicated to the task of mobilizing the Scottish people towards the goal of political independence, this was a geographical disadvantage of considerable importance. In the years between 1920 and 1922, real political contact with Scotland remained tenuous. This was of little account, because the League did not have any policies or objectives detailed enough to appeal to the Scottish populace. The only idea that the SNL could bandy about was the broad objective of Scottish independence. However, a definition of what this was, or how it was to be achieved, received only a minimum of elaboration. This lack of political clarity was a result of the fact that most members had known each other for some time and the early history of the League resembles more that of a private club than a political organisation. In such a relaxed and friendly atmosphere, there appears to have been little pressure to hammer out concrete plans and objectives, which could be practical, and potentially divisive. The situation in Ireland acted as a convenient diversion and absorbed most of the League's early energies and frustrations.[13] All agreed that the plight of their Irish brethren was more serious than their own and, consequently, little beyond propaganda operated in Scotland. Another reason for the League's ideological poverty was the fact that both its leaders, Erskine and Gillies, were not detailed planners. Most of their ideas were abstract and neither of them could be bothered with the elaborate planning required to set up an effective political organisation. Both men were willing to point out the main objective, but not so keen to go into the details of how it was to be achieved. In any case, they believed that propaganda was the most important function of the League, stressing, as they perceived it, the need to alert the Scottish people to their 'true situation'.

John MacArthur was the SNL's most important man in 1920, both for establishing links with Scotland and disseminating the 'essential' propaganda. MacArthur lived in Glasgow and it was from there that he edited and published his journal *Liberty*, which first appeared in December, 1919. Unfortunately, little is known about MacArthur, although it does seem likely that he was initially involved with the Scottish Home Rule Association when he was first approached by Erskine to join the League. To begin with, *Liberty* was advertised as the 'Scottish Home Rule Journal' and its pages contained news of the SHRA's activities. It is not unreasonable to speculate that Roland Muirhead helped to provide funds to set up the journal, but later disassociated himself and the SHRA from it because of its increasingly radical and Sinn Fein sentiments. Indeed, after a short time *Liberty* was to change its title from the 'Scottish Home Rule Journal' to the 'Scottish National Journal' and the Muirhead brothers brought out their own *Scottish Home Rule News-sheet* to fill the gap caused by MacArthur's departure. However, *Liberty* was not really an official journal of the League and there were usually articles in favour of Scottish self government, aspects of Scottish culture and football, as well as plentiful helpings of pro-Irish nationalist news items. An irony worth pointing out was the fact that MacArthur used to sell his newspaper outside Ibrox football ground.[14]

By using the columns of *Liberty* it is possible to glean some information as to the structural apparatus, in so far as it existed, of the SNL in Scotland. The only public meeting organised by the League in 1920 was a demonstration at Arbroath Abbey in October to mark the 600th anniversary of the Declaration of Scottish Independence. The main speaker was supposed to have been Erskine of Mar, who, because of illness, had to step down. His place was taken by John Maclean who, by all accounts, managed to boost the attendance figures.[15] Evidence of the League's weak membership and lack of political direction was given in the speech made by MacArthur at the meeting: 'The League stood for the complete restoration of Scotland's independence and membership was open to all men and women regardless of party, so long as they approved of that object'.[16] Acceptance of members from the Conservative and, to some extent, the Liberal parties went square in the face of their accusations against these people of being responsible for a military occupation in Ireland. Also, for an organisation which was decidely anti-British, their willingness to tolerate as members individuals belonging to political parties which were committed to the unity of the British state, displayed a total lack of realism. However, perhaps due to the nature of the League's propaganda, no-one of any significance from these parties was persuaded to join.

The perennial weakness of the League during the first years of its existence was the failure to attract new members and any amount of public sympathy. This state of affairs, they argued, was the result of English propaganda, which had duped the Scottish people, who now were no longer aware of just how serious their plight was. It was therefore necessary, they maintained, to intensify their propaganda campaign in order to bring about an 'enlightened' Scottish national consiousness. As far as League members were concerned, Scotland, like Ireland, was little more than a colony of England. They asserted that from the earliest times the English had tried to subjugate the Scots to their rule, destroy their culture and economically exploit them. Erskine, Gillies, MacArthur and other members of the League believed that this English policy had almost been totally successful and had just been recognised in the nick of time. They now made it their objective to reverse this process. In the years from 1920 to 1924, the Scots National League began to take steps to build a philosophy which explained and justified the role and necessity of Scottish nationalism. In the initial stages, central to this philosophy was their interpretation and understanding of Scottish history with particular reference to affairs with England. In order to understand the political development of the SNL, it is first of all necessary to elucidate their peculiar and, at times, rather unique and colourful interpretation of Scottish history.

In order to build up Scottish national consciousness and awareness, the League believed, it was important to provide a 'corrective' analysis of Scottish history which, they argued, had been distorted since the Union as part of the plan to destroy the Scottish national identity. The teaching of 'bogus' Scottish history at schools, they claimed, was a favourite Unionist tactic. They complained that 'The two most serious defects in the teaching of Scottish history are the neglect of the more Celtic period on the one hand and the decided Whiggish interpretations given to the later periods of the other'.[17] This, according to the League, was propaganda being used to undermine Scottish cultural unity. As the SNL equated Scottishness with celticism, the absence of attention paid to the early part of Scottish history was not due to any problems connected with historical research, but was part of the plot to diminish the Celtic aspect of Scottish culture while promoting English influences. *Liberty* thundered against this:

> The pernicious stuff labelled as 'history' usually dealt out to Scottish children is largely composed of barefaced lies concocted under the baneful influence of John Bull. Such 'history' affects to regard the ancient Celtic speaking peoples of Scotland as being ignorant barbarians without any distinctive culture, or political ability, and who, because of these supposed defects in their character were, for their own ultimate good, driven into the mountains by a supposed superior 'race', the so called Anglo-Saxons of the lowlands, who are regarded as the bringers of civilization into the darkness of Celtic barbarism. Lies such as these only serve to spread discord among the Scottish people, in fact, they were largely invented for that purpose, and are still propagated for the same reason, although at the same time many well meaning, but unreflecting Scots accept them as Gospel and pass them on.[18]

As one might expect, similar inducements of unfairness and bias were made by League historians on aspects of later Scottish history:

> As regards the later periods of our country's history the usual unhistorical 'history' affects to regard the promoters of 'Union' with England as far seeing statesmen and high minded patriots, dis-interested men with never a thought for themselves, devoting all their energies to the betterment of their country. Genuine history, which is not taught in our schools, exposes these men as mere agents of England, nearly all of them in receipt of English money or other favours of John Bull.[19]

Members of the League believed it was more important to undo the contemporary state of Scottish historical interpretations and replace them with 'corrected' versions than concentrate on the 'petty and transient' aspects of political life. Until this was done, they argued, the Scots would not have the necessary cultural base upon which they could build their national aspirations. Consequently, the years between 1920 and 1922 witnessed members of the League engaging in the task of reshaping Scottish history with considerable relish, anxious to make amends for two centuries of Unionist bias.

In the League's account of history objectivity was often replaced by a desire to illustrate contemporary ideas in a historical context. For example, the Scots were portrayed as an inherently democratic and progressive people, and this could be traced back to the English invasion led by Edward I in the thirteenth century. William Wallace was an example of 'the great Scots patriot and lover of liberty [who] played a very important role in bursting the chains of feudalism and paved the way for the democratic principle in government'.[20] The left wing ideas of the League were also injected into the new history of Scotland. However, the conventional Marxist interpretation of two opposed classes struggling against each other was not deemed applicable in Scotland's case. The reason given for this was that it would imply that the Scots had been divided amongst themselves. Instead a colonial explanation was used to show how the whole of the Scottish people (with the exception of the unionists and Anglo-Scots) were exploited by an alien power. The reason why the exploiters had to come from England was the fact that the Scots were naturally pre-disposed towards communism and socialism: 'The community will be the ruling power and on the sane and stable foundations of Celtic culture and Celtic communism, from which Wallace drew his inspirations, we who share his convictions and speak his tongue, will use both to work out freedom for our beloved land'.[21] Just as the Scots were naturally inclined towards the left, the English tended to be capitalist exploiters and oppressors. These values, so they believed, were attributed to the result of racial characteristics. This argument was used to explain the persistent English habit of trying to conquer her northern neighbour and the latter's ability to resist:

> Scotland has fought over three hundred field battles with England to guard her sovereign rights...the Scottish people never at any time surrendered these...Scotland's position as a self-contained nation with a resourceful and unconquerable people, considerable national wealth, home industries and foreign trade attracted the envy of her southern neighbour, England, who made repeated efforts to conquer her for the possession of these.[22]

It was argued that, in keeping with an evolving imperialist nature, the English were forced to adopt new methods in order to try and gain control of the Scots. In other words 'what England was not able to wrest from Scotland on the battlefield, she set about attaining by chicanery and political intrigue'.[23] As one would expect in a 'communistically minded' nation the King eventually had to let the side down. According to the League, James VI was the lever the English first used in their new strategy of underhand colonization. Scottish hopes that in 1603 'the Auld enemy would cease their cruel and unprovoked attacks' were soon dashed because 'James accustomed as he was to being strictly kept in his place by sturdy Scots, whose outlook was distinctly democratic and republican, was amazed and delighted to find that the English were the exact opposite; servile and grovelling.'[24] The real irony, in the opinion of John MacArthur, being patriotic as ever, was the fact that it took the ability of a Scottish king to set in motion the English policy of insidious conquest. From this point onwards, the League argued, the campaign was stepped up, reaching its fruition with the Treaty of Union. Significantly, the Reformation and the religious conflicts of the seventeenth century receive little attention because of the inability to explain them within the League's concept of the perennial unity of the Scottish nation. However, there did slip through the occasional few swipes at the Protestant church.[25] The essence of pre-Union history in the eyes of the Scottish National League was that of a struggle between a democratic, progressive and Celtic people on the one hand, and an authoritarian, imperialist teutonic people on the other.

Of all the chapters of Scottish history none received such violent and vehement denunciation from members of the SNL as the era of the Treaty of Union. To them, the Union was the root cause of all Scotland's current troubles in that it openly and freely facilitated the colonization of Scottish culture, society and economy. The League did not believe there was any need to justify its termination:

> The so called Treaty of Union is a spurious document in as much as it was procured to be passed as an Act through the Scottish Parliament by force and fraud and in defiance of democratic opinion throughout the country, to say nothing of the laws regulating to the Scottish constitution.[26]

The Treaty was also condemned from the 'socialist' angle in that 'the Scottish nobles had no right or power to sell Scotland and the Scottish people. The latter opposed the Union, but were never consulted'.[27] The Treaty was not regarded as being an equal union between two nations, but rather as an underhand method of incorporating Scotland into England under the guise of the British state. It was argued that the English would not surrender any of their interests for the sake of Union and, in any case, they could always use their numerical superiority in the House of Commons. Erskine of Mar characteristically explained the situation in racial terms: 'The Teutonic character of the English Parliament is not affected by the fact that a small minority of Scots and Welsh cells sit in it...the presence of a few Scottish lackeys in an English household does not constitute that household a British dwelling place.'[28] However, after the Union, according to the League, there rose to prominence the greatest enemy of Scottish nationality; the so-called Anglo-Scot. This group was accused of collaborating with the English in order to undermine Scottish culture and national aspirations. 'Anglo-Scots' were also condemned on account of their capitalist inclinations and their tendency to suppression. It was argued that they were prominent in crushing the 1820 rising and that they exploited the situation for their own ends:

> Want and starvation, aided by a carefully arranged provocation of soldiers let loose on the street with ball cartridge and bayonet by an 'oversight' of their officers, led to the premature rising (assisted, I am led to believe, by the aid of what we now call agent provocateurs) and so, with the usual English - and shall I say Anglo-Scottish? hypocrisy, examples were made of Baird, Hardie and Wilson...[29]

However, as far as members of the League were concerned, the greatest threat posed by 'Anglo-Scots' was their perpetration of the idea of separate Lowland and Highland cultures, which was designed to be harmful to national unity.

The creation of false divisions, the League argued, was a standard practice of English colonial policy, which grouped subjugated people against each other. As one League historian explained: 'The whole of English policy throughout history has been to divide and sub-divide...she has divided the houses of her enemies against each other.'[30] This policy was considered especially loathsome as it was more often than not the Celtic side which got the short shrift of things. What the Scots needed, they argued was unity and they only had to look to Ireland for an example:

> We in Scotland have much to learn from Ireland; in this respect, we are more than ten years behind her. First we must build up our national conscience, and blushing from its discovery, we must set ourselves to build up our nationality from the foundation. The foundation — the bedrock of our Celtic origin — is already there awaiting the builders, and the cornerstone — our Gaelic language; the only national language of Scotland, is already in the hands of the hewers.[31]

As might be gathered from the above extract, during the 'Celtic' period of its history from 1920 to 1924, members of the League had little time for aspects of Lowland Scottish culture. Despite the obvious socialist and nationalist parallels which could have been made, Robert Burns received little attention. People who belonged to the League during this time were, above all, Celtic nationalists and there were many implicit criticisms of Scottish culture which had been tinged with 'Anglo-Saxon teutonism'. The SNL wanted to purge Scotland of all these cultural blemishes, and, using some Irish nationalists as a model, create an unadulterated Celtic state. The Irish were held up as examples because they fitted into Erskine's concept of the 'race struggle' between Celtic and Teutonic cultures. Racial and racist thinking determined much of the League's attitude towards contemporary situations and this type of behaviour was fairly common in many parts of Europe during the interwar years.[32] However, the idea of a 'race struggle' often went to absurd and paranoid levels: 'It was an ill day for the Celtic people when the German Georges and their German Jew supporters got their grip on Alba, Erin and England. We must unite again, clear them out, and re-establish our noble Celtic ideas in place of 'Teutonic Kultur' and its military despotism now trying to rule our nations.'[33] Although in their ambitions to 're-celticize' Scotland members of the League often brought positive cultural values to bear, such as encouraging an interest in Gaelic and Scottish history, they often plunged head first into vulgar racism. Scottish independence was advocated by one person simply because Scots 'hate Anglo Saxon rule as heartily as their brethren in Ireland'.[34] Others claimed that the English were racially predisposed towards lies, deceit, treachery, etc.[35] Much of this vulgar anti-English feeling was fuelled by events in Ireland, which raised many League tempers. The problems, they argued, were caused by the English trying to force colonial rule on Ireland through military means. The British Army was referred to as the 'English Army of Occupation' and *Liberty* regularly disseminated Sinn Fein propaganda. A common example reads as follows:

> They invade a peaceful and prosperous Irish town, they stir up hell and leave it like Ypres, and as they depart after an outrage and murder, leaving blackened and bare walls smouldering fire and death, they raise their drunken throats in the battle hymn of Britain; 'Boys of the Bulldog breed'. Balbriggen will go down to history amongst all the other English atrocities as a particularly outstanding incidence of barbarism.[36]

The Scots, the League argued, should have no truck with the British in Ireland because, as Erskine of Mar explained, 'It is the English and the Irish that are now at feud, as they have been for centuries, and not ourselves'.[37] However, racial obligations dictated which side ought to receive moral support, 'we desire nothing so much as she [Ireland] should 'down' England in her unequal struggle with that power.'[38]

Although most founders of the SNL displayed a close affinity to a vague concept of socialism, their attitude towards the Labour Party was much more ambiguous and confused. Much of this confusion arose from the fact that the Labour Party in 1920 was paying regular lip service to the idea of Scottish Home Rule. William Gillies and several other members of the London branch were also members of that city's Scots Labour Club. Initially, the League's presidency was shared by Erskine of Mar and Govan Labour MP, Neil Maclean, who, after a year's service, resigned because he thought the organisation was far too extremist.[39] It seems very likely that Maclean, like many others, had no idea what the League was about when he agreed to sharing its presidency. Robert Smilie was one of many trade union leaders who, in principle, promised to support the SNL and Scots Labour MPs were invited in 1920 to speak at the League's meetings in London, and a few did.[40] At this time nothing was considered amiss with having members, who also belonged to another political organisation. However, this benign view of the Labour Party was to come under increasing attack because of its association of 'Westminsterism'. Erskine of Mar was the most fervent opponent of this, arguing that to go to the House of Commons was to admit English dominance and sovereignty over Scotland. Independence, he argued, would not be obtained by this method and soon scepticism about the intentions of the Labour Party became evident:

> The possible advent of a Labour Government in so called 'Great Britain' would not give Scotland freedom. The English Labour men would predominate, and being Englishmen, with a natural gift for interfering in what does not concern them, would now and again, as long as the Union lasts, prevent the development of Scottish aspirations.[41]

However, members of the League found a contemporary solution to the problem of reconciling their 'socialism' with nationalism, by questioning the integrity and objectives of English socialists while, at the same time, attempting to persuade their Scottish comrades of the merits of greater detachment from the British movement. Again the Scots' racial predisposition towards socialism was emphasised: 'It is not without significance, that, with scarcely one exception, the doughtiest opponents of capitalist rule throughout England's cracking Empire are men of Celtic blood and Gaelic name.'[42] There were few direct denunciations of the Scottish Labour Party as most members of the League hoped to persuade them of the errors of their ways. Many argued that the current political system and the British parties were of no use and had always failed Scottish Home Rule in the past. The British commitment to Scottish self-government was skin deep, as one member claimed: 'in order that constituents may be properly gulled, a sham Bill is from time to time introduced. After some show of mock heroics the Bill disappears.'[43] Although the Parliamentary system was not considered as a suitable avenue for achieving progress, neither was violence or armed insurrection. In spite of the fact that they were greatly influenced by Irish nationalists, few League members believed anything constructive could be achieved by emulating their armed struggle. In any case, the option was not available because, as they readily admitted, militant nationalism did not exist in Scotland and even if it did, it would simply play into the hands of the British militia: 'We... are not going to oblige with an Amritsar, nor even a Peterloo. Our weapons are not material, but they will be none the less effective.'[44]

What exactly these 'weapons' were received no elaboration and the League's policy of political action languished in a sea of indecision. The Sinn Fein tactic of having elected MPs convening in Dublin and refusing to go to Westminster struck a positive chord among many members. This policy was thought to have potential for Scotland and was named the Lockhart policy after Lockhart of Carnwath who, in the eighteenth century, advocated that the Scottish MPs should withdraw as a body from Westminster and reconstitute the Scottish Parliament. A number of League members believed this to be the only viable option available:

> The only policy consistent with national self-respect and with potential efficiency is to revive and improve the Lockhart policy...Our remedy is the first General Election, when we can have our candidates in the field ready to go to Edinburgh as our representatives. Ireland has done this.[45]

However, in 1920, this was idle day dreaming. The League had neither the public support nor the necessary organisation built up to make this a realistic option. Also, it ran against the views of Erskine of Mar, who was against using even the smallest part of the Westminster machinery. The inability of the League to agree on what political direction to take, opened up the floodgates for most naive and simplistic notions: 'In place of Westminsterism let us engage in constructive work in Scotland itself. By doing so the English government machine may gradually be edged out. Bit by bit, the Scottish people can obtain control of their own affairs'.[46] Members of the League showed an extreme reluctance to face up to the reality of the problems posed by the British political system and by doing so rendered their political ambitions futile.

By 1922, the League had made little progress. They had neglected to develop the degree of political philosophy necessary to appear as a credible political organisation. The chronic lack of realistic policies, the ineffective and limited party machinery, together with half-baked and muddy objectives, had led the League to struggle to maintain the support of its handful of followers. No one, inside or outside, could make up their minds as to what kind of organisation the SNL was. The leadership still regarded detailed discussions of policies, other than general propaganda, as irrelevant. The fact that the League was wandering about like some headless political chicken led to increasing dissatisfaction among rank and file members. Action was demanded, especially, as by now, the Irish question had been resolved:

> What shall we do to be saved? Form up, get shoulder to shoulder, stand together, proclaim our principles, raise the banner of Scotland once again. Talk during the winter months will not suffice. Ceilidhs and picnics will not do, meetings at intervals, without sustained effort is unavailing...Let the Scots National League move, or for that matter, any League that has for its object, the Independence of Scotland. But for God's sake move.'[47]

Many felt an urge for more action because the Labour Party had made significant electoral gains in Scotland. With the Clydesiders proclaiming the necessity of Home Rule many in the League felt they would be left behind in the clamour for Scottish self-government. However, the responses of the leadership to the charges of inactivity were full of self-justification and probably did more to damage their credibility than allay membership fears. Confusion and woolly-mindedness reigned supreme:

> A chief theme...is an absence of any constructive policy on the part of the League...The League has a very well thought out scheme based on the past history, present conditions and future development of Scotland. Connected with the movement, not out of necessity, but prominent on the propaganda side, are writers and thinkers well versed in the peculiar needs of their own country and students of the other national renaissances in other lands, who are eminently qualified to give a lead in the initiation and launching of organised efforts in the special departments for which their experience and research qualifies them so well.[48]

This was vacuous nonsense, more concerned with promoting self-flattery than an attempt to answer the accusations of inactivity and lack of direction. There is no evidence of any such 'experts', and, in any case, their advice, identity and knowledge were never divulged in any meaningful way. The more the leadership tried to justify themselves the more ridiculous they sounded. Members were asked to believe that the League was following an intricate and pre-determined plan:

> A moment's thought also should convince our critical friend that the time for construction has not yet arrived. 'A time to break down', in the words of the preacher, very significantly preceded 'a time to build up'; we are at the first stage now. Attempts to build up our Celtic state while the soil is encumbered by the fallen and still tumbling edifice of post feudalistic cum capitalist masses of crumbling masonry would be worse than futile. There are many well meanimg reformers, who are still endeavouring to do this. Not only are they wasting their own labour and obstructing the pioneer

levellers of the old fabric, but in most cases they are even bolstering up the ruins and making them tenable still longer for the ghouls to infest them.[49]

This philosophy displayed an incredible degree of naivety and arrogance. In pseudo-Marxist terms, Scottish nationality was portrayed as something inevitable, which would triumph as a result of impersonal historical forces in which endeavours to change the political scene were of no account. What was worse still, the League, not content with its own inaction, began to fire off at random at other groups, whose actions were helping to bring public attention to the Home Rule issue. Even the Highland Land League was criticized: 'Our Land League friends are out for the freeing of the soil from the grasp of the stranger, and instead of making all sport in Scotland impossible, they spend money to send candidates to the sportsman's club in Westminster.'[50] As the SNL was not itself prepared to advocate a policy of civil disobedience and disruption in the Highland estates, their criticisms of the Highland Land League were totally unjustified. The Labour Party was also attacked for trying to be constructive: 'Our socialist friends of all shades of opinion follow suit, oblivious to the fact that, patent to all who use their senses, the power to put their laudable schemes to the practical test can never be obtained from Westminster.'[51] The League's attitude towards the Home Rule movement was negative, obstructionist and offered no credible alternative strategy. Few people in Scotland believed there was anything wrong in giving the Labour Party a chance to carry the Home Rule banner and, judging from the contemporary political scene in 1922, they had the best chance of bringing this policy to fruition. Discounting omniscience, the League had no evidence of how the Labour Party would act once in government. Much of the League's leadership's grumbling simply may have been sour grapes because the Home Rule movement had taken off without them and no one appeared desirous of their expert advice. The simple formula of 'First the destruction of alien power and influence where ever it appears on the surface or under the surface, and then it will be time for the measuring tape. The architect's plans will be produced when required'[52] appealed to no one. Apart from colourful metaphors and the prospect of waging a cultural guerilla war, the League, during this phase of its history, had nothing positive to offer the Scottish national movement. This simple fact accounts for their small amount of support.

During its 'Celtic romanticist period', what the League lacked in terms of concrete policies it made up by giving vent to furious anti-English sentiment. Of all things, abstract or otherwise, the English were to receive the most generous helpings of League abuse, which was usually based on the pretext of an examination of racial characteristics. Erskine of Mar described the history of the British Isles as a struggle between two races and cultures, Celtic and Teutonic. The English had gradually become the dominant influence, and as a result of their direct influence Celtic culture experienced a severe setback in 1745. Erskine and others believed this situation was being reversed. Accordingly, the attempts to promote the Gaelic language and the re-emergence of Scottish nationalism were evidence of a 'rising tide of Celtic awareness'.[53] This 'Celticism' was used as the basis to explain the racial difference between the Scots and the English. However, these ideas often spilled over into rampant anglophobia and relegated political considerations to second place. Hence, Scots should not use the British Parliamentary system because: 'it was humiliating and degrading for Scotland to beg for justice in Westminster'.[54] The League was forever reluctant to let bygones be bygones, especially the history of armed conflict between the two nations:

> When the Scots people make up their minds to have freedom again, it will be theirs for the taking. There will be no repetition of England's 'method of barbarism' in Ireland, which she now sees and admits to have been a failure. England would not dare attempt such methods in Scotland. She knows too well what came of her former attempts, and does not want another Bannockburn...we are not afraid of war and do not desire war with England.[55]

Although much of this anti-English sentiment was expressed in the format of 'racial' theories, and in a non-personal way, on many occasions the intellectual trappings fell off to expose a naked prejudice of a less sophisticated nature. In March, 1922, Lewis Spence wrote about 'The English Peril in Scotland'. His main concern was his perceived increase in English immigration and its effect on Scottish society. Spence believed that this was evidence of an attempt to colonize Scotland and destroy the native culture:

> I feel it my duty to warn my fellow countrymen of the danger which undoubtedly threatens them of being absorbed by the swarming thousands of the South...Such conditions, of course, constitute a serious menace to Scots nationality. These thousands have come to stay. Filled with Saxon arrogance and contemptuous of their neighbours and surroundings, they are not content to accept the manners of their adopted country but constitute in themselves a distinct colony — the nucleus of a settlement which if prompt measures be not forthcoming for its suppression, is destined to strike a serious and damaging blow at the entire fabric of Scots Nationality.[56]

William Gillies was just as paranoid, bemoaning the quality of the new immigrants: 'Insidious and increasing, the English peril has recently taken on alarming proportions, as the English cities have to get rid of their surplus population, undesirables and weaklings unfit for the rougher life of the colonies, and from these elements Scotland gets her new citizens.'[57] The social implications of this immigration were claimed to have grave consequences for Scottish daily life. Not only was there a threat to culture, the Scots were also being economically undermined:

> The character of the neighbourhood in which the English reside has undergone a complete alteration. The shops in the district have been taken over by glib English tradesmen, who not only supply the strangers, but by assiduous hat touching, and the sycophantic manners peculiar to the lesser Saxon, have secured the patronage of many Scots people; so that the business of the native tradesmen languish.[58]

Such attitudes put paid to any attempt to make the League a serious political organisation. Despite the garb of racial anthropology, the League's ideas about the English were little more than vulgar prejudice. However, in fairness it must be stated that the League was not racially chauvinistic. They supported Indian, Arabic and African nationalists in their quest for independence within the British Empire on the principle of national self-determination.[59]

Negative and obscure thinking reached new depths of unreality in March 1922, when the leadership decided that members ought to boycott the electoral system:

> Members of the SNL are reminded that in neither general nor particular elections ordered by the English Government to be held in Scotland, is it becoming for them to take any part whatsover. As such elections are held by a usurpal power, as it is in no way obligatory to take part in them, they should be boycotted by all Leaguers. The National Committee hopes that this rule will be strictly observed by all head branches, provincial branches and groups. Further, the National Committee recommends to all nationalists throughout the country that they follow the League's example and abstain from exercising the English Parliamentary sufferage.[60]

Erskine of Mar's pathological disdain for all things connected with Westminster only helped to disenfranchise League members; a move that was unlikely to bring any amount of progress. This motion was another indication of the chronic lack of realism prevalent among the leadership, which was becoming simultaneously more paranoid and ridiculous in its outlook. A lack of concern about ordinary political issues was stemmed by more and more bizarre conjectures. For example, Lewis Spence claimed that the SNL's fortunes were being undermined by an extensive Unionist conspiracy: 'Recent intensive examination of forces at work in Scotland has led me to form the opinion that a secret organisation, the object of which is to destroy the nationality of Scotland, exists in London'.[61] According to Spence, this organisation was responsible for a campaign designed to destroy Scottish cultural, industrial, banking, and railway interests. Whether Spence genuinely believed his own propaganda or not is a matter for contention, but the statement does illustrate the farcical depth to which the League had sunk. Foremost among these conspirators were 'English diehards and Anglo-Scots of vindictive anti-national proclivities, chief among them, it is believed, is Sir Henry Craik, Scotland's Old Man of the Sea. Colonel John Buchan, the novelist, pseudo-Scot and late chief of the English Secret Service is also believed to be implicated'.[62] In spite of all their efforts to evade the issue, the main problem facing the League as a political organisation was its lack of support and credibility. Neither of these two things would be forthcoming to a group as politically barren as the Scots National League. What this meant was that until the League had more concrete and feasible political goals and objectives which were strong enough to enter the political arena and challenge the existing political parties, they would remain an obscure pressure group. The main reason for the League's initial failure was the inability of the leadership to grasp the political realities of the day. Much of the outlook of the early SNL was shaped by 19th Century and pre-First World War ideas about Scottish nationalism, which was romantic, backward looking and largely apolitical. Erskine of Mar, William Gillies and Lewis Spence had their nationalism shaped more by cultural inclinations rather than social, economic and political factors. Likewise, Gillies and Erskine were more influenced by events in Ireland than in Scotland. Pragmatism was not their forte, and it is easier to categorize them among nineteenthth century nationalists such as John Stuart Blackie and John Murdoch, than with people like Roland Muirhead and Tom Gibson, who were firmly grounded in the twentieth century. However, events which happened outside in the real political world were to save the Scottish National League from political oblivion.

When George Buchanan's Home Rule Bill failed its first stage in the House of Commons in May 1924, it sent shock waves through all the nationalist circles. The waves of disquiet were extenuated because there appeared to be a considerable degree of ambiguity in support for the Bill among the leadership of the Parliamentary Labour Party.[63] Although most Scottish Home Rulers held their peace and continued to hold their faith in the Labour Party, several did not, and left the SHRA. One of these people was Tom Gibson, who then joined the SNL and was to have a crucial impact on the development of the organisation. Gibson argued, in clear and precise terms, that the only way forward for Scottish Home Rule was through a purely Scottish organisation dedicated to that principle. This movement ought to have no connections with the established British political parties because, he argued, by virtue of an English numerical superiority, Scottish interests would be subordinated, or over-ridden in favour of the British majority. All these conclusions were based on the experiences he had gained as a member of the Scottish Home Rule Association and its gradual domination by the Labour Party which, in any case, had failed to deliver the goods in May, 1924. Gibson's argument was simple and straight to the point: 'The present political parties are dominated by, and their policies controlled by English majorities in each, and I cannot conceive that Scottish political independence will ever be acquired through the medium of any of the parties'.[64] Gibson, who was more inclined to the centre of the political stage, was sceptical of the Labour Party's future pledges on Home Rule, because they had blown a perfect chance and seemed none too perturbed about it. The tame attitude of the SHRA had shown it was little more than an adjunct of the Labour Party. They were, he argued, 'under the domination of the Socialist Party, a party which is in turn dominated by an English majority'.[65] No British political party, he stated, would ever secure Scottish Home Rule as this went against English imperial aspirations over its northern neighbour: 'The failure in the past of any Home Rule Organisation was, in my opinion, due to the predominance of English elements in these parties'.[66] Although the Labour Party had emerged as a new force in British politics, Gibson did not believe that they would change the situation in any way because they would eventually succumb to the same pressures of British orientation which had affected the Liberal Party in the past. The goal of Scottish independence, he argued, 'would only be obtained through the medium of a Scottish National Party, independent of any of the present political parties and having as its chief objective the attainment of Scottish political independence, but at the same time paying attention to the more pressing problems of the day'.[67] This latter point was very important because Gibson realized that in order to attract support and make it a 'live' political issue, it was necessary to tackle and explain existing social and economic problems within the context of the Home Rule debate. Such problems, he argued, could not be ignored because their ultimate solution would not be obtained without self-government. Although Home Rule as an abstract idea found ready public approval,

Gibson believed that until it was explained to ordinary people in terms of its relevance to bread and butter issues, it would not receive the priority of attention necessary to make it the most important political issue of the day.

However, before Gibson could do any of this, his first task was to help put the League's house in order. As the SNL never had a large following, they suffered comparatively little in the way of contact with the British political parties. Gibson believed that this 'freedom from contamination' would be the League's main source of strength, and was indeed the principal reason for his own enrolment. He was soon made chairman of the Glasgow Area Branch and set to work in an effort to resolve the League's ambiguity pertaining to the question of British parties. Largely at his own instigation, the following branch resolution appeared in December, 1924:

> That any person or organisation attached to, working with, or in any way bound to any party, institution or organisation interfering in any way politically with Scottish affairs and dominated by an English majority, is not competent or authorized to speak on behalf of the independent Scottish nation and any action taken by such a person, party or organisation and not approved by the League, shall be and is hereby repudiated and that branch secretary be instructed to inform the National Secretary accordingly.[68]

After a short period of time, this resolution was accepted in principle by the League and was incorporated into their constitution. Gibson's immediate objective in following this course of action was to isolate the SNL from the SHRA, which, as a result of its involvement in the 1924 Home Rule failure, was now believed to be a discredited organisation. Any members, who belonged to both groups were given the choice of remaining in one or the other as the Association was filed under the category of a British political establishment. League members were urged to hold no sympathies with the SHRA and rumours of a possible fusion of the two groups and the idea of sending a delegation to the Scottish National Convention, were quickly scotched. The National Secretary, Ian Scott, assured members that: 'no overtures have been made by the League concerning a fusion from our side with them. They shall have to join the SNL if they want our help...The Scots National League is going stand on its own feet'.[69] Gibson was confident that the SNL's uncompromising attitude would ultimately be vindicated, and that all those in favour of Scottish self-government would come to realize that the only way to obtain their objective was through the League or some other tailor made Home Rule party. By 1925, there was an air of optimism among members. Although much work remained to be done, membership was on the increase and more realistic modes of operation were being adopted. The first victim to fall to Gibson's quest against League 'collaborators' was Erskine of Mar, who had unwittingly agreed to speak at the SHRA Wallace Day meeting in 1925. At first diplomacy was tried and the situation was explained in philosophical terms, justifying the necessity of isolating themselves from British groups.[70] However, when his appeals to reason failed, Gibson challenged Erskine's position within the leadership of the League in forthright terms. The following Glasgow Branch resolution was threatened:

> Having heard with astonishment that the President of the League has consented to be one of the speakers at a demonstration held under the auspices of the SHRA, believes that the invitation was engineered by the anti-home rule section of the SHRA, in order to embarrass the Glasgow Area Branch in its activities, the Glasgow Area Branch declares that it can no longer have confidence in the Hon. R. Erskine of Mar as president of the League and requests that action be taken forthwith by the National Executive.[71]

Gibson refused to back down over the issue; stating that 'by this resolution I stand or fall'. Few people in the National Executive were prepared to support the erratic Erskine against their most gifted organiser who had built up the Glasgow Area Branch into the largest in the League. Also, if the resolution had been passed it is unlikely that Erskine's credibility would have taken the strain. Hardly anybody in the SNL had any respect left for his romantic notions on Celticism, which was now being challenged by Gibson's reasoned and logical political pragmatism. Shortly before the demonstration was to have taken place, Erskine backed down and Gibson's point had been made. From now on Erskine was no longer able to treat the League as if it was his own private organisation. By the end of 1925, the League had taken the first steps towards becoming a more self-disciplined organisation with all officials having given written affirmation of the constitution, which prohibited contact with organisations, or associations, connected with the established British political parties.

Throughout 1925 and 1926, further moves were taken to knock the League into the shape of a functioning political organisation by instigating regular conferences, making officials and leaders more responsible to the members and streamlining the decision-making process. Objectives and policy were no longer the narrow prerogative of the London Celticists, but were to be formulated by the membership, who elected representatives to give expression to these opinions at annual conferences where decisions were voted on. One of the first objectives expressed in the inaugural annual conference held in June 1926, was to reduce the influence of the London leadership. It was a considerable source of grievance that both the President and the Vice-President, Erskine of Mar and William Gillies respectively, resided in London. Also, the League's unofficial journal the *Monthly Intelligencer* was printed and largely written in London. The appalling lack of success prior to 1926 was blamed on the influence of the Celticists and their lack of real contact with Scotland. However, the June 1926 conference decreed that all members of the Executive Committee now had to live in Scotland. Also the conference voted to establish a chairman, Hugh Paterson, who would act as a focal point for the leadership, while the Presidencies of Erskine and Gillies were demoted upstairs to 'honorary' ones.

Although the League was beginning to tighten up its organisational structure, the day-to-day running of the League left a great deal to be desired. The most urgent need was for an effective Central Office, which could control and administer the network of emerging branches. Gibson wrote to Paterson highlighting their inadequacies:

> I am in perfect agreement with what you say about Central Offices...we could make no progress until we had a secretary at C.O. with time, ability, education and enthusiasm, capable of carrying out the instructions of the Executive Committee. At present the E.C. is most ineffective. We meet, we jaw, we disperse to our various caves until the next meeting...a strong and intelligent C.O. is absolutely essential if we are to open new branches or even keep in touch with the existing ones.[72]

Throughout 1926, Gibson and Paterson made concerted efforts to establish and embellish the administrative framework of the League in order to facilitate its expansion. In addition to more local branches, an informative new journal, the *Scots Independent* was established, which acted as the League's official mouthpiece. The *Scots Independent* kept members informed of organisational progress and was a forum for policy objectives and ideas, which, in turn, helped to attract new members and kept morale high. However, in spite of progress made on the administrative front, the League had to contend with a history of chronic interfactional disputes, of which many were well publicised.[73] The most serious incident was the argument which led Lewis Spence to form a breakaway group called the Scottish National Movement. The SNM, which was set up in the first months of 1926, was created not from ideological or political reasons, but was the result of petty bickering and slandering between Spence and the Treasurer of the SNL, R.M.

Brown. The incident caused dismay among League members because, politically and ideologically, there were supposedly no real differences between the two organisations:

> There is no difference between the objects of the SNL and the 'movement'...There is no doubt that, owing to a few officials in the East taking sides in a petty quarrel - we in the West refuse to take sides or interfere — some interruption in the work of the SNL took place. But that has now been overcome.[74]

Perhaps Gibson was trying to be blasé in this last statement, and underestimated the damage in the interest of morale. However, the departure of Spence considerably reduced membership in Edinburgh and the entire Dunfermline Branch (bar one) of 65 members joined the Movement en bloc.[75] The pettiness of the squabble and its ensuing results, together with the bad publicity which followed the affair, obviously had some demoralizing effect on members of the League. Even in June, 1926, Iain Gillies was complaining of a lack of commitment among some members, who 'presently at least, take too detached an interest in activities'.[76] What was worse, after Spence's departure, the Edinburgh branch sank into organisational chaos, which, as one of the key centres of the League, was potentially disastrous. Even after the 'disruption' petty bickering still continued in the East. Iain Gillies lamented, with perhaps more than a slight touch of Western bias, that 'it is a great pity Edinburgh folk are so lacking in spirit and common sense, presumably'.[77]

Undoubtedly the departure of Spence and his brood was a blow to the SNL, however its effects were harmful in the short-term only. It is important to place these difficulties within the context of a changing and developing political organisation. After all, much of the petty squabbling was a result of the efforts to build the League into an expanding and credible political group. After four or five years of stagnation, such a process was not likely to be easy as it involved considerable re-orientation in an organisation which had been very conservative in its ways. The bickering was symptomatic of the SNL's lack of self-discipline, which was now gradually being brought under control. Although Spence was a colourful and charismatic figure, he was also politically naive and had little time for, nor understanding of, the political apparatus. He was first and foremost a cultural nationalist and failed to take account of anything outside that sphere. Spence was also guilty of some of the League's most virulent anti-English writings and the author of some bizarre ideas on achieving Scottish self-government.[78] In the long-term such an obstreperous and naive leader would have been a positive hindrance to the League's progress, and few pragmatists in the organisation viewed his departure with sorrow.

However, while the League was experiencing negative setbacks, it was also on the threshold of receiving major positive boosts. Perhaps the most important event to change the SNL's political fortunes was the publication of its new journal, the *Scots Independent*. In April,1926, Gibson first drew up plans for a newspaper which would contain articles on such matters as the social and economic problems facing contemporary Scottish life.[79] As mentioned earlier, this was considered vital because it illustrated the importance and relevance of Home Rule to the ordinary person. The Celtic Romanticism of Erskine of Mar had proved a heroic failure and had motivated no one to action. What was now required was a philosophical underpinning of Scottish nationalism which was pragmatic and relevant to the contemporary political issues. The *Scots Independent* was to be the vehicle for the expression of these new ideas on Scottish nationality. The emphasis was now on issues that were positive and forward looking. Social, economic, political and cultural affairs were to be tackled by the new philosophy, which would act as a polemic against opponents of the League. Also, it was hoped that it would attract new members: 'It will be a paper for the man in the street, you will find no highbrow stuff or articles written just for the sake of smart phrasing...What the editor does not want are; long letters with padding, articles breathing hate or jealousy of England; hysterical statements and above all, abuse of persons who may be opposed to us'.[80] The *Scots Independent* was an attempt to dispel the cranky image of the League by the advocation of rational argument which was aimed at ordinary Scots people in order to further their case. Gibson was the *SI*'s business manager, while William Gillies was the editor. Although a member of the London branch and one of the original Celticists, Gillies had acted as one of Gibson's consorts in helping to usher in an era of reform. He had abandoned Celticism as a political idea and had replaced it with a much more positive image of Scottish nationalism. In doing this, he had been much influenced by his son Iain, who put pressure on his father to accept Gibson's directives, because he believed them to be the only way forward for the League. Iain Gillies acted as an intermediary between the two men and had no doubts as to what kind of organisation the SNL ought to be:

> To my mind Scotland's need is a National Party, advocating full self-government; anti-jingo and anti-militarist; strongly radical in its general outlook and prepared to face the question of housing and land on socialist

lines: These two problems at least...I feel that if the SNL object included some such progressive platform, our position would be clearer and greater support would be forthcoming.[81]

Iain Gillies was to be a main contributor to the new journal, and his attitude was to take a modernised Scottish nationalism into the political arena and intellectually challenge the other political parties for support among the electorate. Gillies was inclined to the left and believed that the new dominant political idea in the world would be socialism. Consequently, he targeted his brand of nationalism at potential Labour voters. Also, he believed that it was important to educate people about the 'political realities' of the Scottish situation:

> Convince the Scottish progressive that Westminster action is futile, prove by our radical policy that we are not reactionary and I believe we shall get our necessary support... Attempts at conciliation and cooperation will only encourage them (the SHRA) in a belief of our weakness. Quiet confidence will force them to move along the right road in order that they may not suffer loss of membership...The day will come when the divergence of interests between Scots and English sections of the parties can no linger be ignored.[82]

When that day dawned Gillies wanted the SNL, by virtue of its policies and support, to be in a position to be the most able representative of the Scottish national movement.

An obvious first target for the League to challenge was the authority of the Labour Party in Scotland. The basis and principles of this party were subjected to close scrutiny. The Scottish socialist was called on to take cognizance of the concept of nationality and accept the fact that no truly scientific socialism could fail to take account of it. Indeed, it was argued that any legitimate intellectual foundation for the Scottish Labour Party was lacking because of its subservience to the British Labour leadership. This, it was claimed, rendered all their Scottish aspirations bogus. There was a need, the Rev. Malcolm MacColla argued, for Scottish socialists to subject themselves to considerable self-analysis. 'The circumstances call for a review of the entire position of Scotland by Scottish socialists and especially by those who are engaged in Labour college work. Their textbooks have been English; their study of past history has been confined to England. They have built around themselves a paper wall of English books; no wonder the common Marxist cannot see Scotland'.[83] The lack of independence faced by Scottish socialists was highlighted by drawing attention to the failure of Buchanan's Home Rule Bill and the exclusion of some of Wheatley's Housing Act clauses. The failure in both cases was attributed to English

Labour interests. How, argued the League, could Scottish Labour deliver Home Rule when it did not even enjoy this as a principle within the ranks of the British Labour movement?

> Socialist members! Do you remember that memorable occasion, when fired by election triumphs, you raised your voices in psalm and pledged yourselves to the cause of Scottish self-government...your pledges have been cast aside; the English Government formed by your Party refused facilities for the introduction of a Scots Home Rule Bill, refused to allow in its Wheatley's Housing Act clauses necessary to ensure the provision of houses in Scotland. You have been as neglectful of Scotland as the members of any other Party; you have wasted in futile discussions opportunities that might have been devoted to Scottish affairs. You pay lip service to self-government; you have admitted its urgent need. You have drafted a separate Land policy for Scotland and admit the impossibility of its ever becoming law and its impracticability of operation without prior attainment of a new Scottish Parliament. You have raised no effective protest against any of the many recent insults to Scotland and encroachments on her rights. Can you wonder that in Scottish eyes you are deemed as useless.[84]

The kid gloves were off! Labour was attacked more than the other parties because of the seeming ambiguity in their policies and also, because it was believed the League would be able to steal their support. It was felt that this was a soft spot worth exploiting. As regards to the other parties, the Liberals had become, more or less, a spent force in Scottish politics, and it was thought that they were no longer worth bothering about. The Conservative Party, which had an uncompromising view on Scottish Home Rule, received only the usual habitual condemnation. Apart from theoretical ambiguities, the League seized with a vengeance any dichotomies between Scottish and British Labour interests. The confused approach by the Scottish Labour Party to the threatened closure of the Rosyth naval dockyards was exploited mercilessly. It was argued that the proposed closure was partially the result of the Labour Party's demands for pacifism and disarmament. The SNL accused the Scottish Labour MPs of being little more than Westminster lackeys, while the SHRA kept, as far as possible, an awkward silence about the whole affair.[85] In October 1925, the League organised its first full-scale protest meeting, which pulled in over 1000 people who were anxious as to the future of the dockyards. As a result of this successful activity, several local branches were set up in the area, with the one in Inverkeithing attracting a respectable figure of over 200 members.[86] An extension of the theme of attacking the Labour Party was highlighting the lack of freedom the SHRA suffered. The failure of the Rev. James Barr's Bill in May, 1927, and the almost total lack of enthusiasm with which it was pursued was gleefully reported by the SNL to create tensions within the Association:

> The Bill was introduced with the usual talk by the Rev. James Barr, seconded by Mr. Tom Johnston and talked out by Mr. MacQuisten. The Labour members achieved their objective; they can now return to Scotland and say they have done everything within their power to secure self-government! It was a pity — from his own point of view — that Mr. Johnston showed how little he cared for the Bill by predicting the result of the half hour talk. The mover and seconder well knew that the Bill was doomed to be talked out, and the whole farce would have to be started over again — not this year, but next year or sometime. Surely our Home Rule friends can now realize the futility of all their efforts and tactics — the utter stupidity of putting any trust, so far as Scotland's rights are concerned, in the pledges of any members representing Scots sections of the three English parties. The Scots National League points the right way with its policy of ignoring English politics, concentrating on Scottish issues and endeavouring to rally supporters of Scottish self-government into one democratic and progressive League with the sole object of securing for Scotland this most important and first of all reforms.[87]

In spite of the fact that no official contacts existed between the SNL and the SHRA, many of the Association's members were coming to the same political conclusions as held by the League, much to the chagrin of the Scottish Labour Party.[88] The SNL played on the fact that many members of the SHRA were readers of the *Scots Independent* and tried to foster demands for the creation of a new 'national party'. Also, from inside and outside the Association, more hefty commitments were now being sought from the Scottish Labour Party. Malcolm MacColla's demands were typical: Scottish Labour MPs should pledge to 'work and vote as a Scottish Party. To decline office in any English Labour Government; to demand as English Labour's first use of its power the fulfilment of its pledges in favour of Scottish self-determination'.[89] Few people with any sense of political realism believed the Labour Party would change its order of priorities, and the League concentrated on giving tacit support to those people in the SHRA who advocated the creation of a new 'national party'. Calls for such a party had become more and more insistent and were only defeated by Labour's stranglehold on the policies of the Association.[90] However, the League encouraged these people to persist: 'We regret that the Scottish Home Rule Association has been compelled by an adverse vote to put aside the idea of a national party. We trust that this may only be temporary, and that when the "National Party" is again mooted in that body, the idea will be divested of any connection with the Westminster

Parliament'.[91] As the Labour Party's indifference to the nationalist claims increased, many in the League believed there would soon be an opportunity to lead the Home Rule movement under their own philosophical flag.

The *Scots Independent* was an effective proponent of the new nationalist ideas and had subscriptions placed in over 100 public libraries.[92] Even Tom Johnston's *Forward* had to sit up and take notice of the newcomer, and a defence campaign was launched to protect the record of Scots Labour MPs, although the challenge to intellectual debate was declined.[93] Also, Edwin Scrymgeour MP quoted facts and figures from the *SI* in Parliamentary debates.[94] In September, 1927, the journal carried an article of considerable importance written by Iain Gillies called 'Scotland's need: A National Party'. The article was designed to sway Home Rulers in the SHRA to adopt the League's dictum that self-government could only be obtained by an organisation independent of the British political parties. Gillies was hopeful that, with mounting disaffection in the Association over Labour's policies, the article would receive a sympathetic hearing. His emphasis was on the need for unity among nationalists:

> Various organisations, with more or less success, are spreading the gospel of Self Determination for Scotland. One may well ask what good purpose is served by this multiplicity of bodies that profess the same, or similar objects. But of these there are notably two — the Scots National League and the Scottish Home Rule Association — that show some signs of effective propaganda and durable work in organisation. It is the height of greatness to produce two blades of grass where one grew before; but it is surely the height of folly to perpetuate two organisations where one would do.[95]

Gillies was obviously being generous to the Association in his assessment of their achievements and propaganda in order not to give offence. This was a sop in order to make more palatable his suggestion that the two groups should combine their respective forces into one organisation. He believed that the League's policies and ideological motivation, when combined with Muirhead's finance and the boost that would accrue from the activities of the SHRA membership, would present an effective challenge to the British parties in Scotland. However, there remained a number of differences between the two groups, especially concerning the definition of 'Home Rule' and it was by no means clear that the Association would lie down and submit to the League's ideological domination. Gillies felt that the best way to persuade members of the Association that the SNL had the best policies was to highlight SHRA weaknesses. As the League had not yet undergone any acid test of political importance, this was a safe option to try.

As far as the SNL was concerned, nationalists would now have to stand for election on their own ticket. However, as elections were expensive and required effort and an effective political machine, many believed it was only sensible for all Scottish nationalists to pool their resources:

> To achieve independence it is necessary to bring Scottish politics before the Scottish electors and to organise opinion in favour of Self-government independently of the Scottish sections of the English political parties...The present policy of the League as recently adopted 'by means of the existing electoral machinery to obtain a *majority* of Scottish representatives pledged to remain on Scottish soil and to resume the powers of govern-ment'...Abstention from Westminster is not necessarily entailed by the League policy until such time as a majority of the representatives in favour of independence is obtained.[96]

This was a significant step forward in the League's political thinking, and may well have been designed to motivate members of the SHRA into action because it is questionable if the SNL had, at that time (June, 1927), sufficient resources to fight elections on its own. They compared their own policies to those of the Association:

> In our campaign we are forced up against the vested interests in Scotland of the English political parties and their agents. That fact is often ignored. The efforts of our Home Rule friends to achieve their object by stroking the backs of the Scottish candidates of the English parties is futile. It reminds us of the remark made by the celebrated wit, Sidney Smith, to a little girl who was stroking a tortoise. 'You might as well pat the dome of St Pauls Cathedral to give pleasure to the Dean and Chapter!'[97]

While, at the same time as condemning the Association's policies as futile, the League did offer an olive branch in the form of the idea of a national party. The national party idea was used by the League as an honourable way out for nationalists in the SHRA who, much to their embarrassment, had backed a lame horse. Throughout 1927, the League applied psychological pressure on members of the Association by forcing them to choose between the two modes of operation available. The League's criticism was temperate; it was designed to hurt, but not to provoke hostility:

> In terms of the latest Bill sponsored by the Home Rule Association, it certainly failed in important respects...Its form of presentation to the predominantly English Parliament for approval was acceptance of the implicit English claim to deny, or limit as England pleases, the rights of Scottish self-government. However, if one may judge by public utterances,

our friends in the Association are coming 'up to scratch' — and it may be that there is little now to distinguish the aim of a strong body of opinion in the Association from the aim of the Scots National League.[98]

The SHRA, argued the League, was under 'a two fold spell. It is hypnotised by Westminster and it has the faith of a suckling in the Liberal and Labour humbug'.[99] It was also criticized for the degree of Home Rule they advocated: 'The aim of the Scottish Home Rule Association is not clear. But apart from the practical necessities of Scotland, it is surely incredible that any Scottish organisation would demand for our country a status and powers inferior to these which have been admitted as the right of Canada'.[100] Many in the League believed that, after the failure of Barr's Bill, there would be a fundamental re-orientation in the Association's policies. There was a constant barrage of criticism directed against the SHRA's dependence on the Labour Party and calls for a new 'national party' were, by now, monthly features in the association's news-sheet.[101] Gibson and other members of the League were desperate to influence the state of flux in the SHRA to further their own interests:

> The policy of the Home Rule Association is presumably in the melting pot. There is evidently much keen dis-satisfaction at the cavalier treatment of their Government of Scotland Bill. Faith in the ability, if not also in the sincerity, of members of the Westminster parties is giving place to the realization that there is hope alone in the policy advocated by the League. Scots MPs of the three political parties neither enjoy Home Rule nor attempt to show any independence of spirit within these predominantly English parties. The folly of expecting them to advocate Scottish self-government successfully has long been recognised by the League's policy of a Scottish National Party.[102]

Many in the SNL were hoping that the Association would throw in its lot with a new National Party headed by League members. The National Party, they argued, was ready and waiting to be set up. All that was now required was clarification from the SHRA. To many in the SNL, it appeared that they had won a crucial ideological war over which method of political representation would further the interests of the Scottish national movement. In the meantime, co-operation between the two groups increased.

In June, 1927, the Scotland's day parade and demonstration held in Stirling was organised by both groups and was based on the understanding that, for this occasion, the SHRA would sever its ties with the British political parties.[103] The demonstration was important in that it proved conclusively that the nationalists could work together.

Many in the SNL believed that, when the new party would come into existence, it would fly a banner which had been woven by the League:

> The Scots National League has laid the foundations of a National Party — democratic, progressive and radical minded — with a demand that will gain the support of all Scots save the reactionary who may, with advantage, be left to amuse themselves with the 'red letters' and red herrings of English politics. If and when the Home Rule Association boldly proclaims adherence to this policy, what is to prevent its co-operation in the League's work of putting forward and securing the return of National candidates.[104]

However, the process was not going to be as easy as many imagined. It was to be almost another year before the National Party of Scotland would be formed. During this time, the Home Rulers still persisted with the Scottish National Convention as a forum for political debate and policy options. As the SNL, on principle, boycotted this forum, they were left out of the decision making process. There is no doubt that the options being mooted by the League had a profound influence on other nationalists. However, it was not guaranteed that they would follow without any reservations the line being given by Gibson. Members of the Association displayed a greater sense of imperviousness than many in the SNL had expected. Indeed, as events were to prove the creation of the National Party of Scotland did not happen as many League members had planned.[105]

The establishment of a broad political strategy was an ongoing process and this framework was bolstered from within by specific arguments from the social and economic perspective in favour of Scottish independence. The League's main thrust was that Scottish social and economic maladies were the result of bad government from Westminster and that once Scotland was in control of her own destiny, the economy would flourish. Such discussions were designed both to impress nationalists outside the League and to bring a greater degree of immediacy to the Home Rule debate. The SNL had no doubt as to the economic feasibility of an independent Scotland: 'It is clear that Scotland's area, population and revenues are greater than those of many prosperous European states'.[106] To ram this message home, figures were given to lend authority to their arguments, although it is, more often than not, impossible to tell how these statistics were computed. Comparisons were drawn to show how much different countries earned in their national incomes. Iain Gillies believed that the annual revenue in £ millions for the following countries were; Denmark £18; Switzerland £12; Sweden £40; Holland £51 and Czechoslovakia £63, while Scotland's was £90.[107] Westminster government was condemned for its costliness, which devoured most of the earnings created by the Scottish economy:

> The annual cost of government per head to the independent citizens of Denmark is roughly £4 10/; of Switzerland £3; Sweden £6 15/-; Holland £7 5/-; whilst the hard headed Scot, glorying in his business ability and his position of office boy in the great imperial concern, the cost is £18 per head! If the Scots prefer to be ruled by another nation rather than manage their own affairs, why in the name of shrewdness can't we give the contract to a country more economical than England.[108]

The League regarded Scotland as being part of the British Empire only in the sense that she was a colony, which was being economically exploited. 'The Milch cow of the Empire', they argued, was consistently over taxed and received none of the spin-off benefits from Government expenditure.[109] Scotland, they believed, produced, manufactured, and exported more per head of population than England. This state of affairs, they argued, was necessary in order to pay for the upkeep of Imperial concerns, which, they maintained, were of no practical benefit to Scotland.[110] Current economic phenomena were used to back up these claims especially with regard to the defensive amalgamations which, they argued, did considerable harm to the economy. The SNL used the October edition of the *Glasgow Chamber of Commerce Journal* in 1927, to back up its argument that industry naturally gravitates towards the area of government: 'The significant fact, to which we have alluded, that the area of profitable enterprise is shifting southeastward'.[111] Gibson argued that this was the economic price Scotland had to pay for its political subordination to England: 'Railways, shipping, basic industries are all coming under English control: banking, insurance, trade unions - everything that materially counts — safely into English hands'.[112] It was claimed that self-government was the only effective remedy for Scottish economic problems.

Reform within the context of the Union was not considered as a viable policy option by the League, because they believed that, in many important aspects, the economic interests of the two countries were diametrically opposed to one another. To stay in the Union, they argued, would only mean more deindustrialization, depopulation and unemployment as the English promoted and protected their own economy at the Scots' expense. This was all the more likely, they believed, because of the structural changes that were then shaking the world economy:

> Industries and trade will be sucked dry to keep London going. Its Highlands will be more and more completely depopulated to supply English and

American millionaires with a playground. Its workers will be ground down by the taxation necessary to provide the great navy and the heavy debt settlements needed to buy American friendship. In the end, the prosperity of the new 'little England' will centre round the cities of the South, and Scotland will be as poor and deserted as are the agricultural eastern provinces of Holland.[113]

The only solution to these economic problems, the League argued, was to break the Union which had caused them in the first place. Once this had been achieved it would be able to utilise the natural resources of the nation in order to generate economic prosperity. Attention would be paid to agriculture and rural industries. The models the SNL based their arguments for economic growth on were taken from the small western European nations, particularly Norway, Holland, Belgium and Switzerland:

> We must get rid of our partnership with England...we must get out of it *now*, while the situation is still fluid. Independent Scotland will, of course, have to face the industrial difficulties in which the Union has involved us, but if it faces them alone it will do so with great hope of success. For it will be free to escape the expensive business of being a world power. Moreover, Scotland has far greater resources on which to base a new type of agriculture and industry than England has. Our highlands and southern mountains contain thousands of acres suitable for small holdings and afforestation. They contain waterpower enough to give cheap electricity to many small industries, though not enough to be of great use to such 'big business' as the United Kingdom has come to depend on...We shall be able to embark as a small nation on the sort of economic prosperity that Belgium, Denmark, Norway and Sweden have shown to be so possible and so desirable.[114]

The land issue received a great deal of attention from the League. This was a result of the Highland Land League influence and, more directly, the fact that landownership in Scotland by absentee landlords was the most conspicuous piece of evidence for their claim that the nation was colonially exploited. The SNL demanded that the land had to be used for productive purposes and support a substantial rural population. T.H. Gibson played an important part in developing nationalist land policies, and he also, in an indirect way, helped to shape the Scottish Labour Party's land policy by communicating ideas to J.M. MacDiarmid.[115] For Gibson, the issue was best explained in simple terms: 'It is generally accepted as a basic principle that in the interests of the general community, the fullest use must be made of the economic resources of a country. Therefore, it follows that unless the fullest opportunity is made available to those desirous of working the land — the primary source of all wealth — the economic and therefore, the social life of a country will never be complete'.[116] He believed that small-holding farming would provide the key to a vital redevelopment of the Scottish economy. Forestation and cottage industries would become valuable sources of income as well as providing farmers and their families with part-time employment. Land reclamation, fencing and draining schemes were also advocated as part of the plan to build up the rural economy. The fishing industry was believed to have greater scope for development, and Gibson argued that railways designed for such an economy should be built to help with transportation costs.[117] Why members of the SNL were more interested in agricultural expansion rather than industrial regeneration is not particularly clear. Although industrial problems featured in many of the economic tracts produced by the League, they are not nearly as prominent as ones concerning agriculture. It is possible members of the SNL believed agriculture, particularly small farming, would create a society more conducive to their cultural aspirations. Industry, on the other hand, was impersonal and always brought social problems in its wake. Also, the League was keen to repopulate the Highlands and crofting and fishing seemed the best way to achieve this. Whereas small farms were under individual control, industry was often subject to outside control and capital. The implications this had for economic independence probably led many in the SNL to shun it.

The economic policies of the League set them apart from other nationalists because they advocated, for the first time, projections of what an independent Scotland would look like. The economic reasons for going it alone were put forward only by the SNL. The idea that the two nations' economies were not compatible and that the larger's interests impinged on the smaller's, would be of great significance to future nationalist ideas. By advocating a different and alternative economy, based on the principles to be found in other European small nations, the SNL offered something positive and, to many people, desirable. The old idea of Home Rule being a good thing in an abstract sense but not worth elaborating on was no longer tenable. The League, through its economic policies, tried to illustrate, in a practical way, why independence would be beneficial. By claiming that people would be materially better off, the SNL attempted to bring the Home Rule issue to the forefront of the Scottish political debate. It is also worth mentioning the calibre of the League's economic thinking. Gibson, who was later to rationalize steel production during the Second World War, was a precise and exacting thinker. Evidence of their intellectual quality is to be found in the fact that many of their ideas, particularly concerning land use, were subsequently put into practice and of those that were not, many of them are still in circulation today.

As one might expect, the Scottish National League argued that Scottish social problems were the result of her economic subservience to England. Once there was political and economic independence, so the argument went, social problems would effectively be dealt with. However, in order to convey the idea that the League, as a political organisation, was concerned about the social plight of ordinary working-class people, time was spent on highlighting the issue with an eye to winning their support. The most endemic social problem facing Scotland during the interwar period was the appalling living conditions in the many slum areas. In December, 1926, Peter Fyfe, director of housing in Glasgow, delivered a talk on the issue at a meeting held under the auspices of the SNL. Fyfe backed the League's position concerning the origins of the problems:

> We are too much in the hands of Parliamentary Committees set up from London, composed of gentlemen, who have no knowledge of Glasgow, and never took the trouble to see for themselves the state of affairs and ascertain what the word 'backlands' really means...I sincerely trust you will, before long, be strong enough and influential enough to take the handling of this problem out of the jurisdiction of an English Parliament, and place it untrammelled by the voting power of a parliament sitting in London, before one composed of Scotsmen assembled in the city of Edinburgh.[118]

This was a major coup for the League as Fyfe was a respected and influential member of the SHRA and his speech at the meeting indicated his frustration with the lack of progress being made by the Association. The SNL was keen to point out that the housing problem would have its importance dictated by the House of Commons and although people in Scotland might believe it to be of major significance, this was not necessarily the view of Westminster:

> Whilst the politicians have been wrangling about English politics, the housing problem still remains as bad as ever. All three political parties, Labour, Liberal, and Conservative, have made an attempt to solve the problem, but it is still as acute as it ever was. The real blame for this state of affairs is with the Scots people, who have attached themselves to English parties, for the English governments — of all political complexions — have consistently refused to recognise that Scotland had a problem in any way different from that of England.[119]

As far as the League was concerned all the attempted solutions to the problem failed because the Parliamentary Acts were based on assumptions and information taken from England, which had less of a housing problem than Scotland. The net result of this, they argued, was that the Scots got fewer houses than were needed and worse still, they were usually far too expensive. The Wheatley Housing Act of 1924 was often used as a case in point to back up the validity of their argument.[120] Housing was another issue the League used to bring home to people the relevance of their case for independence.

The questions of immigration and emigration were two issues which were often hotly debated within the ranks of the SNL. Many believed that the greatest threat to Scottish national hegemony was English immigration, which, they argued, was a far greater peril than Irish immigration.[121] However, unlike previous times, the 'Celtic' aspect of this question was not brought up. Attention was focused on the fact that the peak of Irish immigration had passed, while the English were still arriving in increasing numbers at a time when Scottish emigration was high. The question of race brought up by the Celticists received very little attention. Erskine of Mar was, by now, nothing more than a colourful figurehead with no effective say in the running of the SNL. However, this did not prevent him from coming up with the occasional hare-brained scheme. He wrote to Gibson, for example, advocating the idea of 'race co-operation' between Scots and Scots of Irish descent: 'They might be of much use to us and to neglect them would be bad policy...We should seek to strengthen our relations with the race conscious Irish in Scotland'.[122] Gibson, as chairman of the Glasgow Area branch, was only too well aware how such a policy would go down. However, by now he was quite an expert at fobbing off Erskine's schemes. A more serious problem was the question of emigration and depopulation especially when: 'other nationals are coming in and filling the places they have vacated'.[123] This emigration, they argued, was the result of land hunger and industrial depression which could only be solved by a Scottish Parliament with the necessary economic clout.

Perhaps the most fundamental difference between the SNL and other nationalist groups was the priority they gave to the question of national sovereignty. Although the League often talked of Home Rule and self-government, what was really meant by these terms was full political separation of Scotland from the rest of the United Kingdom. Indeed, this strand of thought is the one constant link throughout the League's history that all members agreed on. The 1926 British Imperial Conference was used to highlight their case and the following resolutions were passed:

(1) That at all international and other conferences, Scotland is not represented, despite at these conferences decisions on matters vitally affecting Scottish life are arrived at.

(2) That this humiliating position is again emphasised by the exclusion of Scotland — a mother nation — from the participation in the conference of countries comprising the British Empire.

(3) That the resumption of the Scottish people of their independent status as a sovereign nation is the only remedy for this deplorable state of affairs; and urges all democratic Scotsmen and women to protect their welfare by combining to prevent a continuance of this humble subordination of Scottish interests.[124]

The lack of independent government affected Scots in their everyday life. For example, the herring trade, they argued, was disrupted with Russia because of the break in relations between the two countries as a result of the Bolshevik Revolution. This was given as an incidence of how British foreign policy was carried out without regard to Scottish interests.[125] Until Scotland had independence, the League maintained, her economic and international interests would not receive the necessary attention to make them function properly.

By April, 1928, the Scots National League had over 1,000 members in 15 local branches.[126] In November, 1927, Donald Clark had contested a local council by-election and although he lost, he was able to win it for the National Party of Scotland in May, 1928. In September, 1926, Compton Mackenzie, the novelist, joined the League and in December, C.M. Grieve (Hugh MacDiarmid) wrote in *Contemporary Scottish Studies* that the SNL was 'the most promising Nationalist movement that has been formed in Scotland since the Union'.[127] The same author had also begun to contribute articles for the *Scots Independent* in 1927.[128] The Welsh Nationalists regarded the League as the best representatives of the Scottish national movement by late 1926.[129] On the eve of the formation of the National Party of Scotland in April, 1928, it was clear that the SNL was an organisation that the nationalist movement, as a whole, could not afford to ignore. However, in assessing the performance of the League, it is easy to over-emphasise their effect on the Scottish political scene. The truth is that they were mostly regarded as a nuisance by the three main political parties, although the Labour Party often accused them of trying to split the Labour vote.[130] Their real success lay with the impact they had on the nationalist movement, especially regarding the policy of putting forward their own electoral candidates. In this respect, they broke the mold of nationalist thought, which, up until then, had relied on British political parties to further their cause. Also, by advocating social and economic policies geared for an independent Scotland, the SNL ensured that it was the intellectual vanguard of the nationalist movement during this period.

NOTES

1. The first mention of the League's existence is to be found in *Liberty*, June, 1920. p.6.
2. For a history of the Highland Land League see J. Hunter, 'The Gaelic connection: The Highlands, Ireland and Nationalism. 1873-1922'. *SHR* 1975 pp 178-204.
3. This information is taken from the obituaries of William Gillies printed in the *Scots Independent* September. 1932, p166, p167.
4. For biographical material on Erskine of Mar see H. Hanham. *Scottish Nationalism* (London 1969) pp119-167 and also Hunter op cit. Note *Guth na Bliadhna* was first published in November, 1903, and not in 1904 as stated in the above article page 192).
5. For example, *Guth na Bliadhna*, December, 1904. p.8
6. See the *Scottish Review*, Spring 1919 for the petition in full.
7. *Guth na Bliadhna*, 1906, p.17
8. See *Scottish Review*, 1918 p.177, p.173. See also Nan Milton *John Maclean* (Bristol, 1973) pp. 236-248.
9. op.cit. p.250-259.
10. Letter written by Maclean, 25th of September 1920. Maclean Mss, file 6, Acc.4251.NLS
11. Lenin, it would appear, was ignorant of the peculiarities of the Scottish situation. William Gallacher, who was opposed to the concept of Scottish nationality, slipped off to argue his case for the creation of a British communist party with Lenin, while Maclean was held in prison. Lenin, unable to get Maclean's opinion, opted in favour of Gallacher's partisan view of the situation and decreed the Scottish national question to be of no importance. See Milton op.cit. for details.
12. See *Vanguard* November, 1920 and *Scottish Review*, 1918, p.268.
13. Gillies and Erskine of Mar worked with Art O'Brien to set out the possibilities of founding a Celtic daily paper in Scotland. Art O'Brien Papers, Mss.8427. National Library of Ireland. (I am grateful to Mr. Iain Patterson for drawing this to my attention.)
14. MacArthur was an enthusiastic Rangers fan. He regularly printed articles on League football in *Liberty*.
15. *Liberty*, 2nd, October, 1920 p.102.
16. Ibid.
17. H.C. MacNeacail, *Liberty* 9th October 1920. Also *Scottish Review*, Winter 1919, p.406.
18. Ibid.
19. Ibid.
20. *Liberty* March, 1920. p.28.
21. William Gillies, *Liberty*, June, 1920. p.59.
22. Lindsay Crawford, *Liberty*, April, 1920. p.37.
23. Ibid.

24. John MacArthur, *Liberty*, 9th October, 1920. p.113.

25. See, for example, William Gillies, *Liberty*, March, 1920. p.25.

26. Erskine of Mar, *Liberty*, October 2nd, 1920. p.103.

27. Crean Mor, *Liberty*, October 23rd, 1920. p.137.

28. Erskine of Mar, *Liberty*, October 2nd, 1920. p.103.

29. William Gillies, *Liberty*, October 2nd, 1920. p.105.

30. Seumus Mac Garaich, *Liberty*, July, 1920. p.67.

31. *ibid.*

32. Many of these theories were inspired by Spengler's *Decline of the West* (London, 1931) see *Standard* p.77. for Erskine's opinions of this work.

33. Lindsay Crawford, *Liberty*, April, 1920. p.37.

34. Ibid.

35. Evidence of this runs throughout *Liberty* particularly in the correspondence columns see esp. p.174.

36. Iain MacRuaraidh, *Liberty*, October 23rd, 1920. p.138.

37. Erskine of Mar, *Liberty*, October 9th, 1920. p.117.

38. Ibid

39. Neil Maclean to Lewis Spence, 12th of December, 1920. Spence Mss. Acc 5916 Box1. NLS

40. Documentation does not exist to show who spoke but probably Neil Maclean, E.D. Morel and Edwin Scrymgeour were likely candidates.

41. H.C. MacNeacail, *Liberty*, August, 1920. p.77

42. *Liberty*, June, 1921. p.83.

43. Ibid, October 30th, 1920. p.151.

44. William Gillies, *Liberty*, July, 1920. p.73.

45. H.C. MacNeacail, *Liberty*, August, 1920. p.77.

46. Ibid. p.78

47. *Liberty*, August, 1921. p.124.

48. *Standard*, January, 1922, p.10.

49. Ibid.

50. Ibid.

51. Ibid.

52. Ibid.

53. *Standard*, May 1922. p.77.

54. *Standard*, June 1922. p.82.

55. Ibid.

56. *Standard*, March, 1922. p.41.

57. *Some Arguments for Scottish Independence* (Glasgow, 1920) p.13.

58. Ibid. p.16.

59. For example, see *Liberty* p.141. p.146. p.129. p.121.

60. *Standard*, p.43.

61. *Monthly Intellegencer*, March, 1924. p.2.

62. Ibid.

63. See chapter 1.

64. T. Gibson, memorandum on the SHRA., June, 1924 Gibson Mss. Box 1, Acc. 6058. NLS.

65. Ibid.

66. Ibid.

67. Ibid.

68. Copy dated 1st of December, 1924, Gibson Mss. Acc.6058, Box 1, NLS.

69. Ian Scott to Gibson, 7th of February, 1925, Gibson Mss. Box 1, NLS.

70. Gibson to Erskine of Mar, 7th of July, 1924, Gibson Mss. Box 1, NLS.

71. Gibson to Ian Scott, 7th of July, 1924, Gibson Mss. Box 1, NLS.

72. Gibson to Paterson, 28th of October, 1926, Gibson Mss. Box 1, NLS

73. Spence was a monthly contributor and regular letter writer to the *Edinburgh Evening News*, where he trumpeted his breakaway movement.

74. *Glasgow Evening Citizen*, 21st August 1926.

75. Minute Book of the Scottish National Movement. Dott Mss. Acc. 5927. NLS.

76. Iain Gillies to Gibson, 29th of June, 1926, Gibson Mss. Box 1, NLS.

77. Ibid

78. See chapter 3.

79. Memorandum on the proposed *Scots Independent*, April,1926, Gibson Mss. Box 1, NLS.

80. Iain Gillies to Gibson, April, 1926. Gibson Mss. Box 1, NLS.

81. Iain Gillies to Gibson, 3rd of February, 1926, Gibson Mss. Box 1, NLS.

82. Ibid.

83. Malcolm MacColla, *Scots Independent*, November, 1926. p.3.

84. *Scots Independent*, April, 1927. p.4.

85. The only guarded mention of this from the SHRA is to be found in *Scottish Home Rule*, October, 1925.

86. Taken from the monthly reports 'frae a the Airts' in the *Scots Independent*.

87. *Scots Independent*, June, 1927. p.4.

88. See chapter 1. Also, Muirhead ordered seven dozen copies of the *SI* Gibson Mss 4th September 1927. NLS.

89. Malcolm MacColla, *Scots Independent*, September, 1927. p.2.

90. See chapter 1.

91. *Scots Independent*, June, 1927, p.6.

92. *Scots Independent*, June, 1927, p.7.

93. *Scots Independent*, October, 1927. p.1.

94. *Scots Independent*, June, 1927, p.7.

95. Iain Gillies, *Scots Independent*, September, 1927. p.5.

96. Iain Gillies, *Scots Independent*, May, 1927. pp4-5.

97. Ibid. p.4.

98. Iain Gillies, *Scots Independent*, September, 1927. p.5.

99. *Scots Independent*, April, 1927. p.5.

100. Iain Gillies, *Scots Independent*, September, 1927. p.5.

101. See chapter 1.

102. Iain Gillies, *Scots Independent*, September, 1927. p.5.

103. Gibson Mss, 9th May 1927, also *Scots Independent*, July, 1927. p.1.

104. Iain Gillies, *Scots Independent*, September, 1927. p.5.
105. See chapter 3.
106. Iain Gillies, *Scots Independent*, February, 1927. p2.
107. Ibid.
108. Ibid.
109. Iain Gillies, *Scots Independent*, July, 1927. p.4.
110. ibid.
111. Tom Gibson, Scots Independent, October, 1927. p.4.
112. Ibid.
113. *Scots Independent*, January, 1927. p.2.
114. Ibid.
115. Gibson to MacDiarmid, 3rd of September, 1926, Gibson Mss. Box 1, NLS.
116. Tom Gibson, *Scots Independent*, December, 1926. p.3.
117. Tom Gibson, *Scots Independent*, August, 1927. pp. 3-4.
118. *Scots Independent*, January, 1927 p.3.
119. Ibid, May, 1927, p.5.
120. See the earlier section of this chapter.
121. *Scots Independent*, December, 1926 p.1.
122. Erskine of Mar to Gibson. 11th of May, 1926, Gibson Mss. Acc. 6058, NLS.
123. *Scots Independent*, June, 1927, p.5.
124. *Scots Independent*, November, 1926. p.10.
125. *Scots Independent*, February, 1927. pp3-4.
126. Information taken from the *Scots Independent*.
127. *Contemporary Scottish Studies*, December, 1926.
128. C.M. Grieve 'Neo-Gaelic economics', *Scots Independent*.December, 1927. p.21.
129. Letter to T.H. Gibson. 15th of October, 1926, Gibson Mss. NLS
130. *Scots Independent*, January, 1927. p.6.

CHAPTER THREE

The National Party of Scotland 1928 – 1933

The idea of creating a 'Scottish National Party' in order to unite the various disparate sections of the Scottish national movement into a coherent political organisation was one that had been constantly mooted by a growing number of people from within the various nationalist groups during the 1920s. The impetus for this movement arose from the political vacuum that had come to exist concerning the Scottish Home Rule question. Much of the debate focused on the suitability of using the existing political apparatus to represent and forward Scottish issues. After October 1925, there were more persistent calls for the setting up of some form of 'National Party' which would act as an umbrella organisation for Scottish political interests.[1] As was stated earlier many of the original proponents of this idea believed that the Home Rule question would provide a unifying quality in Scottish politics that would override conventional ideological differences. However, given the nàïveté of the proposals, it is hardly surprising that plans for the new party received little more than a passing interest amongst established politicians. At the same time as these ideas were being mooted, there was a perceptible decline of interest in the Scottish Home Rule question among leading members of the Labour Party, which had been the stalwart carrier of the issue during the early twenties. This forced several members of the Scottish Home Rule Association, including its principal architect and founder, Roland Muirhead, to begin a search for new ways to put the issue of Scottish self-government more firmly on the political agenda.[2] Initially, members of the SHRA thought that the best way to forward their cause would be to sting the Labour Party into action: 'The fact is that the most effective way to get the Labour Party or any other Party to take Home Rule in earnest, is to show it that votes will be lost if neglected. Even if a Scottish National Party never became strong enough to carry Scottish Home Rule on its own effort, its existence might well prove to be just the stimulus required to make the Labour Party move'.[3] An important section of thought involved in the creation of the National Party of Scotland was that which stressed the need for the organisation to be first and foremost a catalyst in Scottish politics. The advocates of this philosophy felt that there was little need for the party to adopt specific policies relating to social and economic

questions because their only concern was to stimulate the demand for
Home Rule, rather than be responsible for its delivery.

However, there were other groups of nationalists, which each had its
own set of priorities and ideas as to the future role of the new National
Party. One group, drawn mainly from the ranks of the Scots National
League and led by Tom Gibson, argued that the new organisation would
have to lead the Scottish people towards the goal of independence.[4] As
far as they were concerned, the National Party would have to emerge
as the strongest political force in Scotland by challenging and defeating
the existing 'Westminster' parties for electoral support. Concurrent with
this view was the belief that votes would only be forthcoming if the
nationalists could firmly place Home Rule, or independence, as some
preferred to call it, within the context of desired social and economic
objectives. Without explaining self-government in terms which related
to issues of political concern such as employment, housing, industry
and social welfare, it was argued, few people would see the relevance of
giving it support. Another interested party were those who saw Home
Rule primarily in cultural terms and viewed it as a way of redressing the
decline of a distinctive national identity and culture. This group of
cultural nationalists were to be found within the ranks of all the various
nationalist organisations and were, more often than not, the least
concerned with political strategy. Perhaps the most influential group in
the creation of the NPS was the gathering of pragmatic young men
from the Glasgow University Scottish Nationalist Association led by
the charismatic and able John MacCormick. These students were new
to the nationalist scene and had little time for, nor understanding of,
the complex arguments that raged between the various factions. For
them the most important thing was to do something positive and leave
behind the disputes on tactics no matter how important the others
believed them to be. In doing so, the GUSNA brought a freshness of
approach and a sense of urgency to the nationalist cause, which had
long been lacking. The raw political material of the future National
Party of Scotland was made up from all shades of ideological opinion
and there was within this a further plethora of divisions concerning the
preferred use of tactics and strategy. However, by early 1928, they were
united in the one belief that, within the present political scenario, there
was no future for their nationalist aspirations other than to take matters
into their own hands.

The process leading up to the creation of the National Party of
Scotland was, by all accounts, a tortuous affair. Although the SNL and
the SHRA had maintained a formal and at times, hostile, distance from

each other, several important contacts had been established during the middle 1920s. The most important of these was the relationship between Tom Gibson and R.E. Muirhead, who discussed possible opportunities for co-operation between the two organisations, and both men tentatively hinted at the option of creating some form of nationalist popular front.[5] However, the main barrier to achieving this was the fact that they each had their own preferred political strategy, which was largely incompatible with the other. Muirhead was convinced that the best way forward was to use and work with the existing political parties, especially the Labour Party. Gibson, on the other hand, believed that this strategy was doomed to failure and he was the strongest proponent of the argument that the only viable option available to nationalists was for a new political party to campaign on the specific issue of Scottish self-government against the 'London controlled' organisations. However, as early as June, 1925, Muirhead was beginning to concede ground to Gibson's argument.[6] He was propelled further along this road by the summer of 1927, when it became obvious that no candidates from the major parties were prepared to give Scottish Home Rule the ultimate political priority.[7] Increasingly, he began to find more common ground with other nationalists and his disaffection with the Labour Party led to his decision to contest East Renfrewshire as a Home Rule candidate at the next general election.[8] Although this action effectively isolated him from the Independent Labour Party, it does appear that it was his intention to provoke a stronger commitment to Home Rule from the Labour movement rather than blaze a trail for the new National Party of Scotland. It was only when the Labour Party refused to endorse his candidature, or give him significant reassurance on the Home Rule question, that he felt compelled to throw his lot in with the NPS.

The National Party of Scotland was not born in a blaze of glory, but rather experienced a slow and painful birth, which was bedevilled by suspicion and procrastination by members from all the interested parties. Initial optimism that 'the time is not far by distant when Scottish Nationalists united in one progressive and democratic National Party will form an unbroken front' was significantly misplaced.[9] Although as an intellectual idea there had been considerable discussion about creating a National Party, the first practical steps were taken by a member of the SHRA, A.L. Henry, who, as chairman of the Scottish National Party group within the Association, contacted members of the SNL and Lewis Spence's SNM and arranged a meeting for the 24th of August, 1927.[10] Muirhead did not attend the meeting, because he was still unconvinced of the efficacy of a National Party going it alone. Also, it would have meant overriding the Scottish National Convention, of which he was secretary, and, as far as he was concerned, it was still the best organisation for putting forward the case for the Home Rule. This was in spite of the fact that many now regarded the Convention as nothing more than a Labour-dominated talking shop. Muirhead was uncomfortably aware of the increasing unease that many were expressing about the viability of the SNC as an effective forum for the self government cause. Lewis Spence wrote to him asking for a clarification of the issue and the reply reveals a man obviously engaging in a political juggling act keeping as many options open as possible:

> With respect to...a proposed Scottish National Party. As hon. Secretary of the Convention I have no knowledge of such a Party, but as a private individual I understand that some of those who brought forward the suggestion of a National Party...are forming themselves into a group...There is, I think, a considerable number of the members of the SHRA, who feel that if a Scottish National Party were formed, the demand for self-government for Scotland would take precedence of all other matters.[11]

Muirhead's confidence in the Convention was put under pressure from the fact that members of the SNL refused to take part in the discussions because of the SNC's association with British parties. The absence of the League from a forum which was either to create a new National Party or to focus pressure on the existing political parties to step up their commitment to Home Rule was damaging to its credibility and authority, especially as the SNL was foremost in the agitation for a new nationalist strategy.[12] Although Spence and the SNM were quite happy with this arrangement largely because of the personal animosity that existed between the two groups, a compromise about procedure was finally reached. The League was allowed to attend the Convention as spectators, although they were not represented in an official capacity. Also in attendance were members from Glasgow University Scottish Nationalist Association who, despite their appeals for calm, could do little to stop the meeting from degenerating into a pointless shouting match. During the debate members of the SNL made their presence and displeasure known by engaging in bouts of continuous heckling, before symbolically storming out in protest at the influence of British political parties at the meeting.[13]

MacCormick and the GUSNA students brought new blood into the Scottish national movement. Their non-dogmatic approach to the problems of nationalist strategy helped to put some of the problems in perspective. As far as they were concerned, the fundamental problem was one of arranging priorities:

One point nearly everyone who has spoken has failed to see is that this motion (calling for the creation of a National Party) does not express any policy on the Scottish National Party going forward. It does not say whether the policy of the Party will be to go to Westminster, or to appeal to the League of Nations, or organise a national plebiscite. It merely states it is time that we had in this movement a united front, and by forming this National Party we shall be forming a centre to which every man who loves his country can come. We will be forming a centre where we can discuss matters of policy.[14]

MacCormick believed that the starting point had to be to find the areas of universal agreement and, consequently, build upon them.

However, the key difficulty was to reconcile the differences between Muirhead and Gibson. Both men were stubborn in their beliefs and Gibson had a tendency to be very abrasive while under pressure.[15] As MacCormick noted, Muirhead was 'dour, intransigent, but sincere', while Gibson had 'a capacity to get so enthusiastic in argument that he almost literally drowned all opposition'.[16] Both men occupied different positions in the conventional political spectrum; Muirhead was a Fabian socialist while Gibson was better fitted to the Liberal mould. Muirhead was an enthusiastic member of the ILP and would hardly be endeared to Gibson for his vitriolic attacks on Labour's connection with the SHRA. Also, Gibson was responsible for a particularly insensitive attack on the Association for allowing a collection to be taken for the widow and family of John Maclean within the premises of one of their meetings.[17] Of the two men, Muirhead was put in a more difficult position regarding the creation of the National Party. He was, after all, very closely involved with the growth of the Labour movement in Scotland. He had provided funding for the *Forward* newspaper and had worked alongside such prominent Labour politicians as Tom Johnston, James Barr, James Maxton, David Kirkwood and Ramsay MacDonald.[18] The prospect of throwing all this over to join with a group of political unknowns with no previous track record in public or political life must have been a daunting decision. Also, some of the more extreme elements within the national movement would have filled him with great reservations about the potential for success of the proposed party. Comments such as follows from Lewis Spence could not have filled him with confidence:

We do not yet advocate taking up the rifle, because that is a course I feel that would hardly appeal to the majority of our fellow countrymen — although it is the method I would prefer. I will not deny that for a moment. I believe the only way to beat an Englishman is to beat him physically. You cannot drive it into the thick head of a southerner by any other means.[19]

Muirhead was not convinced that the new party ought to contest elections and Gibson had to apply considerable pressure before he would change his mind:

> All my efforts were mainly directed to showing the utter futility of the Home Rule Association, and at long last I managed to persuade Muirhead, albeit perhaps rather unwillingly. But it ultimately became recognised that unity would be unity in name only, and not in practice if we did not establish the principle of independence of action, although in the process the negotiations nearly fell down on two or three occasions because people did not want to give up their particular parties.[20]

Another area of conflict between the two men was the proposed policies of the National Party. Muirhead wanted a broad policy and believed that there was no point in going into detailed objectives:

> If I had my own way I would have no constitution, but simply the object stated and leave the body to develop itspolicy as it goes along.[21]

Gibson took the opposite view and believed that, unless the new party could translate the Home Rule issue for the benefit of the man in the street and explain its relevance in bread-and-butter terms, they would never attract sufficient electoral support.[22] Also, a clear social and economic policy was considered necessary for establishing a sense of party indentity and discipline. Eventually Muirhead succumbed to the majority of Gibson's arguments, especially the one concerning the independence of the party from other political groups. However, Muirhead was slow in giving up his hopes that the Labour Party would eventually come round to a more vigorous stance on Home Rule. Indeed, many of his subsequent actions can be explained by the fact that a salient motive in his involvement with the National Party was the desire to stimulate the Labour movement to take nationalist aspirations more seriously.

On the 11th of February, 1928, a meeting of all the main nationalist groups was held under the presidency of John MacCormick with the objective of narrowing down the areas of potential disagreement. Although the SHRA members attended only in an official capacity as representing the nationalist wing of the Association,[23] the following resolutions were passed without too much difficulty:

> (1) This meeting representative of the SHRA; SNL; SNM; the National Party Group and the G.U. Scottish Nationalists Association is agreed in principle to the formation of an independent Scottish National Party and to the merging of the existing bodies into one organisation, subject to the approval of the governing committees of each organisation. (2) The object of the new Party shall be self-government for Scotland.[24]

It was also agreed that 'the object of the new Party shall be attained by putting forward national candidates at Parliamentary and local government elections, independent of the present political parties, and by the presentation of a nationalist programme for Scottish affairs.' After this promising start a provisional steering committee, supervised by MacCormick, was set up to hammer out more precise details on policy and objectives. The choice of MacCormick as chairman was a good one. He was neutral in the eyes of the opposing camps and his pragmatic approach to the problems was backed up with a sense of urgency and a desire to achieve positive results. He was also suitable because of his easy-going manner and an ability to motivate people no matter how difficult the circumstances:

> I cannot say the agreement was easy to reach. All the infinite capacity of the Scots to bicker over definitions, words and even commas was fully displayed throughout the period of negotiation. Often Valentine and I, who represented the University, and who attended the negotiation committee as secretary and chairman respectively, were either privately amused or thoroughly exasperated by the endless arguments which took place. To us it did not seem to matter very much how our objectives were stated as long as we could create an organisation aiming, by and large, at a measure of Home Rule, but to our seniors it seemed as though we were actually framing a whole constitution for a new Scotland.[25]

Unfortunately for MacCormick many at the meeting did believe that they were laying down the framework for a new Scottish constitution. However, he regarded this as mere pedantry, which obscured and detracted from the more vital and realistic issues.

In the main, the arguments revolved around the issue of how much Home Rule the party would fight for and how this was to be defined. According to MacCormick, the problem was to find a way 'as to how our objects could be stated so as to satisfy those who wished to break away completely from England and the others who had slightly milder views'.[26] However, at this point in time, this was not the principal problem concerning the formation of the NPS. The real issue, which had already been decided, was the debate between Gibson and Muirhead concerning the efficacy of contesting elections and it was only when a consensus on this question had been reached, that progress could be made. MacCormick was not party to these discussions and, as a consequence, down-graded their importance.[27] Although the arguments concerning Home Rule or independence were important, most members expected the debate to take place after the party had been formed, with protagonists on both sides of the fence confident that they would win the day. Indeed, many assumed it was an issue that would be developed and expanded as part of the National Party's political growth. However, in the initial phases of the party's career, discretion was considered the better part of valour and members were warned against making the divisions too apparent:

> It is more than ever incumbent on all who wish for Scotland to do everything in their power to prevent the trailing of red herrings across the track. It is still more imperative that those whose names are associated prominently with the National Party give the enemy no chance of making capital out of indiscreet expressions of purely personal opinion.[28]

The debates were to be conducted in an orderly fashion with the principle of contesting elections on the self-government ticket as the party's cohesive *raison d'être*.

On the whole, discipline was maintained and there were no widespread reports of significant differences of opinion during the party's formative period. Although several members of the SNL were reluctant to use the Westminster electoral machinery and believed that if any candidates were elected then they ought to follow a Sinn Fein policy of abstention from London, they were prepared to compromise this in order to achieve unity so long as the NPS was independent from other political parties. Iain Gillies wrote to Gibson highlighting the bottom line as far as the rank and file of the League were concerned:

> It has been discussed briefly with Angus Clark. You already know our general opinion that provided the idea (aim and policy) is safeguarded and upheld we are in support of unity at the cost of the League's individuality ...if Muirhead and Co accept this then all will be OK... but so far as Parliamentary action is concerned our view is that we must stick to our attitude outlined in your Saturday's motion. Muirhead must give up the idea of Home Rule Bills and any such paltry actions that would lead to an understanding with the three English parties.[29]

So long as electoral independence was not compromised the more strident definitions of Scottish self-government held by some League members would be tamed for the time being.

Although Tom Gibson was a separatist, he was also a political realist and was only too well aware that devolution, as a political objective, commanded more support among the Scottish people than outright independence. However, he believed that a politically independent National Party would act as an effective forum to educate people away from the devolutionist point of view:

> The present situation is that there is a considerable number of people interested in a more or less degree of Scottish nationalism, but these people

are divided into compartments with no real connecting link and barred from each other by means of so many organisations. Their organisations are admittedly weak except in petty jealousies and, consequently, there is no effective drawing force. There is also a considerable number of people outside who have given indications that they might come in and help if we could offer them something in the nature of a decided directing force. Then there is a vast number of people who could be forced in simply because they would follow the line of least resistance when we present a sufficiently strong ultimatum. Lastly, there are the people who would never come in whom we would render impotent by reason of our strength and activity'.[30]

The new party was to be designed to appeal to as broad a spectrum of the Scottish people as possible and, consequently, a series of social and economic policies were taken on board which were believed to represent a consensus of Scottish opinion. This also reflected the predominantly radical left of centre stance of most individual members of the NPS. The Sinn Fein policy received only a limited amount of support; most people believed that active work in Westminster would attract more profitable public attention:

> Until such pledged nationalists be a majority of the elected representatives of Scotland, they shall attend at Westminster and endeavour, so far as inherent limitations of that Parliament allow, to protect the national interests of Scotland and to promote the amelioration of social conditions and general standard of living in Scotland and by the pressing of practical schemes of housing and slum clearance, land settlement and afforestation, utilisation of water power, development of sufficient transport by land and water and such other expedients preparatory to the effecting of comprehensive schemes of national development by an independent Scottish Parliament.[31]

Gibson argued that if people could be induced to bite the bait of Home Rule then they would ultimately swallow the hook of independence:

> My line is first of all to break down the compartments in the nationalist movement and get in as many people as we can: people who will be detached from the other and anti-nationalist forces. With this mass we can by means of an effective organisation direct them on to the proper road and constantly shift them onwards. A good many will advance to our point of view and we will be dragging others along with us'.[32]

Gibson's pragmatic approach to the question of Scottish independence and how it was to be defined was essential to provide the necessary degree of unity required to get the National Party off the ground.

Although the NPS was officially founded in April 1928, it was only later on in the summer that it began to function as a proper political party. Both the SNL and the SNM did not dissolve themselves until after their respective annual conferences in June, while Roland Muirhead, who did not have the power to dissolve the SHRA, appealed to individual members of the Association to join the new party. By the 10th November, the party had assumed enough shape and members to hold its first annual conference. R.B. Cunninghame Graham, the veteran radical socialist and Home Ruler, was poached from the SHRA and adopted as the party's president. Although he did not play an important part in the negotiations, his support did lend credibility to the party's image. Muirhead was elected chairman; Lewis Spence, vice chairman, and John MacCormick found room for his organisational talents as the honorary secretary. A National Council of sixteen members was formed, which accurately represented all the various strands of nationalist opinion, of which former members of the SNL were most vocal. The party's brief was:

> The National Party stands for the reconstruction of Scottish national life, including self-government for Scotland with independent national status within the British group of nations. Entirely independent of London controlled parties, the National Party's appeal is to every Scotsman and woman without distinction of class or creed.[33]

The pro-independence lobby won an important point in the wording of the object by insisting that the term 'British group of nations' be used instead of 'British Commonwealth of Nations', which had been preferred by many moderates. As MacCormick was later to recall 'even the word Commonwealth was expunged from our vocabulary'.[34] The conference gave the go-ahead to elaborate on policies concerning social and economic issues, which reflected the prominent influence of radical left-of-centre thinking among the party's rank and file. The comprehensive programme of national reconstruction was a package of reforms which was designed to appeal to Labour and Liberal voters.[35] The plans for reconstruction were not gone into in any precise manner and there was a sparseness of detail concerning financial calculations. Most of the economic policies had been formulated by Tom Gibson during his time with the Scots National League and were adopted by the National Party with little modification. Many of the proposals had a quasi-utopian ring about them, and this was an obvious factor in keeping friction among party members to a minimum. The establishment of a necessary cohesiveness paved the way for the adoption of parliamentary candidates and the creation of a network of local branches, which heralded the entry of the National Party into the Scottish political arena.

By January, 1929, seven parliamentary candidates had been adopted for the forthcoming general election and an analysis of those chosen can give some indication of the state of play within the National Party at this time. Of those whose previous political activity can be traced, four of the seven had connections with a left-of-centre political organisations prior to the formation of the party.[36] Another of the candidates, Lewis Spence, although mainly a cultural nationalist, was identified by many as belonging to the radical stable with his previous connections with the SNL. Along with Spence, Muirhead and MacCormick were the only prominent leaders of the party to stand as candidates. One of the candidates, C.M.Grieve, gave members of the National Executive a hard time by attempting to stand as a Labour Nationalist candidate in Dundee in conjunction with the local Labour Party and in doing so revealed many of the latent tensions which still existed within the NPS. Fortunately for the party's unity, he was persuaded to abandon this project.[37] On the whole, the preference was for urban seats in the central belt, which reflected their weakness outside this area.

The first electoral test for the NPS came during a by-election at North Midlothian in February, 1929. Lewis Spence was adopted as the candidate, but, according to John MacCormick, this was a mistake:

> Nor was our candidate the right man for the job. Lewis Spence is one of the most lovable of men, but he is no politician. Time and again he answered questions so clumsily as to give our opponents handfuls of ammunition to fire against us.[38]

Spence's electoral address reveals many of the ambiguities which pertained to the nationalist cause at this time. Apart from very general objectives, very little was offered to the voter in terms of what a nationalist could achieve at Westminster and how a significant nationalist vote would benefit the populace as a whole. Instead, a negative campaign was run, which highlighted Scottish grievances and whose only solution was a large helping of Scottish patriotism.[39] The result was a poor one and the party's organisation was exposed as being inadequate, with charges of confusion and inefficiency levelled against the campaign coordinators.[40] However, although confidence and pride were dented, their faith in their politics remained firm. The problems lay with 'ourselves and circumstances, not in our cause'.[41]

For some the solution lay with a more dynamic and radical image for the party, which would mean the adoption of a more solid left wing political programme. As has already been mentioned, the NPS was created with a vacuum on issues of post-independence policies with little more than a fragile framework of broad statements of intent. The issue had been left deliberately vague and, although many members of the SNL had felt that there had been a watering down of their principles in the creation of the NPS, Gibson did not believe this to be a bad thing:

> No one need give up their principles by joining this new party. Surely if in other movements there are right and left wings then there can be the same in our Party. It is to the advantage of the left wings that there can be the same in our Party. It is to the advantage of the left wing to have a right wing to work on, or where are the left wing to get their recruits.[42]

Gibson believed that a plurality of political opinion within the party would provide an important stimulus to debate and policy formulation. Others saw it only as an opportunity to win their case and change strategy to suit their own political ends.

Along with the demands for a more radical left wing stance on policies there was also pressure for increasing the profile of independence and separation from England. These demands emanated mainly from former League members, who had the advantage of controlling the party's journal, the *Scots Independent*, which was edited from London by William and Iain Gillies.[43] They were unhappy with what they regarded as the ca-canny policy taken by the party leadership:

> There is a dis-heartening lack of spirit and ideas in the N.P. — in fact a poverty that, like material poverty, breeds suspicion and dislike of possession by others. The cry is moderation; reasonableness, dare not to upset the prejudicies from which nine-tenths of the N.P. are not free. There is no understanding of their function at this stage in two out of three among the leading lights. They should be made to read 'the fool' three times daily...but no we must be content meantime to fight on mainly with appeals and economic arguments that are at least partially false to the future... We are attempting, however, in easy doses to introduce a different flavour — not without an accompaniment of critical growls that the S.I. should be a propaganda paper, not the medium for the expression of individual opinions.[44]

Gillies believed that it was necessary to improve the quality of intellectual debate within the party in order to achieve better strategies and policies. He was also convinced that education in Scottish matters and politics was essential if people were to break free of the prejudicies inculcated by centuries of British political dominance. It was only once this had been achieved, he argued, that the healthy development of Scottish nationalism would take place.

C.M.Grieve was strongly attracted to this element within the National Party and used them as a base from which to push his own political ideas. Although he was not involved in the formation of the NPS, [45] he gradually came to represent to many in the National Party its radical, or fundamentalist wing. This was unfortunate for many radicals, such as Gillies, because it meant that their ideas were associated with Grieve's even though they often held totally different points of view. Grieve acted as an intellectual *agent provocateur* which, essential from an artistic point of view, was, more often than not, damaging in a party political context, especially when it involved promoting fascism:

> It is in the power of a handful to create or recreate in this powerfully spiritually dynamic way, and to convict their antipathetic fellow countrymen of a species of imbecility in the face of the world. The next — or the next — generation will hasten to remove the reproach; and adjust itself to the concept of these few... for still deeper reasons aristocratic standards must be re-erected. We in Scotland have been too long grotesquely over democratised. What is wanted now is a species of Scottish Fascism. [46]

Grieve expressed strongly anti-democratic and intolerant ideas, which resembled some of the more inane early writings of the Scots National League. [47] Whatever his literary merits, politics was not his forte. Grieve became a focal point for Celtic nationalism and he endeavoured to give ideological body to its romantic notions.

Perhaps the most credible and realistic proposal he advocated was Douglas's economic theory of Social Credit, which he bound together with nationalism to challenge the threat of international socialism: [48]

> That is the danger of the socialist championship of a class — as against the Nationalist espousal of the interests of the whole people. Workers are inveighing against capitalism; but their employers are hard put to it. Cannot some economic policy to match the nationalist concern for the whole people be substituted for the socialist concern for a section of the spirit of class antagonism it carries with it? Some such economic policy should be part and parcel of the national genius in the sphere of economics — and it is to hand...The socialists hate it like poison. It reconciles the interests of capitalist and wage earner, rich and poor. Tories, Liberals and Socialists can equally espouse it — although their psychological disruptives make them Tory, Liberal or Socialist, there is no need for them to disregard any longer their common interests in this connection and perptuate the false antagonisms that play into the hands of the bankers — the international financiers — playing off one section against the other. This is the Douglas system of Social Credit. [49]

Perhaps the greatest difficulty facing the historian is placing Grieve and his genre within the bounds of conventional right-left wing politics of the period. Although much of what they advocated is recognisably socialist in tone, they also had much in common with other right wing anti-capitalist movements of the period.[50] Perhaps the most common link between such groups was the heavy emphasis they placed on racial questions. Grieve believed that Irish immigration had been good for Scotland, because it reinforced their Celtic racial stock and Social Creditism was mooted because it fitted in with Scottish racial characteristics:

> It will be easy to show that it is in accordance with the principles of the ancient Gaelic Commonwealth; that it supersedes the economic differences of Conservatism and Liberalism on the one hand and socialism on the other; and that it effectively challenges standardisation and robotisation of humanity towards which international capitalism is now tending towards which international socialism would only more quickly hasten us.[51]

Not only was he responsible for producing policies, which were of a dubious political nature; Grieve was also severe in his criticism of the party's leadership. He was looking for the type of leadership which Mussolini inspired in Italy:

> Fundamental developments inevitably produce big men. That is the main criticism of the National Party so far. There is something wrong with it; it has not produced real leaders - or its organisation is still of such a kind as to frustrate them instead of develop them. What I have said about the need for aristocratic standards, for a species of fascism applies equally here. I feel we will never make any real headway till we cease to imitate English organisations by running the Party on democratic lines or wanting anything similar in organisation or programme to the English parties.[52]

During this period, and it has to be emphasised that Grieve constantly changed his political philosophy, he championed a Scottish nationalism that was proto-fascist, anti-democratic and was all too ready to endorse political violence. The historian is allowed a fascinating insight into his political philosophy at this time by examining an article, in which he gave his vision of how politics would develop in a Scotland of the future. It contains his blueprint for Scottish nationalist strategy:

> The younger people, who had never been subjected to the demoralizing influence of the old Anglo Scottish party political system, specially repudiated the methods and ideology of organised and English controlled democracy then in vogue; and, no longer confining themselves to English precedents, availed themselves readily of the examples of Italy and Ireland, and, powerfully reinforcing the transitional organisation of the Scottish National Party (up until then still deplorably liberal and anglophile) with their militaristic and neo-fascist auxiliary 'Clann Albann', carried the movement to the successful conclusion we know of by 1965, and

reestablished the Ancient Gaelic Commonwealth in Scotland on a modern basis.[53]

Grieve's philosophy was a hotch-potch drawn loosely from Italian fascism, the radical nationalism of some Irish socialists and John Maclean, and the Celtic romanticism of Erskine of Mar. However, it was a political vision which did not strike a resonant chord among other members of the National Party of Scotland.

The initial response of the party leadership to Grieve's advocacy of militant nationalism was one of liberal tolerance, although many profoundly disagreed with him. Arthur Donaldson was one member who was not unduly concerned about these outpourings. He believed it was part and parcel of the intellectual development of the party and saw this as evidence of a more progressive movement within the NPS:

> I am glad to see a more vigorous policy is now in prospect. I realise fully that the leadership of the Party cannot afford to move too far ahead of the bulk of the membership, but it seems to me from my imperfect knowledge of events in Scotland that matters are now beginning to move rapidly and that a stronger more spectacular policy is now justified.[54]

However, Donaldson did express some concern that Grieve was trying to push things too far too fast, especially after he announced the creation of a militaristic organisation 'Clann Albann' in 1930:

> I note also that there were some unfriendly remarks about the cautious character of the Party's leadership. Some folks, of course, look for beards on infants and the more irresponsible they are the freer they talk. Grieve's announcement of Clann Albann was not very politic. Such an organisation, I believe, will be necessary but announcement of it at this time is too premature.[55]

However, Party chairman, Roland Muirhead, was furious at Grieve's behaviour:

> Mr Grieve is a very clever man and some of his matter is very apt. I agree with his view that it is to the young men of the party that we must look for vigorous leadership in the future, but I do not agree with Grieve in his idea of fascism, further I think it will be time enough to consider underground methods of organisation after we have made an earnest endeavour to make use of the powers we have. The Scots are not held down by a Coercion Act such as the Irish were held down and we are free to take whatever propaganda methods we feel most likely to achieve our end'.[56]

This was the start of a bitter dispute, not only over the party's political objectives, but also over questions of strategy and tactics, which was ultimately to culminate in the expulsion of Grieve and his accomplices.

It was an intrinsic fault built into the NPS at the time of its creation which assumed that such questions would be able to be dealt with in an orderly and intellectual manner. No one raised the possibility that the party could contain elements which differed on such fundamental issues as to make compromise impossible. It is an all too common assumption to see this dispute as a straight fight between those committed to the fundamentalist position of total independence on the one hand, and those of a more moderate stance on the other. The reality of the situation was in fact much more complex. Many of those on the moderate wing of the party did share some of the same values and objectives held by the Fundamentalists. However, they were separated from each other and their commonly held assumptions were forgotten as the dispute galvanized, sometimes as a result of personality clashes, and forced members into one of two camps in which they often felt uneasy. While many, such as Muirhead, Gibson and, to some extent, MacCormick, shared the belief that the National Party ought to campaign for a Scottish Parliament with full sovereign powers, they were, however, uneasy as to the effect the Celticists and Fundamentalists were having on the image of the party among the electorate. They were also concerned that the Celticism that some advocated would, electorally, have an adverse effect on the NPS as it was more likely to frighten potential support away.

Although Gibson had done much to bring Celtic romanticism in the SNL under control, by 1929, it had broken out again under the leadership of Erskine of Mar and C.M.Grieve. Erskine was once again letting fly with bouts of political gibberish, which this time round replaced Celtic communism with Celtic aristrocracy:

> Its spirit or genius is aristocratic not democratic, though the principle of popular election runs through all its institutions. Celticism contemplates no office that is elective, no rule that is not aristocratic by nature...The important point to note is that the Celtic people should be ruled on Celtic principles and to that end is Celticism instituted.[57]

Although Erskine was regarded as eccentric, Grieve was believed by many in the party to be dangerous. Both men caused anxiety with their anglophobia, which was believed to be excessive and damaging to the NPS's credibility. On the issue of separation from England they were emphatic:

> 'We are out for Scottish independence in the fullest sense of the term and the abrogation of English ascendancy alike in our imperial, internal and international relationship, and in every other objective or subjective connection... Any refusal to give Scotland free choice to remain or go out

of the Empire, to associate freely or dis-associate itself at will from England, to share a common financial and economic policy with other nations, or pursue a separate policy of its own, is to subject Scotland to a species of slavery, involving the assumptions that Scottish people are so stupid that they cannot be trusted for themselves for fear they jeopardise 'wider interests'.[58]

Although many in the NPS would agree in principle with what was said, they did not like the excessive way Erskine and Grieve laboured the issue because it was believed that this would not bring them any political capital. Most members of the NPS felt that a softly, softly approach was the best way forward on this issue. Also, the Fundamentalists were inclined to take the view that they should have nothing to do with England, which most party leaders believed was an unrealistic attitude and one which tainted the movement with vulgar anglophobia. Muirhead believed that Grieve and his fellow writer, Compton MacKenzie, were having a disruptive influence on the party's progress:

> I cannot share the opinion he (William Gillies) holds of Grieve and MacKenzie. The goal of the Celtic dictatorship is not in my opinion one that many Scots have sympathy with...we are getting in more and more members and doubtless if Grieve and MacKenzie do not frighten them away we may gain a number of young men and women holding normal Scottish nationalist ideals.[59]

Other moderate nationalists were likewise unimpressed with the Fundamentalist wing which was tarnishing the party's image.

The initial tolerance of the party leadership towards the Fundamentalists can be partially explained by the fact that the National Party virtually held a monopoly over nationalist political aspirations until the creation of the Scottish Party in June, 1932. Up to that time, most leaders of the NPS viewed the activities of the Celticists as little more than a nuisance which embarrassed them in thier efforts to be taken seriously as a political party. The Celticists, although active in the columns of the *Scots Independent,* were not strong in the branches and were largely confined to the London area. In any case, most members of the National Executive were far too busy building up the party's organisation and contesting elections, to be bothered with refuting fundamentalist claims.

The initial optimism about the NPS's electoral prospects were soon confounded. This was a considerable disappointment, especially after MacCormick's spectacular challenge in the 1928 Glasgow University Rectorial contest where R.B. Cunninghame Graham, the nationalist candidate, was only narrowly defeated by Prime Minister, Stanley Baldwin, by a mere 68 votes.[60] The result was a shock to everyone concerned and the campaign showed off MacCormick's flair for organisation and also his talent as an orator of great skill. As was previously mentioned, Lewis Spence's performance in Midlothian was a disappointing failure and further problems dogged the party's electoral strategy, especially concerning finance and suitable candidates. The number of prospective Parliamentary candidates for the 1929 General Election was slashed from seven to two; R.E. Muirhead in West Renfrewshire and J.M. MacCormick in Camlachie. However, many moderates considered it a stroke of luck that C.M. Grieve had to cancel his candidature in Dundee:

> It was felt that Mr Grieve would have secured a reasonable number of votes but it was recognised that he stood no chance of winning the seat on this occasion. It was accordingly regretfully decided that it was not advisable to spend so much money to secure an inconclusive result.[61]

Both MacCormick and Muirhead polled less than 5% votes cast in each contest at the election. Organisational and campaigning weaknesses were blamed for the poor result and also the fact that the party could not expect to be taken seriously as a major political force while only contesting two seats.[62] However, despite the disappointment, there was no challenge to the efficacy of contesting elections and it was also recognised that valuable experience had been gained.

By June, 1930, the National Party had begun to make electoral inroads by securing 10.1% of the vote at a by-election in Shettleston and subsequently secured a respectable 13% in November at East Renfrewshire. This by election resulted in the party saving their deposit and was seen by many to herald a new era in Scottish politics. Nationalist aspirations were further raised by the victory of Compton Mackenzie in the Glasgow University rectorial election in 1931.[62] However, this momentum was not carried over to the General Election held in November, 1931. The party contested five seats and the results were a mixed bag of failure and only moderate improvement. Three of the candidates saved their deposit with MacCormick doing best in Inverness where he secured 14% of the vote. The other two, which included Roland Muirhead, only managed to secure about 10% each.[63] However, it can be said that in the confusion created by Ramsay MacDonald's decision to form a National Government, the nationalist vote held up fairly well. The creation of a more effective political organisation had begun to pay small dividends in by-elections held the following year. In Montrose and Dumbartonshire the party was able to maintain its normal level of support by securing 13.5% and 11.7% of the vote, respectively. However, the main problem facing the party's organisers was that their vote seemed to have reached a plateau, which showed no signs of rising above the normal 12 to 13 %. Several members of the NPS believed that the way out of this situation was to exploit the opportunities which opened up following the Labour Party's split with MacDonald. It has already been noted that several members of the National Party believed that one of the organisation's prime functions was to maintain pressure on the Labour Party with regard to the Home Rule issue. Arthur Donaldson was convinced that the adverse effect the Nationalist vote had on the Labour Party's fortunes was of more significance in the short term than the unlikely prospect of a nationalist win. This was how he analysed the result of the East Renfrewshire by election:

> Probably the most important and significant feature of the result is the division of the votes. Had the Labour man polled the total nationalist in addition to his own vote, he would have made as good a show as the Labour candidate in the General Election. As it was the nationalist vote made it impossible for Labour to win. I am sure that this aspect of the matter must be giving serious thought to many of our Home Rule Labour members whose hold on their seats could ill stand the strain of a Nationalist attack. It may lead them to reconsider carefully their Home Rule stand.[64]

The same form of argument was used at the by-election in Dumbartonshire in March, 1932, in which Tom Johnston was kept out of Parliament by the Nationalist vote. Muirhead was jubilant at the result because the NPS had 'saved our deposit...and kept Tom Johnston from Westminster for the present. This may cause some of our halfway Scottish Nationalists to reconsider their position'.[65] Johnston himself had no doubts as to the fact that it was the NPS which had ensured his defeat, while, at the same time he admitted that the result would make Labour candidates more wary of the Home Rule issue.[66]

This negative form of political pressure was keenly advocated by Roland Muirhead who never lost faith in the Labour Party's ability to take up the cause of Scottish self-government. He believed that the formation of the National Government and the ensuing electoral collapse of the Labour Party presented a prime opportunity for the formation of an alliance between the National Party and Labour Home Rulers. However, the bottom line for such an agreement was that the principle of self-government must take precedence over all others:

> I would certainly not like to oppose him [Tom Johnston] or men like the Rev. James Barr, but one must carry on with the Party to secure the best interests of the movement and having assisted to carry the National or

Home Rule Party, that, of course, will have, by far and away my chief interests. I am sorry that David N. MacKay, Tom Johnston, and the Rev. James Barr do not see their way to stand for an independent Scotland.'[67]

Muirhead kept in contact with several of his old ILP colleagues, who did their best to get him to leave the NPS and to rejoin his old party. For his part, Muirhead reciprocated the compliment, but likewise found no takers willing to join the National Party. Indeed, few in the ILP could understand his motives and J.M. MacDiarmid took a grim view of Muirhead's activities:

> I am sorry to tell you that a Home Rule Party in Scotland which cannot command the support of men like Tom Johnston, James Barr, D. MacKay and men of that type is doomed to futility. I am doing what I can to assist you entirely out of personal regard to yourself and I am quite convinced that working on your present lines and a policy of abstention from all other issues except Home Rule is ploughing the sands. Now that MacDonald has ruptured his Party a new orientation of the Scottish Home Rulers should be aligned by which the S.N.P. (sic) could save its face by walking over to the Labour Party and impregnating it with the S.H. Rule principle. Now is your opportunity.[68]

Muirhead believed that this policy was not feasible because no matter how many Home Rule supporters there were in the Scottish Labour Party, their aspirations could be circumvented by the numerical superiority of their English colleagues. He tried in vain to interest Scottish Labour politicians and failed to read how the tide was turning against Home Rule:

> Unless my logical faculty is mixed, it seems to me that what Maxton said in 1924 is about as strong support as we could get for the demand which is being put forward by the National Party of Scotland, and, as far as I am concerned, I will do all I can to get such men as Maxton to help us get Scottish control of Scottish affairs.[69]

Muirhead had high hopes for Maxton especially after the latter's decision to split the ILP from the official Labour Party. 'In view of the fact that Maxton's supporters are practically all Scotsmen, the commonsense plan for him would be to join up with the Nationalist Party in order to achieve his goal in the quickest possible way'.[70] However, such hopes were forlorn as the philosophy, which was now beginning to harden among Labour members, stressed the primacy of the United Kingdom as an economic and social unit. According to Maxton and others, the national question was of little importance. 'The general social problem always takes the premier place in my mind, before the nationalist or political changes, and I do not think that I am likely to change in that respect'.[71]

The Labour Party's attitude, if anything, hardened towards the NPS because it was seen as fostering unnecessary divisions and was responsible for an electoral wrecking policy which benefited no one but the National Government. According to one member of the ILP:

> If the National Party persists in a policy of injuring and opposing all who aim at Scottish management of Scottish affairs unless they abandon all other causes than Home Rule, then I can safely predict the youngest members of the N.P. will be mouldering in their graves and Home Rule still in the future.[72]

Others in the Labour Party, who were less sympathetic to Home Rule, regarded the National Party as little more than a political nuisance which was, according to Patrick Dollan, 'a mutual admiration society for struggling poets and novelists and of no use to the working class'.[73] Although the policy of contesting elections made Labour politicians more aware of the potential dangers of ignoring Home Rule, it had a long-term effect of alienating former sympathizers and helped to move the issue to the periphery of Scottish political life.

The failure of the National Party to make any significant electoral breakthrough in the early years of the 1930s, coupled with a decline of interest amongst the political mainstream Home Rulers, led to an exacerbation of the inherent divisions within the NPS. The leadership's initial tolerance of the Celticists began to wane as the party failed to project itself as a serious challenger in the political arena. Likewise, there was an increasing output of criticism from Grieve and others about the National Party's timid approach to politics. Many moderates believed that the Fundamentalists, or the 'wildmen of Scottish nationalism', were seriously damaging the party's image, especially as they had a flair for attracting public attention. One observer expressed many of the doubts which were held about the National Party and its political ability and, consequently, believed them to be unsuitable for anything other than local government:

> In many quarters the National Party is suspected for the good reason that the people who have made most noise about nationalism till now have been cranks, more or less incompetent woolly witted creatures. That is why I advocate infiltration: If there was a majority of nationalists in every local authority in Scotland we would not need Home Rule. We would have it.[74]

Another feature at this time was the willingness of many moderates to court the 'right type' of people. John MacCormick was aware that many such notables were beginning to take an interest in the ideas and progress of the National Party and, in view of this fact, he was keen to manoeuvre the party into as favourable light as possible without compromising the ideals and objectives of his organisation. For some months there had been rumours circulating in the National Executive and elsewhere that a group of prominent people were ready to join the party.[75] A further stimulus for emphasising the party's moderate image came from the interest that was shown by *Daily Record* editor, David Anderson, who was willing to give coverage to their ideas and activities:

> Mr Anderson informed us that he was not yet convinced that Scotland would be better off economically under Home Rule which the Nationalists advocate. Mr. Anderson is friendly to us although he is much more interested in the cultural side of our movement than the political or economic and while it will be a good thing for us if he will increasingly give us publicity, it will be valuable to him and his owners.[76]

Although Anderson gave coverage to the party's activities, he also raised alarm at the prospect of compulsory Gaelic, border posts and other such 'sinister activities'. Muirhead, MacCormick and Gibson were quick off the mark to dispel and play down such fears, much to the chagrin of Grieve and his clique.

Increasingly, attempts were made to present the party as one consisting of moderate and reasonable people, whose prime objective was to secure a more efficient system of Scottish government. Moves were undertaken to emphasise the positive aspects of the party's programme in order to divert attention away from some of the wilder aspirations held by several members. However, this added fuel to the claims of the Fundamentalists that underhand methods of conniving were going on and that the party was straying from its original course. This led Tom Gibson to urge MacCormick to adopt a more restrained approach towards moderation: 'I was asked if I had heard that we were out for the conservatives on the basis that they would give us some committees and that Sir Iain Colquhoun had been invited to join on that basis'.[77] He also warned that in courting such people there should be no indication that the National Party would change its policy. What was needed, he argued, was a more open policy to prevent the development of rumours, which only helped to further an atmosphere of paranoia and suspicion. Should any prominent people want to come in, he argued, then they should do so only as ordinary members:

> G. Malcolm Thompson, Dewar Gibb or Buchan [John]. Let these people come in as ordinary members of the Party, not as dictators. What we must watch out for is an attempt by interested parties to use us for their own

ends...our ship must be carefully sailed through the troubled waters of political intrigue and do not be too much impressed by the distinguished or notorious people...By all means, have new people in, but let them come in as acceptors of the ideals we have the Party for.[78]

However, MacCormick did make a special effort to recruit figures from the establishment and one success was Lord Dalziel of Kirkcaldy, the former Liberal MP.[79] He also set about establishing contact with the Duke of Montrose, who agreed to support Compton MacKenzie in the Glasgow University rector's election. However, the Duke was unsympathetic towards the Celticists within the National Party and would not accept an invitation to join. Indeed, after his initial contact with the NPS he lent his support to the Liberal candidate at the next election.[80] In spite of MacCormick's attempts to clean up the party's image, including the removal of the editorship of the *Scots Independent* from William Gillies, who was susceptible to the intrigues of Grieve, into the more sober hands of the Rev. Walter Murray, by the summer of 1930, the NPS was still not attractive to the establishment nationalists. Although most moderates were prepared to accept this as a fact of political life, they were shocked into a dramatic reappraisal of their political strategy when in June, 1932, the Scottish Party emerged to challenge the National Party for control of 'moderate' nationalist opinion.

The origins of the Scottish Party can be traced back to 1930, when George Malcolm Thomson and Andrew Dewar Gibb set in motion a process which aimed at establishing a right wing nationalist pressure group.[81] Although both men broadly sympathized with the aim of setting up a Scottish Parliament, they were alarmed at some of the tendencies evident within sections of the National Party of Scotland. For them, Scottish nationalism and Scottish control of Scottish affairs would be an important facet in maintaining and strengthening the unity of the British state and Empire and as such, they were totally opposed to the separatist claims of some members of the NPS. Also, they wanted to pose a challenge to the socialist leanings of the National Party, believing that, as a philosophy, nationalism was the intellectual property of Conservatism: 'Nationalism for Tories, that's our proposal — a synthesis of Toryism (real Toryism) and nationalism'.[82] Within this loose grouping of individuals, there was a thorough distaste of the Celticism which was advocated by Erskine of Mar and C.M.Grieve:

> When you utter the name of Erskine of Mar you hit the nail on its head. This man is mad and bad and dangerous, an arch intriguer... a Pan Celt, a person who believes in madness for madness sake... Grieve too is

dangerous...After all it is he and Bell between them who have made Douglasism a strong thing in the NPS'.[83]

Conservative nationalists were alarmed at the prospect of the National Party adopting Social Creditism as an official economic policy, which they regarded as a turn towards left wing extremism. They believed that they had a duty to prevent 'certain Douglasites who wish to use nationalism for their own ends' from taking over the leadership of the Nationalist Party.[84] Both Dewar Gibb and Thomson were anti-Roman Catholic and disparaged the people of Irish descent as racially inferior to Scotsmen.[85] This anti-Irish feeling spilled over onto questions concerning Scotland's Celtic past, something which the NPS was actively supporting. Thomson described the *Scots Independent* as a vehicle only for Gaelicism and Douglasism and 'To describe it as Scottish Nationalist is a farce. It should be kept out of the hands of all prospective Nationalists'.[86] Gaelic could be tolerated; however, it had to be kept in its place. [87] Another facet of the NPS which attracted criticism from the embryonic Scottish Party was its lack of distinguished leadership, which Thomson described as 'those despicable old women... The NPS reminds me of the British Army — Lions led by donkeys'.[88] The impetus towards the creation of the Scottish Party was largely fuelled by the desire of some conservative Scottish Nationalists to produce an alternative strategy which was more in keeping with their other political ideals.

Initially, Dewar Gibb and Thomson wanted to get together a group of prominent, like minded nationalists to join *en bloc* the National Party and in doing so, they would be able to give effective leadership and guidance to the rank and file, who, they believed, were being led astray by wild socialist Pan Celts. However, the first task was to seek out the right sort of people necessary to give a qualified lead to Scottish nationalism:

> Our job is to collect a few men all of whom have a certain reputation or position and who agree to act together and, when the time is ripe, to make a spectacular embarrassment of the NPS...The idea would be to form a little group which would go over to the NPS or issue a letter to the press. The group might continue even in the NPS with the special mission of getting at the universities and the middle and upper classes.[89]

Once the group had been established, it was decided to approach the Duke of Montrose with a view to him being the figurehead of the new organisation. The letter Gibb wrote to Montrose in connection with this enterprise is of considerable value in the way it sheds light on the political approach favoured by this group:

I have been authorized by a group of some half a dozen Scotsmen who are seriously interested in Scottish nationalism to approach you in connection with the following suggestion, since your interest in the question is well known. Those for whom I speak are united in feeling that Scotland is about to launch out upon a course which, properly directed, will lead her once more to taking the place in the world to which she is entitled. But in that statement of belief we lay stress upon the words 'properly directed' and we consider that at the moment there is no proper direction for the wholesome aspirations which are undoubtedly latent and widespread in modern Scotland. A true national movement is one which affects the whole outlook of the people both spiritually and materially. The propriety of such a proposition is not self-evident. The rank and file require to be guided, instructed and shepherded towards the proper course.[90]

This élitist approach to politics was obviously calculated to make sure that any populist nationalist movement was led along the right road. Gibb and others believed that the main British parties were not interested in Home Rule and that the National Party would become the focal point for popular support on this issue. However, they were not convinced that the NPS in its present form was capable of fulfilling the duties and responsibilities that would fall upon it:

This Party, ever since its foundation, alternatively repelled and attracted us. It attracts us by its main purpose and by the sincerity of its rank and file. It repels us because it appears to have no properly stateable or at least properly stated plan...It suffers from divided councils and certain of these councils (the more extreme) seem positively objectionable.[91]

In order to assist the healthy development of the National Party it was proposed that some form of watchdog should be created to ensure that proper policies were given a good airing and support. At this stage, the question of joining the NPS was left open and was not a precondition for membership of the new society. Montrose was favourable to the idea and put Gibb in touch with other like-minded individuals.[92] In any case, the majority of those who were attracted to the informal grouping were repelled by the policies and objectives of the National Party, especially concerning the thorny question of separation from England. By September 1930 any impetus to join the NPS had vanished due to both a lack of interest and a fear of the extremist tendencies of Grieve and others, and indeed, by June, 1931, Thomson was advocating the Liberal Party as the best means of attaining Home Rule.[93]

However, the National Party forced itself upon the attention of the establishment in the Spring of 1932, when both the *Daily Record* and Beaverbrook's *Daily Express* gave fairly extensive coverage to the party's campaign in the Dumbartonshire by-election. It would appear that the

NPS was the prime beneficiary of a circulation war in which each of the newspapers tried to outdo each other in terms of proving their Scottishness.[94] Home Rule, especially as Tom Johnston was the Labour candidate, became a political issue in the press and Beaverbrook gave the National Party considerable encouragement, although he ultimately backed his own candidates.[95] Interest in moderate Home Rule was given a further boost in 1932 when Gibb published his book *Scotland in Eclipse*, which outlined nationalist grievances. This was followed up by Sir Alexander MacEwen's *The Thistle and the Rose*, which put forward the moderates' case for self-government. [96]

John MacCormick was in constant touch with such people outside the National Party. He had established contact with the Duke of Montrose during the Glasgow University Rectorial campaign in October, 1931, and about the same time he moved in the same circles as Sir Alexander MacEwen and Andrew Dewar Gibb, who both were friendly with Neil Gunn, a NPS activist in Inverness.[97] The message MacCormick received from all concerned was that the National Party was far too extreme in its views and policies, and could not count on their support. Although he did his best to persuade such people to join the party by giving them his own moderate interpretation of his organisation's policy, the inherent degree of ambiguity and the activities of the Celticists within the National Party meant that few of these moderates would stomach joining such a group. This was especially the case after Grieve's Clann Albann fiasco which sought to create a paramilitary nationalist organisation dedicated to extra-Parliamentary activities.[98] Although Grieve was expelled from the party, the stigma of extremism was not so easily removed. MacCormick believed that the party's unruly image and reputation was costing them potential moderate Home Rule support. The trick was, as he saw it, to remove fears that the National Party was out for complete separation from England while, at the same time, to ensure that their policy was not emasculated into some form of devolution. It was to this end that MacCormick was to spend most of his energies in the period following the Dumbartonshire by election.

From the outset MacCormick's task was made difficult by the fact that it was becoming rapidly apparent that the National Party was fundamentally and irrevocably divided over certain key issues. Tom Gibson was singularly unimpressed by the devolutionist stirrings and argued that the party should take no cognisance of these developments.[99] Others warned that the devolutionists had the objective of destroying nationalist aspirations:

The increasing success of the National Party's propaganda is calling forth many expressions in favour of Home Rule or devolution from people who formerly manifested little or no interest in the subject...there are real dangers which cannot be ignored. The big danger in the immediate future is that devolution may be used to dish nationalism. Mere devolution may be presented in such a guise that many unwary may suppose that it will satisfy the demands of Scotland and solve all her national problems. But devolution would leave Scotland in the position of an English province, unable to move forward in any important way without the consent of England.[100]

Although MacCormick himself did not believe there was a need for a devolutionist 'stepping stone' policy towards self-government, he was prepared to try and find some common ground with moderates in spite of the hostility this would arouse among the more hard line members of his own party. However, the main area of confrontation was over the interpretation of the party's objective with regard to relations with England and the British Empire. Contradictory views on this issue emerged with rapid frequency and, for example, in March, 1931 Compton Mackenzie argued that an independent Scotland would be able to conduct its own foreign policy without regard to England, while at the same time, Walter Murray, in an effort to persuade Sir Daniel Stevenson to join the party, talked about self government allowing Scots to participate 'in her full natural freedom within the British Commonwealth'. [101] The latter view was, in all probability, the one that most members of the rank and file agreed with and it was also the one which was most likely to strike a resonant chord with the electorate. MacCormick believed that the main priority was to clear up the ambiguity which surrounded this sensitive issue.

The first moves in this direction occurred in February, 1932, when, at the half-yearly annual conference, a short restatement of policy was issued. This was carried out on the pretext of clarifying certain issues which were emerging during the campaign at the Dumbartonshire by-election. The restatement of policy was the response of the party to the goading they were receiving over the question of separation from England. The NPS claimed that their objective was independence within the context of the British Commonwealth, and as such, they tried to allay fears that they were out to destroy the unity of the Empire.[102] Although this provoked some degree of controversy at the conference, it was accepted without too much difficulty and illustrates how weak the Fundamentalists were, in a numerical capacity, among party members. Also, there was a changing balance in the make-up of the party leadership, which started to move away from the preponderance of left-of-centre ideas and personalities. The candidates in the 1931 General Election and subsequent by-elections reflected this movement with former Conservatives and Liberals out-numbering those with any history of a socialist pedigree and one of those, John MacCormick, could scarcely be accused of having any overt left wing tendencies.[103] In an effort to encourage Andrew Dewar Gibb to join the party, a member of the National Executive, Charles Black, offered him the candidature of the Universities' seat. He also claimed that the 'wildmen' 'are in a rapidly diminishing minority, and will become quite ineffective when broadminded folk like yourself (Gibb) join us'.[104] Although the restatement of policy, which was yet to be enshrined at the proper annual conference in May, failed to win over the embryonic Scottish Party, it did not have the effect of throwing down the gauntlet to the Fundamentalists, who would from now on devote all their energies to forming a strategy of opposition to moderatism. As if this was not bad enough, the party now faced a challenger for moderate Home Rule support in the shape of the Scottish Party, which was initiated by a breakaway section of the Cathcart Unionist Association led by Kevin MacDowall. With its pro-Empire sentiments, the new organisation mopped up all the 'prominent' men who had been expressing an interest in the National Party.

The first challenge issued to the National Party resulting from this development was a questionnaire sent out from the *Daily Record*, which attempted to establish the notion that the NPS was a separatist group. At the same time, a conference of Moderates organised by the *Daily Record* brought out their own plans, which were then set out against those of the National Party. The *Record*'s proposals disappointed many, even in the Scottish Party, which was soon to bring out a set of much further-reaching policies because they did not go as far as the Statute of Westminster and would have left Scotland with less self-government than most of the Dominion nations.[105] This worked to the advantage of the National Party which went on the offensive. In October, 1932, MacCormick denounced the Scottish Party and claimed that the NPS was the only organisation capable of representing nationalist aspirations. He attacked the ambiguity of the Scottish Party's relations with other British political parties and emphasised that Home Rule was only an issue because of the endeavours of the National Party:

> I believe that first among the things which has made our success possible has been our determination to cut right across the political divide and create a completely independent party standing for self-government alone...of no less importance has been our determination to have no pact

or alliance whatever with the older parties. Self- government can only be won by our independent action. During the next three years attempts will no doubt be made to persuade or drive us from our determination. But if we remember that this policy alone has been responsible for forcing the issue of self-government to the forefront of Scottish politics we shall not be likely to give up this essential of our faith.[106]

MacCormick astutely recognised this area as the Scottish Party's principal weakness, because the National Party was the only organisation which was prepared to fight elections on the self-government issue, and until their nationalist opponents resolved to do otherwise, they could be no more than impotent vocal detractors; a condition that was not conducive to gaining mass support. With a recent opinion poll in the *Daily Express* showing considerable support for Home Rule, the stakes were high.[107] As the Scottish Party was unable as yet to challenge the NPS for electoral support, MacCormick proceeded to then take the wind out of the sails of their criticisms by arguing that the National Party was in favour of maintaining the Imperial *status quo*: 'We have always made it clear that we want complete self-government within the Commonwealth, and that we insist that only an elected Scottish Assembly will in the long run have any right to determine how far membership of the Commonwealth shall limit our exercise of the rights of nationhood'.[108] He further strengthened his case by getting approval from the party to commit themselves to a policy which would maintain joint cooperation with England in foreign and defence matters. Also, it was agreed that there should be no tariff barriers between the two countries and that the administration of British colonies should be a joint affair.[109] On the whole, the restatement of policy should have been enough to quell criticisms from the Scottish Party; however, the battle MacCormick and others had in getting these ideas accepted by members of their own party was enough to maintain suspicions about the integrity of their moderatism. In addition to the hostility of the separatists, the restatement of policy caused unease among many stalwart party activists who were not altogether convinced of the efficacy of such a move. Many believed that the restatement would be interpreted as a concession to the pressure for moderation, which was mounted by the Scottish Party and, as such, would only encourage them to make more demands. Tom Gibson believed that if this was to happen it would only help to give credibility to the devolutionist stategy. Gibson, who at that time was living in London and often out of the party's leadership activities, was afraid that individual members of the Scottish Party were exerting too great an influence on members of the National Executive. He cautioned against strenuous efforts being made to win them over to the National Party's point of view and believed that it was only their attention which enabled them to keep going. Although Muirhead shared some of Gibson's unease he did not believe in isolation:

> I note that you do not quite know what is taking place within the Party re policy judged by the newspaper reports. I believe I am myself no less interested than you are to see the policies of the National Party of Scotland are not altered to meet the wishes of those outside the Party. The constitution of a self-governing Scotland will be formed along the lines advocated by Sir Alexander MacEwen, so far as his views are in line with our policy, but no further...Sir Alexander admits our case to the hilt but says he believes in devolution as a first step.[110]

Muirhead was in favour of establishing a nationalist consensus and believed that the Scottish Party members could be won over and could see no harm in informal contacts between the two groups. Gibson, however, believed there were inherent dangers in such an approach that could lead to concessions being given which would undermine the credibility of the National Party.

MacCormick further increased anxiety in the National Party when he put forward the idea of launching an all-party Scottish Convention.[111] The logic behind this proposal was that it would be a short cut to establishing popular support for Home Rule without the problems of contesting elections. MacCormick made approaches to prominent Home Rulers and the Scottish Party with the aim of drumming up support for the idea. Sir Alexander MacEwen and Sir Henry Keith were asked to sit on a joint committee which would set up a Scottish National Covention. They were also to review the present political situation and consider a short draft bill which would form the basis of a Parliamentary Bill to be presented at Westminster. MacCormick was adamant that his involvement with this project in no way contravened his duties to the National Party:

> This does not in anyway modify our policy. In this first place, if the non-nationalists persons will not agree to join the committee unless we modify our position then we will do without them. Further if the National Convention will not accept our short draft Bill unless our Policy is modified, then we shall just refuse to accept. It must be kept in mind, however, that it will be the business of the nationalists to see that the convention is composed of a majority holding the nationalist's outlook. It must be kept clearly in mind that there is nothing to prevent devolutionists supporting our draft Bill for a constituent Assembly to modify the proposed constitution of Scotland into a devolutionist one, but it will be for the nationalists to see that this does happen.[112]

MacCormick was a political pragmatist and was willing to face up to the reality that the NPS did not automatically command the support of all nationalist sentiment. He was especially concerned to make the National Party the most credible vehicle for nationalist aspirations and, consequently, this would involve challenging and converting devolutionists from their old ideas on Home Rule to the more radical approach favoured by the NPS. As a political idea, devolution would not go away and MacCormick believed the best way to discredit this approach to self-government would be to show its supporters that among the public, the policies advocated by the National Party were gaining more and more support. He was hopeful that the NPS would be able to increase its influence by scoring electoral successes in local and Parliamentary elections. He argued that:

> There is no reason why devolutionists should not be willing to support our short draft bill in the Convention, unless they refuse to permit the ultimate decision to the Scottish people and the MacEwenite type of devolutionist admits that the Scottish people and not the London Parliament must have the final decision... Personally I am satisfied that an attempt should be made to call the convention early next year. Before that time we hope to have some more of our members in town, country and district councils and other administrative bodies.[113]

The proposed convention never got off the ground. MacCormick did not win sufficient approval for the project among members of his own party, and devolutionists were likewise reluctant to be tied down to a convention. In any case, the NPS failed to win anything like the electoral support that would have been necessary to pressurise the moderates into believing that the National Party had the virtue of public opinion on its side.

Although MacCormick was convinced of the logic behind his proposed strategy, for many members of the NPS he was moving too far, too fast. Gibson wrote critically to Muirhead about the idea for a convention: 'You state that it will be for the nationalists to see that it does not happen that a modification in policy takes place. But I am afraid that circumstances will compel you to consider modification and unfortunately there are people in our Party still willing to modify our policy'.[114] Gibson believed, correctly, that the Convention was not a feasible alternative to the more mundane policy of contesting elections and that the only way that the NPS could claim a mandate for self-government was when it held a majority of Scottish Parliamentary seats. As far as he was concerned, the idea of setting up a convention was merely a dubious shortcut whose main purpose was to avoid hard work:

I think it is bad tactics and I am opposed to it... My own view is that you should be paying attention to Parliamentary constituencies with a view to placing the largest number of candidates in the field and considering ways and means of raising money.[115]

Gibson and several others linked the Convention idea with the restatement of policy, which was taken to be firm evidence of a move towards conciliation and greater cooperation with devolutionists and as such, he demanded an immediate repudiation by the National Council. MacCormick was unimpressed and merely informed Gibson that 'there is no cause for alarm'.[116] Compton Mackenzie likewise expressed doubts about the desirability of associating with devolutionists.[117] Although much of the flak was aimed at MacCormick, the hon. National Secretary was himself totally opposed to a devolutionist policy:

> For four years the National Party of Scotland had gone up and down Scotland preaching not devolution, not the erection of some glorified county council in Edinburgh...Devolutionists, who argued for what they called a measure of internal Home Rule — whatever that might be - wanted whatever they wanted, according to their own declaration, not for Scotland's own sake but because poor Westminster was congested with work. In order to relieve the Parliament of Great Britain and Ireland of this congestion of work let us in Scotland do a little for ourselves. That was the attitude of nine-tenths of those who call themselves devolutionists.[118]

At this point in time it is important to emphasise that very few in the NPS were in favour of devolution as proposed by the Scottish Party. However, a further area of dispute was developing over the question of how to approach and diffuse the threat of moderate Home Rule.

By the time of the half-yearly conference in November, 1932, clear lines of demarcation had been drawn within the ranks of the NPS. The Fundamentalists, who had begun to organise themselves, were positively aghast at the apparent collaboration with the devolutionist enemy. MacCormick's attempt to clarify the Party's position *vis à vis* the Empire brought stern condemnation:

> You will probably share with Angus Clark feelings of disquiet at the Schoolboy tactics of the executive of the NPS - numbers at any price; please everybody; contempt of public intelligence; naive assurance of ability to outmanoeuvre experienced professional politicians; telegrams to the King; contradictory restatements of policy; constitution making, indecent galloping at Dalziel.[119]

The recruitment of Lord Dalziel to the ranks of the party was one indicator that perhaps MacCormick's drive towards improving the image of his organisation was beginning to work.[120] However, the divisions, which had become increasingly bitter, now spilled out into the open and the public bloodletting undid much of MacCormick's work. The former chairman of the SNL, Hugh Paterson, put forward the case against the restatement, arguing that with regard to imperial affairs Scotland was 'best left out of it altogether and should cast herself adrift entirely'.[120] In reply, MacCormick stated that, whether they liked it or not, Scotland had been a partner with England in building the British Empire and, as a consequence of this, Scots had certain obligations placed on them. He argued 'It was accordingly necessary to face up to these obligations, and in the restatement of policy no aspect of sovereignty was given up'.[121] Angus Clark challenged this and demanded that the Scots should have no less freedom in their foreign policy than was enjoyed by the Dominion states. MacCormick agreed with this and claimed that the restatement in no way impeded this , although they would have to face up to the political realities of the situation which made such propositions unlikely. He believed that the antics of the Fundamentalists were mere hairsplitting and told them to face facts: 'The old Home Rule parties never got anywhere with their theoretical propaganda until the National Party came along with a realistic aim'.[122] MacCormick accused the separatists of advocating policies which were unrealistic and unlikely to cut any ice with the electorate, while at the same time, he stressed that the restatement would rid the party of the 'separation' bogey:

> The moderate Home Rulers are continually protesting that they don't want separation, but they rarely say what they mean by separation. Home Rule without separation is unthinkable; it is a contradiction in terms. It is customary to condemn the National Party as separatists and therefore hopelessly impractical people. Separation is the bogeyman of the Home Rule controversy. The National Party had never advocated the separation of Scotland from the British Commonwealth.[123]

MacCormick went on the offensive and advocated ideas that stressed the similarities in principle among nationalists rather than harping on about their differences in policy: 'The National Party, like all Home Rulers, believes in separating the affairs of Scotland from those of England, and placing them under a Scottish government'.[124]

The NPS also produced a six point charter for Scotland, which was designed to present, in simple terms, the basic demands of the party and put further pressure on members of the Scottish Party to abandon their futile gesturing: 'Some leading members of the Scottish Party such as Sir Alexander MacEwen and Andrew Dewar Gibb, if we have not misread their writings, seem to accept all these points and we wonder why they did not throw in their lot with the National Party'.[125] Although MacCormick had to face the fact that many in his party were unhappy at the moderate image he was trying to project, he was able to hold the NPS together and furthermore, he was astute enough to use the restatement of policy to counter claims made by the Scottish Party and others in the Unionist establishment.[126]

The most significant factor to affect the direction of the National Party's leadership since the inception of the Scottish Party was their electoral performance. At the beginning of 1933, the announcement of a by-election in East Fife presented the NPS with the opportunity to convince moderates that their policies were electorally popular. If they could poll a significant number of votes, it would undoubtedly strengthen their hand against the argument for maintaining the Scottish Party as a separate organisation. However, the choice of candidate and the campaign probably did more damage to the National Party's credibility than any other event in its short history.

The novelist Eric Linklater was chosen as the candidate because, according to R.E. Muirhead:

> After careful consideration I came to the conclusion that of the possible candidates for the constituency Eric Linklater was the most likely to do the best for the Party ...First impressions of him make me quite satisfied with the selection, although of course I do not know how he will develop in the campaign. There is certainly some risk in nominating someone who has not been through the rough and tumble of our movement but I believe that it is worth taking the risk. Some nationalist friends who know him and whose judgement I respect spoke well of him. It is likely that our candidate will get a better press than would have otherwise been given...He is a writer and that to my mind is perhaps his weakest point.[127]

It was thought that Linklater with his reputation as a novelist would attract more attention than an unknown candidate and his undogmatic approach to politics was likely to appeal to moderates. The National Executive was confident that the election would leave the Scottish Party politically impotent and it was thought that in order to highlight this, there should be no connections or contacts between the two groups during the campaign. From the beginning, this line was pushed hardest by Tom Gibson:

> I suggest strongly that the announcement be made at once that we are contesting without the Montrose group — we must act independently of them. I am also — as strongly as I can be definitely opposed to permitting on our platform any person belonging to that group.[128]

However, as the NPS campaign began to bog down, it soon became evident that no one from the Scottish Party had any intention of indentifying themselves as supporters of Linklater's candidature.

MacCormick gave his verdict on the performance of the party: 'Whatever Linklater's merit as a novelist, he certainly was no campaigning politician. From the start of the campaign the Press refused to treat him seriously and only used him as a source of light relief'.[129] Linklater, who was troubled by what still seemed to be the inherent ambiguities of NPS policy, answered questions awkwardly and without confidence, and only helped to add fuel to Scottish Party accusations of separatism. His style of campaigning at times showed an undisguised contempt of the electorate.[130] To make matters worse, the Duke of Montrose challenged Linklater over NPS policy towards the Empire, to which the reply was lacking in both clarity and confidence.[131] The party's organisation and the commitment of some of its members was likewise a factor in producing a disappointing result. MacCormick's attitude towards electioneering and his obsession with fraternizing with the well known and powerful was not one that would engender confidence:

> Part of our secret was that although we were serious about our cause we had no political ambitions and did not therefore need to take ourselves so seriously. Every campaign was to us a gay affair and whereever we went we were sure to find some howff where after meetings we could ceilidh till the small hours.[132]

MacCormick had also, prior to the election, been strung along by Beaverbrook who had urged him to contest municipal, rather than parliamentary elections. Beaverbrook revealed his true support of the NPS at East Fife, where he sponsored his own Agricultural Unionist candidate. This episode revealed a significant weakness in MacCormick's political ability. Not only was he guilty of not taking the election seriously, he also failed to read the opposition's sincerity on certain critical issues. The result was a humiliating defeat for the National Party, with Linklater coming at the bottom of the poll behind four other candidates.

The most serious effect of the poor showing at East Fife was that, at a stroke, much of the party's previous hard work in building up credibility was wiped out. Questions were raised regarding the validity of their own strategy, and their previous self-confidence was shattered: 'The first and most obvious lesson of East Fife is that Scotland is still not ready for national freedom'.[133] A further hard lesson was that the Scottish Party was not an impotent force as was hoped and indeed, it was castigated for its negative influence: 'East Fife should finally destroy the folly of the Scottish Party with its feeble claims for Scotland.... A party which will not take an independent stand for Scotland will never do anything effective'.[134] Although many regarded the Scottish Party with nothing more than contempt, they could not escape the fact that the Liberal Home Rule candidate, David Kerr, had managed to secure twice as many votes as Linklater and, consequently, were forced to come to the uncomfortable conclusion that a moderate approach to the national question was electorally more popular than their own more stringent demands for self-government. At the same time, the result had given both a moral and intellectual boost to the Scottish Party claims that the NPS was extreme in its claims for Scottish independence and that such views had no popular support.

The event was a signal for more polarisation within the rank and file of the National Party and both sides of the divide claimed that the result should be interpreted as evidence for a swing to their particular standpoint. Some members wanted to take the party back to what they claimed was its original aim. Arthur Donaldson wrote to Muirhead complaining of the direction in which the party was moving:

> It seems to me that since the inception of the Scottish Party and still more since the statement above mentioned (the so called 'ragman's roll') our propaganda has lost punch. Maybe it set in when the movement began to gain respectability. At any rate, it has seemed to me that there has been a distinct tendency to depart from our original creed and try to straddle far enough to reassure our 'respectable critics'...Something of this seems to come up at Inverness and there are indicators that it will be the principal issue at the next conference. I hope so that it will be carried to a conclusion. The attempt to 'moderate' our policy means emasculation and failure. There seems to be an impression among some that the 'Empire' in the English sense of the word is an asset to which Scotland must not sacrifice its claim. Instead it is a liability which we should be glad to have got rid of. I can see no way in which Scotland can assume responsibility in any measure for the Empire, any more than Canada does, without sacrificing control of her national policies to England.[135]

Donaldson's letter captures the mood of discontentment building up among the party's Fundamentalists perfectly. It also draws attention to the fact that many of those, who were unimpressed by the arguments for moderation, were not the 'wild men' as was often portrayed by MacCormick. Donaldson was one of those who believed that the party should hold out for complete independence even although, in the short term, this would not prove electorally popular. He and others argued that the process of independence might take a long time and that the party should take the lead in educating people to the nationalist cause. Donaldson had also put his finger on the crux of the problem by stating that before the NPS could make any more progress, it would have to resolve these outstanding issues once and for all. He was also correct to suspect the Inverness branch was behind the movement towards a moderate policy, as it was here that the key figures behind the demands for some kind of rapprochement with the Scottish Party were to be found.[136] As far as the Fundamentalists were concerned there could be no compromise:

> The place for moderates and Imperialists is with the Duke of Montrose and his crew. That kind of stuff has been tried and proven barren in over 50 years of Home Rule agitation...I am for Scottish nationalism without qualification or impediment of any kind, my support will always be for the element which seeks independence, with freewill association with England as a possibility later.[137]

The arena for the forthcoming battle was the annual conference of Inverness on May 27th, 1933. The moderate element most in favour of cooperation and, ultimately, some form of union with the Scottish Party were aided by the fact that Sir Alexander MacEwen's son, Robin, was a close friend of Neil Gunn. This allowed them to engage in covert discussions without the knowledge of the rest of the party, and allowed them a coordination in their strategy that otherwise they would not have been able to achieve. Although Muirhead expressed concern over Donaldson's claims, he did not suspect anything to be amiss:

> I shall enclose a copy of the resolution proposed by Inverness branch so that you will see exactly the nature of the proposals and while a number spoke in favour of the scheme, I feel we would be quite wrong in adopting it. Since the East Fife election there has been amongst some of the members an evident attempt to join with the Montrose moderates. I account for that through the fact that before the moderate Party came into existence, practically all those who were in favour of a national Parliament for Scotland had joined the National Party, although a proportion of our members would have preferred something like a devolution scheme. Those members are now suggesting an amalgamation with the Scottish Party and I see there is likely to be considerable discussions on the subject in the near future, probably culminating at the annual conference.[138]

What Muirhead did not know was that informal discussions had been taking place since the 10th of December, 1932, before the East Fife by-election. MacCormick had attempted to find a platform which would serve as the basis for negotiations for amalgamation. Initially his demands were basically the ones which were already enshrined in NPS policy and his early efforts were attempts to get the Scottish Party to agree with these, while he would guarantee a commitment to maintaining connections with the British Empire.[139]

Before the East Fife by-election, MacCormick was hopeful of the NPS electoral prospects and this in turn helped to determine his unwillingness to compromise to Scottish Party demands:

> In accordance with circumstances I am prepared to consider any method, direct action included, of attaining self-government. But the circumstances of the time seem to show that straight parliamentary electoral methods have a chance of being more rapidly successful than any of us would have believed a year or two ago. If that is true, it is our duty to concentrate on that method, and do everything we can do in our power, constituent with honesty, to strengthen our electoral position. To that end it is necessary for us to do everything we can do to get the moderates to join with us (on our essentials) and bring with them the prestige and the hope of financial support which undoubtedly they command.[140]

MacCormick was also keen to rid the party of those he regarded as extremist and whose ideas and actions, he believed, were bringing the name of the National Party into disrepute. He also came to the conclusion that he now had more in common, politically, with those in the Scottish Party than with some in his own organisation, especially as this group was making more and more criticisms, often of a personal nature, against MacCormick in the Social Credit journal, the *Freeman*:

> We are already being called traitors (Freeman) but I believe the real treachery at the present time would be to indulge in the self-gratification of calling ourselves irreconcilable resolutions something republicans and all the rest. I am certain we can beat the Grieve MacColl element and I am certain of it because I believe that it is they and not us who are ready to betray the cause for their own self-conceit.[141]

The negotiations were kept secret from other party members because it was known that should they learn about such activities, the Fundamentalists would gain valuable ammunition to bolster their claims that the leadership was engaging in a sell-out of principles. There is no doubt that MacCormick was quite unprincipled in his underhand manoeuvrings and he displayed an arrogant tendency to treat the National Party as if it were his own private organisation. The following extract is a perfect example of his ability to disguise his real intentions under a cloak of well-meaningness:

> I think you are right about a small preliminary talk with the Duke and Sir A.M. [Alexander MacEwen] on the 14th but I am still in doubt about the wisdom of R.E.M. [Roland Muirhead] being there. He knows that we are

keeping in touch with the Scottish Party and agrees that it is necessary. But in the meantime it is desirable that these talks should be strictly private or we'll at once have an idiot like Grieve or MacColl starting a row in the press and trying to create distrust in the Party. Now R.E.M. I suspect would immediately want to report every word of such a conversation to the whole council (a dangerous thing with N.K.W. and such others there). I could no doubt persuade R.E. of the unfortunate necessity for security till further developments but know he would feel uncomfortable...I should not dream of taking any step without his advice and counsel for I have a boundless respect for him, but you well understand that the position would be a little awkward. Besides he is our chairman and should be, as he is, above all the talk of treachery etc. which we can certainly expect, no matter how completely they accept our terms, nothing would be more completely a sickener to me than to hear a fool like McColl accusing Muirhead of fraternising with the Philistines'.[142]

The prime reason for MacCormick wanting to keep Muirhead out of the discussions was the fact that the latter was not at all keen on encouraging links between the two groups and indeed, he and others, like Tom Gibson, blocked the Inverness motion, which called for a recognition of the fact that the NPS and the Scottish Party were working for the same objective. This was replaced by a less accommodating motion, which called for nationalists to stop stressing their differences and try to concentrate on the opponents of self-government.[143] Although MacCormick had been defeated on his original aim he was, however, gauche enough to claim the credit for this motion which, to his political advantage, helped to isolate the Fundamentalists who were branded as the most guilty perpetrators of sectarianism.

The failure of the East Fife by-election caused MacCormick to review the position of the NPS, especially its policies and image:

> Since the East Fife election and its disappointing result, a few of us here have been talking over our whole position very seriously...The question that is therefore uppermost in our minds is whether our whole position as a Party must be overhauled. Within the Party itself there is no getting away from the fact that there are many branches which we would be better without, and a large number of our members are of a disgruntled type with whom it is very difficult to work. Have we attracted this disgruntled type because so much of our propaganda has necessarily been a recital of grievances rather than concrete constructive proposals? Does our difficulty in making headway at elections reflect our failure really to appeal to the imagination and aspirations of the electors?[143]

MacCormick's introspective questioning led him to conclude that the National Party's first priority was to put its own house in order. Any further contact with the Scottish Party was unlikely to be productive given the NPS's disastrous showing at East Fife, which would have weakened MacCormick's ability to drive a hard bargain. The real crux of the problem, he believed, was the image of the party and the influence the separatists exerted over it in the public's mind. MacCormick had little sympathy with, nor understanding of, those who wanted to allay social grievances and political discontent under the banner of nationalist aspirations and, instead, believed in a more positive Scottish nationalism. His objective was to try and harness the NPS to what he thought was a policy which reflected the political consensus of the Scottish people. MacCormick was not an ideological politician and this was reflected in the policies he advocated, which were a peculiar mixture of pre-war Liberal radicalism, romantic nationalism and the more populist objectives of the Scottish Labour movement. He paid little heed to the more concrete economic arguments for independence as propounded by Tom Gibson, for example. MacCormick believed he would win Inverness at the next election:

> Not only because I stand for self-government but also, whether consciously or not, I have given the impression, particularly in the West, that I am, as it were, a kind of crofter's candidate standing for the rights of small holders and the improvements of his chances in life. As you know my own outlook in politics is radical, and I know I cannot help letting that radicalism show through my speeches. Is it not possible then that we should be more radical as a Party? Is there not something to be said for the frequent suggestion that we should boldly proclaim our policy for a self-governing Scotland and indicate that even before we get self-government our members in Parliament will be irrespective of Party divisions unfailing in the progressive side.[144]

It is paradoxical that many of the most committed supporters of the idea that the party ought to adopt a more radical stance were the Fundamentalists, whom MacCormick was most intent on removing. However, MacCormick's radicalism was in reality a shallow political concept, which meant all things to all men and, as such, had little relevance in a society which was increasingly drawn into the orbit of class-based politics:

> I believe that radicalism is the only political bent of the Scottish people and that in expressing it, we would only be expressing our national character...I know the feeling of our members pretty well, or those who are worth anything to us, former Conservatives as well as former Socialists, and I believe they are all radicals. I mean by radical that they favour neither capitalism as we now know it, nor socialism as expressed by the Labour Party. They believe in the private enterprise of individuals but are suspicious of monopolies, trusts or combines or anything which, in short, though still privately owned, has reached dimensions too great for individual

responsibility in ownership. They believe in small holdings, in small towns, in small independent business, in everything that is the reverse of either large scale capitalism or socialism. It would not be difficult to formulate in actual political proposals what is at present merely a state of mind, and to do so might be the making of our Party.[145]

Much of this merely echoed previous ideas, again a lot of it coming from the Fundamentalists. However, without detailed explanation and in era of pre-Keynesian economics, such proposals were mere pipe dreams. Although MacCormick was an able Machiavellian in his political manoeuvring both inside and outside the National Party, he was badly hindered by indecisiveness and a tendency to adapt new ideas to a situation and then just as quickly abandon them as new developments arose. Throughout his political career, MacCormick consistently wavered in his political commitments and, more often than not, this was a result of his opportunist tendencies. After the East Fife election there was a crying need for the NPS to dramatically improve its political fortunes and MacCormick's advocacy of radicalism was no more than an opportunist response to this:

It is possible that a National radical Party might make a more immediate and wider appeal to the electors than a National Party which, however positive in its great conception of a new Scotland, must, none the less, be negative in its attitude to the questions which, whether we like it or not, the ordinary elector is primarily interested in.[146]

The reason MacCormick turned his attention towards this new radical image for the Party was that he was still smarting from the East Fife humiliation, which closed his preferred avenue for progress — greater cooperation with the Scottish Party: 'We have come to the conclusion that the time is not ripe for any further approach to the moderates as the East Fife result would appear to have rather weakened our position in any negotiations that might take place'.[147] Evidence that MacCormick's radicalism was nothing more than a short-term opportunist reaction to failure was the fact that within one month he had forgotten all about such notions and was again pressing for further talks with the Scottish Party. A stimulus for this volte-face can be partially attributed to the noises being made by the Fundamentalist wing of the party, which was trying to pressure the leadership into a more genuinely radical posture.[148] MacCormick was becoming increasingly bitter with this section of the party, which was more and more engaging in outbursts of personal abuse against him. He was determined to get rid of this group once and for all and set about organising a campaign to ensure their expulsion:

I believe therefore that the time has come for decisive action on our part, and I suggest conversations regarding the resolution which I sent up last week should be put to the council at this forthcoming meeting. I am certain that we can carry practically the whole council with us, but I feel there is going to be a break with a certain small minority, and to tell you the truth, I welcome the prospect. The division of opinion, to my mind, is not between moderation and extremism at all, it is between those who want to get somewhere within a reasonable time and those who don't care what happens so long as their own vanity is satisfied.[149]

MacCormick moved a series of resolutions for the May, 1933, annual conference which:

> In view of the differences within our own ranks, it is desirable to set the objectives of the Party as simply, briefly and as clearly as possible.[150]

The resolutions called for negotiations with the Scottish Party and accepted the principle that an independent Scotland should cooperate with England in running the Empire and also coordinate joint defence and foreign affairs.[151] The motions moved by MacCormick were devoid of any ambiguities and consequently produced the showdown which the leadership had anticipated.

The resolutions were symptomatic of an intensification of the debate concerning the aims and nature of both nationalist parties and the degree of common ground between them. George Malcolm Thomson argued that there were no real differences in the objectives and policies of the two groups and that the only way forward for Scottish nationalism was through union:

> There has been some misunderstanding of the position of the Scottish Party. Its members have been called the 'moderates'. It is a title that some of them have possibly coveted. But if 'moderate' is taken to be synonymous with devolutionist, then members of the Scottish Party have certainly no right to it. In that respect — and it is the fundamental respect — they are extremists.[152]

Thomson tried to persuade members of the NPS that the Scottish Party was not devolutionist while, at the same time, he endeavoured to allay moderate fears about the National Party's commitment to the British Empire. He pointed out the fact that both parties were committed to the principle of the Scottish Parliament having full control over finances and argued that given this area of mutual agreement, all other differences between them were of only minor importance. He concluded that 'There are in Scotland two parties pursuing what is fundamentally the same object'.[153] This view was heartily opposed by the Fundamentalists and many others who believed themselves to be poles apart from the Scottish

Party. Claims that the two parties shared the same objectives were dismissed as a fraudulent attempt to lead the party astray from its original aims:

> That a confusion of thought exists may be seen from the view which has been frequently expressed that the devolutionary proposals of the Duke of Montrose and his followers do not constitute such a fundamental difference between us that they need to be stressed, but like our own proposals, aim at Scottish self-government and Scotland reaffirming her nationhood. We believe this view to be wrong and subversive of our constitutional position and therefore bound to confuse the public and mislead our own mind.[154]

As far as Fundamentalists were concerned, the Scottish Party was a bulwark of British imperialism which was out to circumvent true national independence. They argued that the devolutionist proposals would leave Scotland with a political status similar to that of Ulster and as such, they believed, was incompatible with the party's objective to secure 'independent national status within the British group of nations'. They were especially angry with MacCormick, who redefined, or restated party policy with regard to the British Empire, which had been left out of the original draft. The notion that there should be joint executive control and coordination of defence and foreign policy was, they argued, 'a clear breach of the objectives and spirit for which the National Party had been created'.[155] It was claimed that these proposals were nothing short of a sell-out to the devolutionists and were incompatible with both nationalist aspirations and even fell short of the Commonwealth ideal:

> The important element which all these proposals overlook is that they do not correspond to the British Commonwealth constitution. It is precisely for this reason that they have long since been unequivocally rejected by the free democracies of the British Commonwealth themselves'.[156]

The Fundamentalists were unhappy with any imperial connections.

MacCormick's manoeuvrings in May, 1933, had two objectives. The first of these was to remove those from the party whom he regarded as 'republican'. Having done this the way would be open for the attainment of his second objective, which was to take the wind out of the sails of moderate criticism. MacCormick was hopeful that once the Fundamentalists were silenced, Scottish Party members would join the National Party, or remain in political oblivion:

> There are today two parties in Scotland each working for self-government. However much we dislike it, that is a fact and we must face it; we cannot shut our eyes to the existence of the Scottish Party nor refuse to admit that its appearance will affect the progress of our work...We must examine

our position, get right down to the fundamentals of our cause, and, for the purposes of clarifying our own minds, clear away anything that is not essential from our dogma. We must look at realities not phrases...We must learn anew what it is that unites us in spite of our differences of temperament and political sympathies. And having done that, we must use our privilege as the older and stronger Party and say to the new Party: 'Here is our aim, here is our policy. We have shorn it of everything that concerns mere detail. By this we stand or fall. We cannot depart from it. But we believe if you examine it in the spirit in which it is prepared, you will find it logical and reasonable, that it seeks to afford Scotland power to set her own house in order, essentially regeneration of our country'.[157]

Such blatant overtures to the Scottish Party alarmed many in the NPS, who were not necessarily associated with the Fundamentalists. MacCormick also had a tendency to categorise too readily those who disagreed with him on policy matters as being against him and his position in the party. Although he was convinced he could carry the majority of the rank and file with him, many were undoubtedly uneasy about the political implications of such moves towards the Scottish Party. There was criticism of MacCormick's action and it was not all delivered from the Celtic Fundamentalists as he frequently asserted. For example, Arthur Donaldson believed the party faced two choices:

Either the Party will come out definitely for Scottish independence, adopt a definite political programme for political, economic and social organisation of Scotland, not omitting a definite cultural side, accepting the loss of its 'cannier' members to the Scottish Party; or it will continue at present, becoming more and more emasculated and see its most desirable and vigorous elements break away to form a new and independent group carrying the standard which the National Party will have let fall.[158]

Donaldson tried to emphasise that the party was facing a choice over its future political direction and this was being denigrated in a competition which had increasingly been about personalities and tirades of pesonal abuse. In the April edition of the *Freeman* harsh things were said about the National Council and MacCormick was branded as a careerist and a liar. The London Fundamentalists abandoned political argument and used a host of strong arm tactics to convince others about the merits of their case. One potential ally who was largely sympathetic to much of their claims and who received this treatment was Tom Gibson:

For some time now I have been subjected to strong pressure from Angus Clark and Iain Gillies to throw my lot in with them, and been, by the pair of them, inundated with lies and misrepresentations of what has been happening in Scotland. At the same time, with their support and approval,

I have been subjected to a perfect stream of abuse from McColl because I refused to believe these lies and did not approve of either their tactics or policy.[159]

This policy failed to impress Gibson, who previously had expressed concern at the activities of MacCormick's dealings with the Scottish Party.[160] The strong-arm tactics of the London Fundamentalists swayed away moderates not so much in favour of a rapprochement with the Montrose Party, but against the activities of the extremists. Gibson, who was very uneasy at the drift to moderation, felt that it was the lesser of two evils and was resolved to back MacCormick's policy of expulsions:

I do feel that it is essential that this crew should be severely defeated at conference, as apart from differences in policy, if people have to reinforce their muddle headed thinking with lies and abuse and misrepresentation, then sooner we get rid of such people the better for the whole movement.[161]

The Fundamentalists' campaign failed in its objective, and merely drew attention away from the activities of MacCormick who was conducting illicit negotiations with the Scottish Party. However, it is important to emphasise that many in the National Party did not link the attack on the Fundamentalists with overtures of moderation to other groups. For Gibson, the defeat of this group was only the first part of a campaign against fringe elements within the Nationalist movement and part of a long-term strategy to put the National Party in better shape to defeat the Scottish Party as the champion of nationalist aspirations. It was not, he argued, a way to secure greater cooperation with devolutionists.

The constant internal bickering within the ranks of the National Party led many to believe that there was a crying need for a consensus on the self-government issue. One example of this phenomenon was Neil Gunn, who, although initially sympathetic to the Fundamentalist wing of the party, soon came to accept the efficacy of MacCormick's claims, especially when the NPS became electorally bogged down. For Gunn, the fundamental issue was the need for unity among nationalists from all persuasions and until this had been achieved there would be no progress. He believed that pragmatism would have to take precedence over ideological considerations and this led him to conclude against the claims of the Fundamentalists:

That extremism in general stands for purity and courage and is a species of self deception practised by the ego on itself all for its glory. Division has been Scotland's arch fiend and has always stood on 'doctrinal purity'... At any rate we should by this time have learned from our history that if we are ever going to achieve a national aim it can only be by a major harmony that refuses to be wrecked by a minority discord. Now I maintain that this major harmony can be achieved in Scotland today, but it can be achieved only on a basis of broad principle and will inevitably be wrecked by over early definition of detail or machinery underlying the principle...such a broad attitude has nothing to do with compromise.[162]

Gunn argued that the Nationalist movement ought to go back to basics and establish a solid foundation which was built from the minimum amount of policies and objectives. This could then be used as the platform from which a substantial political party could erect itself. Obviously such an achievement would only be possible if members could subordinate personal ideals and dogma to the long-term strategy and objective:

> First of all, then, establish points of contact. And apart from that, work out to the solution of disagreements...Presumably our prime concern in the whole affair is to see Scotland get self-government. Anything that stands in the way of that realisation, whether doctrinal purity or canting heresy, must be damned. If e.g. it could be proved that insistence on such words as 'republicanism' or 'Sovereign independence' would result in our never rousing the Scottish people to take control of their own country, whereas some such word as self-government would so result, then it strikes me that our duty is plain'.[163]

Gunn's pragmatic approach was indicative of a new mood of realism that was beginning to ripple through the ranks of the National Party. Although many of the problems were oversimplified, his analysis of the political situation was commendable for its logic. The real problem, according to Gunn, lay with the nationalists themselves and those who were dogmatic were the real barriers to progress. Any member who was unable to face facts and respond to new political realities was best left out of the party:

> It is rather disheartening to think of our efforts resulting than giving satisfaction to extremists a century hence as they proceed, complete with sporran, to lay wreaths on Scotland's final Culloden. And in saying so I am not considering England at all. England has nothing to do with this affair. The idea of England trying to prevent us realizing a united aim is merely amusing.[164]

Gunn formulated a plan of strategy for the national movement as a whole, which contained two fundamental aspects. The first was to 'give us national status' and the second was to gain 'maximum appeal' to our people 'now'. Gunn rejected any idea of advocating a Scottish Republic and believed that Scotland ought to remain part of the British Empire:

I say straight away that Republicanism (or similar separation) is antipathetic to the overwhelming majority of the Scottish people and cannot today be realised either by forceful or peaceful methods. Whether Republicanism is good or bad I am not discussing. I merely know that Scotland will not have it now — and less and less as time goes on with anglicising influences. (What she might ultimately do as an individual member of the Empire is another matter for then her national consciousness would have been awakened and if she thought Republicanism good; she'd simply adopt it).[165]

Gunn believed that the party would have to accept that the majority of Scots wished to remain a part of the British Commonwealth and that cooperation with moderates and devolutionists, no matter how unpalatable that might seem, was a necessary fact of political life if the nationalist cause was to make any progress.

The inevitable showdown came at the annual conference of May, 1933, which was by all accounts a noisy and chaotic affair.[166] The Fundamentalists had mustered all their supporters and engaged in a campaign of rowdyism and heckling opposing speakers. Despite the disorganisation, the conference approved the restatement of policy concerning remaining part of the British Empire, however they narrowly threw out MacCormick's resolution calling for negotiations with the Scottish Party. This illustrates the fact that although a majority of members disapproved of the Fundamentalist position, they were not yet prepared to go the whole way with MacCormick, and still remained suspicious of the Scottish Party. However, the scenes at the conference gave the leadership an opportunity to begin a campaign of expulsions against the Fundamentalists who were accused of organising 'obstructionist' policies within the party. A special meeting was called by the National Council to discuss the question of party discipline. MacCormick read a letter from a 'prominent official', who wanted the expulsion of the South East Area chairman and secretary for obstructionist behaviour and Angus Clark and W.M.McColl from the London branch for letters and articles containing personal abuse of office bearers of the party. The meeting approved of such action because 'There could be no progress while Clark and McColl were at liberty to call the Hon. Secretary a liar and a careerist'[167] The council authorised immediate action to be taken against these people and any others deemed to be obstructionist. Neil Gunn was also of the same opinion:

The *Freeman* has just come in with Clark and McColl's attack on MacCormick and the Executive. This is really damned bad. If the Party has any guts at all surely it will hit out at this sort of thing. If we cannot support our men - while admitting their weakness and errors in judgement and anything you like - from this sort of slander, then the game is pretty miserable.[168]

Muirhead and the National Executive were convinced that the disruptive scenes were a premeditated attempt to prevent the passing of the resolution on the restatement of policy: 'By organised obstructionism and rowdyism, the proceedings degenerated into a fiasco, and many delegates became so disgusted that they left the meeting long before its close'.[169] The subjection of members to abuse and insults would not be tolerated:

> Such behaviour, on the part of a minority, unless effectively challenged will, if it has not already done so, be bound to have a serious effect on the standing of the Party, and do untold damage to the general cause of Scottish nationalism. In addition, an impossible strain will be put on the loyalty of members and on intolerable burden placed upon the shoulders of officials, Council members, Propagandists and other workers in the Party.[170]

Muirhead then asked members to support the expulsion of 'undesirable elements', who were in the process of being thrown out of the party. The mechanism for this was a special conference which was to be held on the 1st of July to sanction the procedures taken by the leadership. MacCormick and J.M. McNicol wrote to all the members urging them to support the disciplinary action which, they claimed, was not the result of a personal vendetta, but in the interests of the party. The problem arose, they stated, because certain elements:

> have shown that they are not prepared to accept or respect the elected officials of the Party as their leaders. They appear to both despise and distrust us and to view with the utmost suspicion any proposal emanating from official quarters in the Party. That being so, it is perfectly obvious that we should find it impossible to carry on with any useful work in the Party so long as they are able to stir all kinds of suspicions against us...What you are to choose between on the 1st of July is not whether you are going to expel certain members or allow them to remain in the Party. Rather you are to choose which set of members you intend to expel, for our position is such that if you decide to retain the members impeached by the National Council, by that very act you expel us, together with nearly all the officials and active propagandists of the Party. We have irrevocably, though regretfully determined to resign from office and membership of the Party unless once and for all freed from the constant unjust criticism and suspicion which the gentlemen named have engaged.[171]

This was a masterpiece of political manouevring by MacCormick who channelled attention away from the political content of the dispute and turned the issue of expulsions into one of party discipline, against which the Fundamentalists had no defence. Also by threatening resignation, the whole question was given a gravity that it might not have otherwise merited.

Against these charges there was little defence. Iain Gillies, with a considerable degree of truth, claimed that the only offence McColl and Clark had committed was 'to maintain the original aim and policy of the Party against attacks by a section of the National Council. We consider the article written by these two men (*Freeman* 1.4.33.) is a fair and just criticism of those members of Council who have sought to emasculate the Party's policy and effect a compromise with the devolutionist groups'.[172] Embarrassingly for the leadership, Gillies blew the whistle on the fact that Tom Gibson, one of the signatories to the demand for expulsions, had informed them of the unauthorised discussions between certain members of the council and the Scottish Party. However, it was not enough to prevent McColl and Clark from being thrown out of the National Party. With this thorn removed from his side, MacCormick was able to make more strident overtures to the Scottish Party while, at the same time, other 'obstructionists' were systematically purged from the party's membership.

NOTES

1. The progress of this debate can be followed in the columns of the SHRA news-sheet, *Scottish Home Rule*.

2. See chapter 1 for details of Muirhead's growing disaffection with the Labour Party.

3. Robert F. Muirhead *Scottish Home Rule*, August, 1926, p.17.

4. See chapter 2 for the development of Gibson's ideas.

5. See the correspondence of the two men on this issue. Gibson Mss Acc 6058 NLS.

6. R.E. Muirhead to T.H.Gibson, 10th of June, 1925, Gibson Mss Acc 6058 NLS.

7. See chapter 2. Also David Howell's analysis of the development of Wheatley's political strategy with regard to the question of Scottish Home Rule sheds much light on the way the Labour Party in Scotland became less interested in the self-government cause. David Howell, *A Lost Left: Three studies in Socialism and Nationalism.* (Manchester 1986).

8. See chapter 1 and Muirhead's statement to the *Scots Independent April, 1928*

9. *Scots Independent,* December, 1927

10. See Gibson Mss Acc 6058 and Spence Mss Acc 5916 NLS.

11. R.E.Muirhead to Lewis Spence, October, 1927 Spence Mss. NLS. Also on the 9th of January, 1928, Gibson stated that Muirhead was ready to throw over the SHRA. In May, 1927, discussions between Muirhead, Gibson and Erskine of Mar about a proposed Constitution for the new party had taken place. Gibson Mss Acc 6058 NLS.

12. See chapter 2.

13. Report of the Scottish National Convention (SNC) Muirhead Mss NLS. There is also an account of the event in J.M. MacCormick's *Flag in the Wind*, pp. 20-21.

14. MacCormick's speech in the SNC report of November, 1927, Box 81, Muirhead Mss Acc. 3721, NLS.

15. There are a number of references to Gibson's outbursts of temper in the correspondence between the two men.

16. MacCormick, *Flag in the Wind*, pp. 23-24.

17. Gibson complained to Muirhead about this. June, 1924 Gibson Mss. Acc. 6058, Box 1, NLS.

18. For a short biography of Muirhead and his role in the Scottish Labour Movement see Helen Corr's contribution to William Knox (ed), *Scottish Labour Leaders 1918-1939* (Edinburgh 1984).

19. Quoted in the 29th of May, 1927 SNC report p.13. Muirhead Mss, Acc. 3721 , Box 81, NLS.

20. Tom Gibson to Neil M. Gunn, 1st of April, 1933, Gunn Mss Dep 209, Box 15, file 2, NLS.

21. R.E.Muirhead to M.A. McCrouther, 8th of October, 1928, Muirhead Mss Acc. 3721, Box 6, NLS.

22. See chapter 2.

23. They were unable, because of the domination of the Labour block vote, to represent the SHRA as a whole. See chapter 1 for details.

24. Muirhead Mss. Acc. 3721, Box 15, NLS.

25. MacCormick, *Flag in the Wind*, p.22.

26. Ibid., p.22.

27. For an alternative view of the events leading to the formation of the National Party see the article by Tom Gibson "The National Party: The true story of its origin", *Scots Independent*, January, 1932. p.36.

28. *Scots Independent*, July, 1928, p.136. Editorial comment by William Gillies.

29. *Scots Independent* to Tom Gibson, 31st of December, 1927. Gibson Mss. Acc 6058 NLS.

30. Tom Gibson to Erskine of Mar, 21st of March, 1927. Gibson Mss. Acc. 6058, Box 1, NLS.

31. Iain Gillies to Tom Gibson, 31st of December, 1927, Gibson Mss. Acc 6058, Box 1, NLS.

32. Tom Gibson to Erskine of Mar, 21st of March, 1927. Gibson Mss Acc 6058, Box 1, NLS.

33. 1st Annual Conference Report. Douglas Young Mss Box 44. Acc. 6419 NLS.

34. MacCormick, *Flag in the Wind*, p.22.

35. *Scots Independent*, December, 1928. pp. 21-22.

36. They were R.E. Muirhead, John M. MacCormick, C.M. Grieve and George Sims. See *Scots Independent*, January, 1929. p.25.

37. Tom Gibson to Neil M. Gunn, 1st of April, 1933. Gunn Mss, Dep 209. Box 15, file 2, Dep 207.

38. MacCormick, *Flag in the Wind*, p.39.

39. *Scots Independent*, February 1929 pp. 37-8.

40. *Scots Independent*, March, 1929, p.58.

41. Ibid

42. Tom Gibson to Erskine of Mar, 21st of March, 1928. Gibson Mss. Acc 6058, Box 1, NLS.

43. For an account of the development of the *Scots Independent* see chapter two.

44. Iain Gillies to Neil M. Gunn, 7th July, 1929 Gunn Mss, Box 15, Dep 207 NLS.

45. The main role played by Grieve was a speaker at the Scottish National Convention. He was not party to any of the negotiations between the various nationalist organisations and did not contribute in any way to the formation of the N.P.S. political strategy. He has exaggerated his own role in his autobiographical works and historians have all too readily believed him.

46. C.M. Grieve, *Scots Independent*, May 1929, p.90.

47. See chapter 2

48. Grieve contributed several articles on 'Neo Gaelic Economics' to the *Scots Independent*.

49. *Scots Independent*, February, 1929, pp. 42-43

50. As far as I am aware little has been done on a comparative study of right wing anti-capitalist groups in Europe in the interwar period. However, a number of similarities can be gauged from the following books: Walter Laqueur, *Fascism* (1979); Fritz Stern, *The Politics of Cultural Despair* (1961); and Richard Griffiths, *Fellow Travellers of the Right* (1983).

51. C.M. Grieve, *Albyn: Scotland and the Future* (1927). Note also the influence of Spengler's *The Decline of the West* on Grieve's thinking. This book was an important work in determining right wing proto-fascist thought in Europe: *Scots Independent*, February, 1929, pp. 42-43.

52. *Scots Independent*, May, 1929. p.90

53. *Scots Indepemdent*, June, 1929. p 103

54. Arthur W. Donaldson to R.E. Muirhead, 1st of June, 1930. Muirhead Mss Box 5 Acc 3721.

55. Ibid

56. R.E. Muirhead to A.W. Donaldson, 16th of June, 1930. Muirhead Mss. Box 5 Acc. 3721

57. Ibid

58. *Scots Independent*, June, 1932, p 116.

59. Muirhead to Tom H. Gibson, 14th of May, 1930. Gibson Mss Box 4 Acc.6058 NLS

60. See MacCormick's *Flag in the Wind* and Compton MacKenzie's *My Life and Times* for details of the campaign.

61. G. Chambers to Neil Gunn 20th of June, 1929. Gunn Mss Dep 207, Box 15, NLS.

62. *Scots Independent*, December, 1931, p.125. The results were as follows:- C. Mackenzie 849 Sir Robert Horne (Unionist) 762 Prof. Gilbert Murray (Liberal) 581 Tom Johnston (Labour) 110 Sir Oswald Mosley (New Party) 21

63. *Scots Independent*, December, 1931 p.19 The results of the General Election contests where the N.P.S. stood candidates were as follows: Inverness-shire Sir Murdoch MacDonald (Liberal) 18,702 David N. MacKay (Labour) 5,941 John M. MacCormick (Nationalist) 4,016 East Renfrewshire Marquis of

Clydesdale (Unionist) 27,740 James Strain (Labour) 12,477 W. Oliver Brown (Nationalist) 6,948 West Renfrewshire H.T.S. Wedderburn (Unionist) 17,318 Mrs Jean Mann (Labour) 10,203 Roland E. Muirhead (Nationalist) 3,547 Dr.Robert Forgan (New Party) 1,304 Glasgow (St.Rollox) William Leonard (Labour) 13,545 Fred Shoesmith (Unionist) 12,734 Elma Campbell (Nationalist) 4,021 Edinburgh East D.M. Mason (Liberal) 17,372 Dr. Drummond Shiels (Labour) 10,244 Rev.T.T. Alexander (Nationalist) 2,872

64. The by election was held in November 1930. A.W. Donaldson to R.E. Muirhead, 8th of December, 1930. Muirhead Mss. Acc 3721 Box 5, NLS.

65. J.M. MacDiarmid to R.E. Muirhead. 6th of April, 1932. Muirhead Mss. NLS.

66. The result was A.D. Cochrane (Tory) 16,739 Tom Johnston (Labour) 13,704 Robert Gray (Nationalist) 5,178 Hugh MacIntyre (Communist) 2,870 *Scots Independent*, April,1932 p84

67. R.E. Muirhead to J.M. MacDiarmid, 29th of March, 1931 Muirhead Mss. Box 5, NLS.

68. J.M. MacDiarmid to R.E. Muirhead. 1st of October, 1931. Muirhead Mss. box 5, NLS.

69. R.E.Muirhead to T.H.Gibson. 7th of July, 1928. Gibson Mss Box, NLS.

70. R.E. Muirhead to J.M. MacDiarmid. 29th of March, 1931. Muirhead Mss. NLS.

71. J. Maxton to R. Scott. 2nd of May, 1928. Copy held in the Gibson Mss, file 79. NLS.

72. J.M. MacDiarmid to R.E. Muirhead. 6th of April, 1932. Muirhead Mss. NLS.

73. Patrick Dollan. 29th of June, 1929. Copy held in the Muirhead Mss, file 100. NLS

74. George Malcolm Thomson to George Dott. 19th of July, 1929. Dott Mss Acc. 5927 NLS.

75. Both Tom Gibson and Iain Gillies were aware of this. See Gillies's letter to Gunn, 14.1.1930, Gunn Mss NLS.

76. R.E. Muirhead to T.H. Gibson, 14th of January, 1931. Gibson Mss, Box 1, NLS.

77. T.H. Gibson to R.E. Muirhead, 14th of December, 1930. Gibson Mss, Box 1, NLS.

78. T.H. Gibson to R.E. Muirhead, 15th of January, 1930. Gibson Mss, Box 1, NLS.

79. See *Flag in the Wind*, Chapter 11 esp. pp 68-71.

80. For the by election in East Fife. see chapter 4.

81. The correspondence detailing this process is to be found in the Gibb Mss, Box 1, Dep 217, NLS.

82. G.M. Thomson to A.D. Gibb. 19th of August, 1930. Gibb Mss NLS.

83. G.M. Thomsom to G. Dott. Undated, although, in all probability, from the same period as above. Dott Mss. NLS.

84. Ibid

85. See Thompson's *Scotland:That Distressed Area* (Edinburgh 1937) and Gibb's *Scotland in Eclipse* (London 1930) for sporadic outbursts of nationalist anti-catholicism. See also Gibb's file of Unionist correspondence (folder 6) especially the article "Tories on the Clyde". P.25 contains the most virulent anti-socialist comments and writing to the Duke of Montrose in August,

1930 he had not altered his opinions: "I am still generally speaking as a conservative and a hater of socialism". Gibb Mss, Box l, NLS.

86. G.M. Thomson to G. Dott, 30th of August, 1930. Dott Mss Box 2, NLS.

87. Ibid, also same correspondence of 26th of September 1930.

88. G.M. Thomsom to G. Dott. 16th of September, 1930. Dott Mss Box 2, NLS.

89. G.M. Thomson to A.D. Gibb 19th of September, 1930. Gibb Mss Box 2, NLS.

90. A.D. Gibb to the Duke of Montrose. 30th of August, 1930. Gibb Mss, Box 2, NLS

91. Ibid

92. Duke of Montrose. 1st of October, 1930. Gibb Mss, Box 2. NLS.

93. G.M. Thomson to A.D. Gibb, June,1931. Gibb Mss, Box 2, NLS.

94. See MacCormick, *Flag in the Wind*, chapter 11.

95. See previous section.

96. MacEwen, *The Thistle and the Rose* (Edinburgh 1932)

97. See chapter 4 for Gunn's role in the creation of the S.N.P.

98. Nothing came of the 'Clann Albann plot' although Grieve did not contact various people in connection with the organisation. Little evidence survives as to the proposed role and function of this paramilitary unit which was supposed to dress in Celtic military fashion and take part in land raiding exercises in the Outer Hebrides. See the letter from A.W. Ramsay to G. Dott. 26th of June, 1930. Dott Mss NLS.

99. T.H. Gibson to R.E. Muirhead, 6th of July, 1932. Gibson Mss NLS.

100. *Scots Independent*, March, 1931 p.67.

101. *Scots Independent*, March, 1931 p.68 and November, 1931 p9.

102. *Scots Independent*, April, 1932 p.90. "The main points were the securing of independence for Scotland within the British Commonwealth of Nations...and where necessary separate diplomatic representation".

103. C. Stewart Black to A.D. Gibb. 11th of May, 1932. Gibb Mss. Box l, NLS.: "of our candidates at the recent election Miss Campbell and Rev.T.T. Alexander came from the Tory camp, Brown and Grey are Liberals, MacCormick is ILP and Muirhead is some sort of Fabian". Note. Oliver Brown subsequently became politically orientated towards socialism.

104. C.S. Black to A.D. Gibb 10th of January, 1932. Gibb Mss. NLS.

105. See Andrew MacEwen, *The Thistle and the Rose*, pp126-132, and the Duke of Montrose, *Self Government for Scotland*, February, 1933.

106. J.M. MacCormick in the *Scots Independent*, October, 1932. p.186.

107. J.M. MacCormick, *Flag in the Wind*. Beaverbrook also expressed his support for Home Rule: see *Scots Independent*, August, 1932 p.146 and the *Daily Express*, 14th of July, 1932.

108. J.M.MacCormick in the *Scots Independent*, October, 1932 p.186.

109. C.S. Black, *The Policy of the National Party*, p.188 Pamphlet, October,1932.

110. R.E. Muirhead to T.H. Gibson, 12th of August, 1932. Gibson Mss, NLS. Muirhead echoed MacCormick's ideas on the subject.

111. See chapter 1 for details of earlier Nationalist Conventions.

112. R.E. Muirhead to T.H. Gibson, 12th of August, 1932. Gibson Mss, NLS.

113. Ibid.

114. T.H. Gibson to R.E. Muirhead. 15th of August, 1932. Gibson Mss NLS.
115. Ibid
116. J.M. MacCormick to T.H.Gibson, 18th of August, 1932. Gibson Mss NLS.
117. *Scots Independent*, October, 1932 p.186. "The measure of devolution suggested by moderate opinion is like trying to cure consumption with a bottle of soothing syrup".
118. Speech at Ediinburgh 30th September, 1932 quoted in the *Scots Independent*, November, 1932. p.8
119. Iain Gillies to Neil M. Gunn. 20th of October, 1932. Gunn Mss, Box 15, NLS.
120. *Scots Independent* half yearly conference report, January, 1933. p.36.
121. Ibid.
122. Ibid.
123. *Scots Independent*, January, 1933 p.34.
124. Ibid.
125. *Scots Independent*, January, 1933 p.33.
126. For Scottish Party fears see chapter 4.
127) R.E. Muirhead to T.H. Gibson. 21st of December, 1932. Gibson Mss. NLS.
128. T.H. Gibson to R.E. Muirhead. 9th of October, 1932 Gibson Mss. NLS.
129. MacCormick, *Flag in the Wind*, pp. 77-78.
130. See the press cuttings of the campaign. Acc. 7295 file 2. NLS.
131. Ibid.
132. MacCormick, *Flag in the Wind*, p.40.
133. *Scots Independent*, March, 1933, p.65.
134. Ibid.
135. A.W. Donaldson to R.E. Muirhead. 20th of February, 1933. Muirhead Mss. Box 5, NLS.
136. The Inverness branch was the centre of MacCormick's activities. See chapter 4.
137. A.W. Donaldson to R.E. Muirhead. 20th of February, 1933. Muirhead Mss. Box 5, NLS.
138. R.E. Muirhead to A.W. Donaldson. 8th of March, 1933. Muirhead Mss NLS.
139. See chapter 4.
140. J.M. MacCormick to Neil M. Gunn. 10th of December, 1932. Gunn Mss. Box 15, NLS.
141. Ibid.
142. Ibid.
143. *Scots Independent*, January, 1933 p.36 and July, 1933 p.135. "Recognising the immediate need of securing the utmost unity in the fight for Scottish nationhood, this Conference of the National Party of Scotland instructs its council officially to approach all or any Scottish organisations which believe in Self-government, and in the event of their accepting the principles of the National Party of Scotland as now defined by this Conference, to take whatever steps may be necessary to achieve that unity".
143. J.M. MacCormick to D.H. MacNeil (NPS Organising Secretary). 8th of February, 1933. Gunn Mss. Box 15, NLS.
144. Ibid.

145. Ibid.
146. Ibid.
147. Ibid.
148. This call was echoed in the *Scots Independent*.
149. J.M. MacCormick to D.H. MacNeil. 7th of March, 1933. Gunn Mss. NLS.
150. J.M. MacCormick to members of the National Council, 21st of M a r c h , 1933. Gunn Mss. NLS.
151. *Scots Independent*, July, 1933 p.135.
152. *Scots Independent*, April, 1933 p.87.
153. Ibid.
154. Angus Clark, Hugh Paterson and W.D. MacColl, the *Scots Independent*, April, 1933, pp. 92-93.
155. Ibid.
156. Ibid.
157. J.M. MacCormick in the *Scots Independent*, May, 1933 p.102.
158. A.W. Donaldson to R.E. Muirhead. 10th of May, 1933. Muirhead Mss. Box 5, NLS.
159. T.H. Gibson to Neil M.Gunn. 1st of April, 1933. Gunn Mss. Box 15, NLS.
160. See the previous section.
161. Gibson to Gunn. 28th of April,1933. Gunn Mss NLS.
162. Neil M.Gunn to T.H.Gibson. 3rd of April, 1933. Gunn Mss NLS.
163. Ibid.
164. Ibid.
165. Ibid.
166. See MacCormick's *Flag in the Wind*, pp. 82-87 for details.
167. Quoted from the minute book of the NPS and SNP 1933-1942. McIntyre papers, private collection.
168. Neil M. Gunn to T.H. Gibson. 3rd of April, 1933. Gunn Mss. Box 15, NLS.
169. R.E. Muirhead to all Party members, June, 1933 (writing in the role as chairman).
170. Ibid.
171. J.M. MacCormick and J.M. McNicol to all Party members, June, 1933.
172. Iain Gillies to all Party members, June, 1933.

CHAPTER FOUR

The Formation of the SNP 1933 – 1934

The removal of the Fundamentalist wing from the National Party was a great personal victory for MacCormick. In many ways, it vindicated the direction in which he had been moving the organisation and it can also be seen as a vote of confidence in his own abilities by the party members. However, as was explained in the previous chapter, the rank and file did not necessarily regard the impetus for the expulsions as being a method for obtaining a rapprochement with the Scottish Party which, in time, would lead to the creation of a new united nationalist movement. Rather, it was seen as an unfortunate, but necessary, method of improving party discipline and removing a rather unsavoury bunch of undesirables. Evidence that there was an ambivalence over the connection of the two issues is to be found at the May conference of 1933, where the party voted for a resolution in favour of a restatement of policy, which went against the claims of the Fundamentalist position, but narrowly rejected a proposal for greater cooperation with the Scottish Party.[1] A special disciplinary conference was held the following month, which was carefully loaded against the Fundamentalists and was the mechanism by which the expulsions were to be secured. MacCormick effectively tied the two issues together by obtaining the passage of his resolution which called for all nationalist bodies to increasingly combine their efforts.

The first action taken by the disciplinary conference was to dismiss prominent Fundamentalists such as William Gillies and his son, Iain, Hugh Paterson and Angus Clark for 'obstructionist' behaviour.[2] Many of their supporters resigned from the party in protest at the leadership's activities before the disciplinary axe had a chance to fall. Although no precise records exist to the exact number of people who were expelled, the effect was considerable enough to close down the London Branch, which was, ironically, one of the largest, and also to suspend the activities of the South East Area organisation. The latter incident was particularly bitter with recriminations abounding over financial misdemeanours.[3] The powers granted to the special disciplinary committee, which was set up after the conference in June, were considerable and they did not hesitate to use them, as Miss C. B. Cameron, Secretary of the Wallace Day Commemoration Committee, was to find out:

...in view of the nature of her letter and the open antagonism of Miss Cameron to the elected representatives of the Party for some time past, it was decided to suspend Miss C. B. Cameron from membership of the Party.[4]

The process of expelling 'obstructionists' was an ongoing one and it produced a series of resignations from many members, not all of whom could be described as Fundamentalists.[5] The purges were condemned as anti-democratic and were certainly not conducive to open debate with regard to the future development of the party's political strategy. Most of the resignations were a result of people believing that the National Party had departed from its original objectives and principles. [6] However, perhaps the greatest effect of the intrigues was to demoralise many of the most ardent and gifted members of the NPS.

With the removal of the Fundamentalists and, more importantly, the authority from the party to step up negotiations with the Scottish Party, MacCormick now believed the way was open for a unification between the two organisations. However, although many were unhappy about the activities of the Fundamentalists, they were likewise concerned about the leadership's uncritical flirtation with the Home Rule establishment. Even before May, 1933, Tom Gibson was pointing out the anxieties that were now abounding in a party which was both demoralised and divided:

> I note that the Executive have been aware of disturbing rumours circulating throughout the Party. I should state that I have been aware for sometime of such rumours not only within the Party, but also outside the Party. It appears that many are aware of conversations between some members of our Executive and one or other of the so called Scottish Party leaders or officials, and whether such conversations are official or unofficial, is not taken into account by the rank and file of the Party and the general public, all that matters to them is that conversations are carried out. A rumour had reached me that members of the Executive have been heard to say that an amalgamation with the Scottish Party was now inevitable ... I had, however, a conversation with a member of the Council who indicated to me that feelers had been put out to the Scottish Party and that indeed, one member of the National Executive had actually written in suggesting that such conversations with the Scottish Party had been discussed by the National Council, although it was not definitely stated that such conversations had actually taken place in an official meeting of the Council.[7]

Gibson's fear that the National Party might be sold out to moderate Home Rule interests intensified after the expulsions, although the leadership dismissed such concerns as the result of Fundamentalist scare-mongering. He was convinced that it was of utmost importance that the purges should not be interpreted as a sop to Scottish Party opinion and it was precisely for this reason that he opposed MacCormick's resolution in favour of greater cooperation with other nationalist groups.

> I am not at all keen to push the resolution through and I think that it could quite well be dropped ... to press it would give that crowd (the Scottish Party) more importance than they would perhaps have. If the Party and the Council discipline themselves as proposed by us, from the tactical point of view it would be desirable ... Our opponents will seize on this resolution, incorrectly state, as Dott stated, that we are going to give up a lot, and probably get support they otherwise would not get.[8]

Gibson argued that having removed their extremist wing, those in the Scottish Party who had feared the Fundamentalists could now safely join the National Party. Those who would not, he believed, were not worth bothering about and the NPS should not make any concessions in order to attract them.

However, what Gibson did not know was that MacCormick, Neil Gunn and D. H. MacNeil had since February, 1933, well before the expulsions, been engaging in establishing points of contact with members of the Scottish Party. They had given assurances to Gibb that they were prepared to modify the National Party's policy and expel the Fundamentalists in order to attract defections from the Scottish Party.

From the outset, MacCormick had regarded the removal of the Fundamentalist wing as part of a package designed to create a more moderate nationalist movement which was attractive to the establishment. In March, 1933, Gunn was engaged in a dialogue concerning these issues with Gibb:

> ...let me confidently give you an idea of the position. You may see the statement is a statement of general principles (the proposed restatement of policy) that only once mentions, but does not qualify, the word machinery. One qualifying phrase, explaining or limiting, can damn the whole effort. That is the position of anyone anxious for union. That is what I argued. The whole cause will be lost if we cannot surmount the Scottish failing for discussions in detail ... and of course there will be heavy weather with the extremists at either end. I make no doubt. But surely there is a sufficiently strong body of realists capable of realising the situation in all its aspects ... Remember a short statement on policy giving general principles I showed you. If we carried out these, then it would be up to you to work for agreement on your side.[9]

Gunn believed in establishing a minimalist framework around which nationalists of all shades of opinion would agree to work together in order to achieve a basic set of political objectives. In order to make this possible, he argued that it was necessary to remove all areas of potential dispute and, in the case of the NPS, this meant the removal of the Fundamentalist wing and the tapering of policy in order to narrow the differences between the National and Scottish parties. Gunn had a pragmatic approach to politics and believed that moderates such as Sir Alexander MacEwen and Andrew Dewar Gibb would attract more support to the nationalist cause than the 'republicans' in his own party. From his, and a covert group within the NPS, point of view, the restatement of policy and the expulsion of the Fundamentalists were an attempt to secure the approval of the Scottish Party, which had the ultimate aim of establishing a political unification. However, the success of such manoeuvres was very much dependent on Gibb's ability to secure a similar compromise within the Scottish Party.

The initial reluctance of members of the right wing nationalist camp to support the NPS was a result of their concern at the separatist and anti-British Empire tendencies expressed by the Fundamentalist wing of the National Party. However, such a loose sense of identity of interests meant that the Scottish Party displayed a whole series of ambivalent attitudes when it came to offering themselves as the alternative, moderate nationalist party. Indeed, most of their political ideas were delivered purely as an expression of individual opinion and most of what was stated was usually a negative critique of the National Party.[10] Alexander MacEwan saw little value in what was on offer from the NPS and highlighted the fact that the Fundamentalists and C. M. Grieve were, more often than not, seen as representing the real character of the National Party. The Scottish Party reinforced their criticisms by giving the Fundamentalists more prominence than was really the case. This included ignoring the fact that C. M. Grieve had been expelled from the party for sometime prior to the main purges in June, 1933. MacEwen tried to emphasise the confusion that emanated from the National Party in the public's mind and pin it on a supposed lack of direction:

> It is a little difficult to ascertain the real aim of the National Party and their literary wing. When one seizes on some passage in the writings of an author, avowedly nationalist, and proceeds to discuss it, one gets the disconcerting reply that either the author is not a member of the Party or that he represents no one but himself ... I can only plead that I have made every possible endeavour to ascertain the official programme of the Party. But I am yet without the inner light.[11]

Moderates largely ignored official National Party policy and instead, turned the spotlight on maverick elements, which made intelligent dialogue between the two camps impossible. MacEwen initially wanted to ignore the NPS's social and economic policies and did not consider the respective strengths and weaknesses of their electoral strategy which were both key areas of political life in which the Scottish Party had little to offer.

The fact that the Scottish Party was primarily a loose collection of individuals, whose only cohesive *raison d'être* was the vague idea of some from of Home Rule which would not impair the unity of the British Empire, meant that, in many ways, they were a hopelessly inconsistent group. Indeed, at the outset of the Scottish Party's history, there were at least three key versions of what was meant by moderate Home Rule, and they were by no means all totally compatible with each other.[12] On the one hand, Andrew Dewar Gibb and George Malcolm Thomson advocated a strident, racially oriented nationalism which was politically to the far right and had quasi-fascist tendencies. [13] This contrasted heavily with the pre-war Liberal Home Rule ideas held by both MacEwen and the Duke of Montrose, who were both very enthusiastic about the Gaelic contribution towards the Scottish identity and were more to the centre of mainstream political ideology. However, both of these men differed in their ideas of how far Home Rule should be taken. [14] Yet, this was an area that the shell shocked National Party failed to exploit, principally because, as the Scottish Party was propelled more by personalities than policies, few in the NPS sought to challenge their intellectual validity. One of the main component parts of the Scottish Party was the frustration that neither the Liberal nor the Tory party was giving sufficient attention to the devolutionist argument. Although the National Party believed them to have a significant political pedigree, most members of the Scottish Party were on the periphery of Scottish politics and it may be the case that Home Rule was seen by some ambitious men as the ticket which would catapult them into political prominence. Andrew Dewar Gibb had been for some time fed up with contesting seats for the Tory Party in which he had little chance of winning and was only driven on in the hope that one day he would receive a safe seat for loyal service.[15] However, an apparent lack of progress in that direction and the fact that the nationalists had been doing well in the Glasgow University Rectorial elections may well have prompted him to believe that his combination of nationalism and Toryism would stand him in better stead in contesting a seat of his own choosing for the nationalists, rather than representing the Conservative cause in Red Clydeside.[16]

Alexander MacEwen belonged to the paternalistic, socially aware wing of the Liberal Party and was, in many ways, the living embodiment of the prewar 'new Liberalism'. [17] His ideas on public service and cooperative democracy tied in with his belief that the issue of Home Rule was a strong enough cohesive element which would unite all like-minded politicians and public figures in pursuit of the self-government goal. However, MacEwen was a notary and a committee man rather than a high ranking political figure who could command the respect of the establishment. His role in the Scottish Party, should Home Rule crystallise into the fundamental political issue in Scotland, would give him a prominence that he was unable to attain in the Liberal Party. The Duke of Montrose was likewise an unimportant figure who, although holding the Tory whip in the House of Lords, played no active role in political life. If the self-government cause took off , his stature would be enhanced, in spite of the fact that according to George Malcolm Thomson 'his name is of greater importance to the cause than his abilities'.[18]

The Scottish Party offered little in the way of a clearly defined set of objectives and no effort was made to differentiate the Home Rule ideas in circulation from devolution. Indeed, there was an apparent consensus that devolution was a necessary first step for the subsequent achievement of Home Rule. Unlike the National Party, the issue was not considered to be important, with principle, rather than method, being what counted the most. According to Gibb:

> I believe in our camp, as in yours (the NPS) there are different shades of opinion as to what we primarily want for Scotland. In our lot there is a group who, as it were, are devolutionist by nature - but there are others I don't care how it comes: whether in a leap or in a series of steps. They are at least all in the same direction.[19]

MacEwen believed that a 'stepping stone' policy was essential to secure the necessary stability and ensure a peaceful transformation to Home Rule. [20] Both he and Gibb believed that a 'Scottish Parliament' should not interfere with the existing British procedures for foreign policy and Imperial and defence matters:

> As regards Foreign Policy, Defence, etc., it was proposed that these should be reserved matters to be dealt with by the present Parliament until such time as a United Kingdom or Empire Council was created ... The Nationalist view is, or was, that first of all Scotland must be given her full independent status, and then negotiate a treaty with England for the regulation of these things.[21]

However, they disagreed with Montrose in arguing that the Scottish Parliament ought to have final sovereignty over all issues. As far as the

Duke was concerned, this smacked too much of separatism and in any case, it was not necessary as the Scottish Government could exercise control in those areas by virtue of their command of Scottish finances, although he gave no indication as to how potential disputes could be resolved. Montrose was especially sensitive on the issue of separation from England and was distrustful of the National Party, which he regarded as extremist. His description of the NPS was hardly flattering:

> It happened that about four years ago a small body of enthusiasts decided to form a new party - or rather, an amalgamation of small existing groups — into the Scottish National Party [sic]. In their early days, the Nationalists were largely swayed by idealism. Novelists, essayists and poets, rather than businessmen, were found in their ranks. Hence the insistence on such terms as 'sovereign power and independence', without much consideration as to what these ideals meant or how they were to be attained. Other extravagances, such as 'separation from England', 'kilted sailors in Scottish ships', and 'Gaelic speaking ambassadors', got mixed up with their utopian ideals, and certainly put off much support which the Party's energy and enterprise would have otherwise obtained. Today the national spirit is sponsored by another 'Scottish Party', based on principles moderate, reasonable and free from all hatred of England.[22]

The Scottish Party, in the final analysis, was united more by what it did not want pertaining to Scottish nationalism, rather than existing as an organisation propounding concrete proposals. They flatly rejected diplomatic separation, although MacEwen argued that Scottish commercial attachés in British Embassies would be a way of bolstering economic interests.[23] In this respect, they were at complete odds with the NPS, which advocated a diplomatic status similar to the Commonwealth nations. The Scottish Party rejected this idea on the grounds that as Scotland was a mother nation of the Empire, they would not be downgraded to a 'colonial state'. They argued that as Scotland had played such an important role in the creation of the Empire they would have to accept joint responsibility with England for its administration. Indeed, members of the Scottish Party were fervent admirers and supporters of the British Empire ideal. Montrose believed that self-government would help maintain the Scottish contribution to imperial affairs:

> If Scotland obtains self-government, and has the three estates of the realm set up once again within her borders, then for the first time in modern history she would be able to play her part with pride as an Empire builder enveloped in the robe of nationality. The step would not be retrograde: it will be an advance. As self-government would apply purely to domestic affairs, it would not weaken the United Kingdom. It would strengthen it.

Out of plurality will come a greater unity than ever before, and the freedom given for self-expression will be in keeping with the spirit which has proved so successful and binding throughout the whole British Empire.[24]

This quote illustrates how clearly their Scottish nationalism was a sub-section of a wider, and more dominating, British nationalism. Gibb saw the link in racial terms, believing that the Scots, as a race, complemented the English in the task of 'Empire building'.[25] He also argued that imperial connections would have to be maintained for practical purposes:

Scotsmen today are occupying positions both eminent and humble throughout that Empire, and Scottish interests are bound up with every colony in it. It is necessary that Scotland should continue to assert her unique status, side by side with England. That unique position cannot be maintained by her assumption of what is called Dominion Status: an unthinkable decline.[26]

The predominant ethos behind much of their Home Rule demands was the desire to strengthen the British Empire by highlighting the Scottish contribution to its creation and administration.

MacCormick was not so much interested in the policies of the Scottish Party, but rather, its personalities and was quite often willing to turn a blind eye to the political differences between the two organisations. He was convinced that his nationalist opponents were after the same goals as himself:

The confusion of issues which has lately hampered us in our progress will disappear when the National Party becomes sufficiently conscious of its own strengths to hold out a welcome hand to all others who are groping their way towards the same goal as ourselves.[27]

MacCormick's conciliatory approach to the Scottish Party failed to appreciate the significant political differences that existed, and even while writing in the 1950s, he seemed to show little understanding of the nature of the debate. In a significant passage from the partially auto-biographical *Flag in the Wind*, he attached more importance to psychological factors, rather than identifying the nature of the political divide that existed between moderate Home Rulers and full blown nationalists:

There was, in fact, a subtle and scarcely definable dividing line which separated one section of the nationalists from another ... it had little to do with moderatism or extremism or with statements of policy. It was rather a difference in mental approach which made itself felt in discussion of any kind. On the one hand, there was what I call a kind of cantankerousness, as though those who displayed it felt themselves, however unconsciously, to belong to a defeated and conquered nation and must therefore always stand on their dignity and look for every slight. They seemed to me to look at Scotland through green spectacles and despite complete lack of historical parallel, to identify the Irish struggle with their own. On the other hand, there were those whose nationalism was a perfectly healthy and normal desire for a better form of Union with England than that which had been freely negotiated in 1707, and who never, either consciously or unconsciously, thought of Scotland as having anything other than equal status with England, however unfortunate the incorporating Union of Parliaments might reflect itself in modern Scottish life.[28]

Although MacCormick was writing at a stage in his political career which placed him poles apart from his previous position in the National Party, a number of interesting consistencies remained. He was always most comfortable with, and most impressed by, sympathetic elements in the Scottish establishment and, as his subsequent career was to show, the thought of being a member of a rogue political party was not one that he would have found appealing. Indeed, when it became apparent that the SNP could not be tamed into holding the establishment values forced upon it by MacCormick, he left, believing that his position was untenable.[29] The passage is also interesting in the way it highlights MacCormick's reluctance to accept that within the nationalist movement there were legitimate arguments about strategy and policy. It was a trait of his to simplify disputes into ones revolving around personalities rather than politics. MacCormick was only too ready to castigate those who disagreed with his version of events as belonging to 'the defeated and conquered nation'.

He ignored the protestations of members of his own party and left a rather confused and confidence-shaken R. E. Muirhead to defend the recent events to Arthur Donaldson, who had resigned in protest at the expulsions:

> You (Donaldson) say the Party has gone back to the exploded Home Rule programme. If that means it has departed from the claim for independent national status: it is not true. The new policy does not commit us to, as the Union now does, the sacrifice of freedom of action on the most important aspects of national sovereignty. There is no reason why modification or revision which Scotland might insist upon the Act of Union, though superficially more drastic, is not essential, as there is no limit on the amount of revision that might be insisted upon... The statement that tariff barriers are undesirable and that Foreign policy etc., should remain matters of joint concern between England and Scotland is certainly new but it does not commit us to anything definite and was adopted merely to satisfy the Scottish Party leaders that antagonism to England, and refusal to recognise

the desire for cooperation with England in matters of joint concern are not objects of the National Party of Scotland. It does not mean that Scotland is not to be independent.[30]

Muirhead could not disguise the fact that the expulsions and changes in policy over the last few months, whether he realised this at the time or not is another matter, were part and parcel of a policy of appeasement towards the Scottish Party. What were once tenets of the National Party's faith were now only matters of interpretation and wishful conjecture. However, the most significant feature about these political manoeuvres was the fact that the NPS sacrificed a lot in terms of policy and internal harmony without achieving any guarantees that it would produce a positive response from the Scottish Party. Indeed, the leadership displayed a culpable weakness in bending to pressure from a group which had, if any, even less influence on Scottish politics than the NPS.

MacCormick was the weak link in the chain and the Scottish Party targeted him from an early date as the most suitable candidate to steer the NPS in the direction which best served their ends. A. D. Gibb felt that the more pressure they were able to put on the National Party, the more pliable they would be to the Scottish Party demands. It was for this reason that they pursued a wrecking policy in the East Fife by-election against the National Party and Gibb and Thomson were not slow in realising the opportunities that were afforded to the Scottish Party should the NPS run into difficulties:[31]

> I think we must get MacCormick into our ambit. Can you do anything to get in touch with him. He is under Gunn's influence now. But he is susceptible to the ideas of others ... The NPS have run into heavy weather in East Fife. They will be ridiculed and maybe open to more reason.[32]

The poor showing of the National Party in the East Fife by-election meant that they would have to use the first opportunity to redeem their electoral standing. It was hoped that their blatant, moderate image would pay off dividends and, in any case, this would be essential in order to justify the recent traumas and raise morale in an organisation which had just completed a punishing course of self-inflicted wounds. Such an opportunity presented itself with the announcement of a by-election in Kilmarnock in the Autumn of 1933. However, the National Party's chances of political redemption were wrecked by the appearance of a Scottish Party challenge in the shape of their intended candidate Andrew Dewar Gibb. Such a clash of rival nationalist bodies would, in all probability, cancel out any improvement in the National Party's share of the vote that might have been won as a result of their recent modifications. However, because they were operating against a party which was starting from a base line of zero and, consequently, had little to lose, the NPS could have found their share of the vote reduced significantly by the split in the self-government support. Also, the resulting confusion that would have ensued from the fact that there were two candidates representing the Home Rule cause was more than likely to have an adverse effect on the nationalist movement as a whole.

Although there was now the possibility of an outright electoral confrontation with their principal nationalist opponent, which could have given the NPS an opportunity to inflict a heavy defeat on the Scottish Party and establish themselves as the main bearers of the Home Rule standard, few had any stomach for a fight which, it was believed, would only lead to further disunity in the self-government cause. The Scottish Party had chosen its moment well and was acutely aware of the fact that the NPS was at the weakest point in its short history. The application of such pressure at this critical juncture meant that the National Party was even more desperate to reach an accommodation with their rivals. In short, the 'appeasers' had been well and truly outmanoeuvred.

Neil Gunn, who had acted as the principal go-between, could not contain his dismay when he heard about the Scottish Party decision to contest the Kilmarnock election, especially as Gibb had been his closest confidant. He wrote to him pointing out what a fragile position he and his fellow moderates must now occupied within the NPS:

> I hope to lay certain matters before you in their final aspect, when the (Daily) Record came in with the announcement of you as a Scottish Party candidate for Kilmarnock. This is certainly a severe shock The National Party decision to fight Kilmarnock is months old and weeks ago schemes were drawn up. In view of recent troubles, never has it been so essential for the NPS to fight an election, and not for any tactical good in itself but for the advancement of the cause for which it has so strenuously fought. The NPS has been accused by many of its followers in recent days of watering down its policy, of making overtures to the SP, in short of stultifying its essential being in order to achieve harmony in the fight for self-government. If it has done so then manifestly it has not been very successful and those concerned must feel rather foolish.[32]

For those in the NPS who advocated a policy of moderation and accommodation with the Scottish Party, their humiliation must have been quite considerable. However, the principal question which must be raised concerning this sorry episode is not about the strategy MacCormick and others pursued, but rather its execution and the implementation of the 'grand plan'. They had totally underestimated what would be necessary to bring the Scottish Party into a united movement, while at the same time, they committed themselves to a policy of unilateral appeasement without firstly establishing safeguards to protect their own political interests. The net result of this process, which it has to be remembered was largely established without the knowledge of the membership of the NPS, was that they were left hopelessly exposed and had to face the option of further sell-outs to achieve the unity they originally had envisaged or back-pedal and lose credibility with their own party. In either case their position was a weak one.

The NPS announced that they would fight the election and in contrast to Gunn's disillusionment, MacCormick was strangely optimistic about the whole affair, which smacked of a total lack of realism:

> I rather think the outcome will be that the Scottish Party will now approach us in order to make a bargain but I think their action has put us in a position of good advantage if they want us to do a bargain. One thing I am determined about is that we must not waver or show any unwillingness to withdraw McNicoll's candidature. The only bargain we can make is for them to withdraw their candidate.[33]

As always MacCormick was the eternal optimist and looked forward to the event as a means for securing the unification of the two parties. However, he was oblivious to the political realities of the situation and showed no evidence that he was aware of the tightrope he and his party were walking. MacCormick believed that if the NPS stuck to its guns they would be able to force the Scottish Party to withdraw for fear of the intensive campaign that would be waged against them. His assessment of the situation was hopelessly out of focus because he believed that the Scottish party would consent to stand down, not because they lacked the organisation necessary to fight an election, but rather, as they were gentlemen and as the National Party had made all the concessions to date, they would be under a moral obligation to make the next move.[34] The naive belief that a party of 'gentlemen' would act in the correct manner, coupled with their refusal to come to terms with the complex political problems and differences which existed between both organisations, reveals exactly how inexperienced the NPS leadership was in the world of realpolitik.

It was a gap in MacCormick's planning which gave the Scottish Party a legitimate opportunity to field a candidate in Kilmarnock as he had failed to notify them of the National Party's intentions.[35] He, along with the rest of the leadership, had under-estimated the Scottish Party, believing them to be a pressure group which would not contest elections.

After all, the SP did not prevent its members from belonging to another party and in their literature and political programme they gave no indication that they would enter the electoral fray:

> 'One other point of difference between the Nationalist and Scottish Parties requires to be mentioned. The National Party claims that it is 'entirely independent of the London controlled parties'. The Scottish Party are [sic] willing to cooperate with members of any other Party who are prepared to accept their policy. This is not a matter of principle but of election policy.[36]

Whereas MacCormick and others believed the Scottish Party was composed of nationalist bedfellows, Alexander MacEwen argued that there were enough significant differences between the two organisations to justify putting up their own candidate. In many ways he was the principal architect behind the decision to contest Kilmarnock. His objectives were to strengthen his hand in any negotiations with the National Party and also to render ineffective what he saw as the more dangerous aspects of the NPS's advocacy of Scottish nationalism. At this point in time MacEwen was not yet convinced that a fusion of the two parties was inevitable and the election in Kilmarnock was for him as much about establishing the Scottish Party as a credible political force as it was about pressurising the National Party:

> They cannot have it all their own way and must not be allowed to think that we can stand aside whenever we had decided to fight this election.[37]

Unlike Gibb, who was working with Gunn to establish a nationalist consensus around which unity could be forged, MacEwen wanted to keep the Scottish Party as a right wing counter-part to the NPS. Initially his objective was to secure an electoral pact with the National Party which would prevent Scottish nationalist claims from being represented solely by the left of centre. Indeed, MacEwen had toyed with the idea of undertaking similar consultations with the Liberal Party. G. M. Thomson was in no doubt about the forceful role MacEwen played in the organisation:

> I am certain that he is an ambitious man who is determined that the Scottish Party shall be his Party and nobody else's.[38]

Gibb and Thomson blamed MacEwen for keeping the Scottish Party from moving over to a full-blooded nationalist programme and consequently, of holding back a union with the National Party.[39]

However, MacEwen was not prepared to fuse with a party of which he was still suspicious. Although he took comfort from the fact that the

Fundamentalists had been expelled, he was not yet convinced at the sincerity of the National Party's new-found moderation and he still harboured fears that a unification would simply be a way of smothering the Scottish Party's 'saner' nationalist aspirations. He was not impressed by the way in which Tom Gibson had secured a boycott on assisting Scottish Party activities, especially their projected Summer school:

> Some months ago MacCormick, Neil Gunn and MacNeil came to lunch here. We had a friendly talk and they were all for cooperation. They were anxious to help in the Summer school. Since their last conference their attitude has changed and hardened. Nearly all of them cold shouldered the Summer school and showed no desire for future co-operation.[40]

MacEwen was aware of the latent hostility towards the Scottish Party among sections of the NPS and he was determined that his organisation would command some respect. He had little time for Gunn's argument that the National Party leadership had to ensure some distance from the Scottish Party in order to calm fears about a sell-out of principles. As far as MacEwen was concerned, the NPS no longer had a monopoly of nationalist aspirations. He was out to secure the best deal for his type of nationalist philosophy and was aided by the fact that his son, Robin, was a member of MacCormick's inner circle and was able to supply him with the relevant information necessary to keep his finger on the pulse of both parties. He knew the National Party was in a difficult situation and he kept the pressure on:

> I agree with you that it would be unfortunate if we were to end up fighting each other. I have inferred to Gunn, through my son, that we will only withdraw from Kilmarnock on condition that this is part of a general agreement as to future association of constituencies to be contested.[41]

It is difficult to ascertain MacEwen's intentions as to the prospect of a union of the two parties and how genuine his threats really were. However, he was prepared to give the National Party a run for its money so long as it suited his own political ends. It is also clear that he was playing with the idea of leading a new nationalist party which might emerge from the ashes of the Kilmarnock 'Gotterdammerung';

> While I have been working all along for ultimate fusion, I am not sure that a straight fight might not clear the air. It would make extremists on both sides see how futile it was. If we made a good show our Nationalist friends would treat us with more respect and would not expect us to follow their trail on all occasions.[42]

However, as the difficulties of contesting an election with limited resources and a mockery of an organisation became more apparent,

MacEwen was forced to preserve the National Party in order to achieve his own political ambitions.[43]

This process became more pronounced when it started to appear as if the National Party was willing to accommodate MacEwen's concerns. Space was made available for him to air his views in the *Scots Independent* while, at the same time, George Malcolm Thomson wrote a series of articles which claimed that the differences between the two parties were more cosmetic than real.[44] Although the NPS was on a sticky wicket, MacCormick was unrepentant about the situation and became more and more convinced that their actions were justified. The main theme of his argument was that had the National Party followed his advice earlier then the moderates would not have felt the need to form their own party:

> A lot of trouble appears to have been caused by the Scottish Party. Well I have never disguised my attitude towards it. In the first place I did my best to prevent its formation at all, if it had not been for R. D. Anderson I would have succeeded. Knowing that I had failed in that, I did my best to secure that their statements on policy would be as advanced as possible at the time, and I had considerable success in that I have kept as friendly as possible with several of its members as I know, with the result that I generally know what they are going to do before they do it ... to my mind our policy must be to do our utmost to bring the Scottish Party along with us, consistent with maintaining the realities of our own policy.[45]

MacCormick, who was never one for pedantry, believed that there was a parallel with the situation which led to the creation of the NPS in 1928. He believed that dogmatism had been the principal barrier to the formation of an independent nationalist party and that important figures like R. E. Muirhead were brought along more by gentle persuasion rather than naked aggression. He argued, consequently, that the National Party would have to operate the same 'give and take' policy with the Scottish Party:

> If during this year we can get the Scottish Party to dissolve and its leading members to join with us, without cutting away from our fundamentals, we shall have brought self-government visibly nearer.[46]

However, the problem facing MacCormick was that in order to recruit members of the Scottish Party to his movement he would have to depart from some of the National Party's 'fundamentals'. Enough of the SP luminaries had made this plain from the start. Also, he grossly over-estimated the value of his cordial relations with the moderate opposition. As the Kilmarnock by-election clearly illustrated, the Scottish Party only told him what they wanted him to know, which, more often than not, left him at a distinct disadvantage.

The ambitions of Alexander MacEwen were much aided and abetted by the fact that he was greatly admired by many in the National Party, who did not realise the pivotal role he played in the running of the Scottish Party. Tom Gibson, who was one of the stalwart opponents of any form of accommodation, was especially impressed by his qualities:

> Sir Alexander MacEwen would be a most valuable asset to the National Party. Indeed, I would not offer any objection if, after joining, he was to become Chairman.[47]

It was MacEwen's reasonableness which tended to single him out from others in the Scottish Party and this was an advantage of considerable importance because MacCormick had to work in a climate in which many members of his own party could not stomach any relationships with the opposition. In spite of this admiration for MacEwen, Tom Gibson was vehemently against his party. As far as he was concerned, there could be no unity or compromises with the Scottish Party, only a long drawn out campaign of attrition which would force those worthy elements to join the NPS:

> There was no need for the Scottish Party. It created disunity and pursued a wrecking policy preventing people from joining the National movement.[48]

So long as people such as Gibson accepted that there were capable members within the ranks of the Scottish Party, MacCormick was free to follow his plans under the guise of attempting to recruit them for the NPS. However, the real barrier to unity was that there were many in the National Party, like Gibson, who recognised the fundamental political differences between the two organisations. The principal problem with the Scottish Party, they argued, was that it was not completely independent from other political groups in the same way as the NPS was. Also, it was pointed out that the SP had yet to give a united statement as to the status a future Scottish Parliament would have in relation to Westminster and Gibson was suspicious that it would not have the same powers as the one advocated by the National Party. While most critics could agree with MacCormick on the need for unity, it was believed by many that if they joined with the Scottish Party, they would simply take on board another extremist wing which would replace the Fundamentalists as the political thorn in their side. According to Gibson:

> Their tactics were as bad as the tactics of the self-styled extremists in our own mob. When the opposing factions, as I sincerely hope they will do, decide to unite (and I am not only referring to the Scottish Party) let us

hope that it will be real unity. I do not think that the Scottish Party realise that we took a big risk in endeavouring to make our position more clear, and there has been no appreciation of our work ... after all, if they ask us, as they do to restrain our extremists, then we have a perfect right to ask them, in return, to restrain the muddleheadedness of such as Kevin McDowall ... I am fighting for unity — but to attain this I am hoping for real cooperation from the reasonable faction in the Scottish Party. There has been, as I think you will admit, no sign that this cooperation is to be forthcoming. The final question is whether the Scottish Party would declare themselves on the issue of English parties, and as you say the majority of members of this party are prepared to bargain with these parties ... if they give up this silly English Party idea, we will modify our attitude.[49]

As far as Tom Gibson was concerned, until the Scottish Party could present a political programme which clarified these sensitive issues, there could be no progress towards unity.

With regard to the by-election in Kilmarnock, the initial response of the Scottish Party was to request that joint negotiations take place in order to secure some degree of cooperation. To a large extent, the hardline response of the NPS towards the candidature of Gibb paid off because they were able to impose a number of conditions on the talks from the outset. Firstly, it was pointed out that as they had a branch organisation in Kilmarnock, there could be no question of them standing down. Also, as it had always been National Party policy to contest elections, they could not withdraw in favour of a body which had yet to give a firm commitment to the efficacy of such a strategy. In addition to these conditions, they had to take account of internal party pressures which could not permit a climbdown from the challenge posed by the newcomer. The Scottish Party appeared to accept these conditions and at a meeting of representatives from both organisations held on the 5th of September, 1933, Montrose gave assurances that they would accept the four-point policy of the NPS, with only a few minor additional safeguards.[50] They also accepted in principle that local nationalists ought to choose their own candidate, which, in all probability, given the numerical superiority, would have been the NPS candidate, J. M. McNicol.[51]

Perhaps the principal reason for the Scottish Party's pliability can be traced to the fact that they had little or no organisation and their initial attempts to formulate a campaign ended in chaos. With few or no members in the constituency, the Scottish Party could not undertake any of the conventional fieldwork normally associated with electoral politics. Evidence of their total lack of any kind of order is to be found in the fact that one of their members claimed to be the local candidate and set about campaigning on this premise. This was done without the authority of the SP's Executive and the correspondence reveals an organisation which was totally at sea as to what was going on. [52] Further evidence that the Scottish Party was in a state of utter confusion was that within a week of the negotiations, they had a volte-face and completely rejected the National Party's demands and instead put forward their own statement which, as it stood, was deemed unacceptable by the NPS. This was a severe shock to MacCormick and the talks seemed to be disintegrating into a shambles:

> We started today at 3 p.m. and were at once confronted with Sir Alex's report that their Executive had met this morning and turned the whole thing down. In its place they suggested a short statement which was totally unacceptable to us. Our representatives at once withdrew to see whether we could again save the day and win them over.[53]

MacCormick believed that a short simple statement upon which both parties could agree was the only way out of the impasse. As he had advocated before, this had to be stripped of all frippery and contain only 'absolute essentials' which according to MacCormick were 'the right of the Scottish people to determine Scotland's status' and 'the right to control taxation and finance'. [54] The Scottish Party accepted this streamlining and secured, by way of a compromise, a section which advocated the reform of the Treaty of Union, instead of its abolition, in order to achieve the objectives of the nationalists. Both MacCormick and Muirhead concluded that this was a safer and better agreement than the one initially proposed by the NPS.[55]

However, not all members of the National Party were happy with the way the negotiations were going, especially Tom Gibson, who accused them of a sell-out of principles in accepting the agreed statement.[56] Further problems were to arise concerning the thorny question of a joint candidate. Initially, MacEwen put forward the suggestion that both existing candidates should withdraw and that a neutral person acceptable to both parties should be put forward. He strongly suggested J. M. Bannerman, who had apparently been vetted by the Scottish Party in advance. Bannerman, who had strong connections with the Duke of Montrose and a long-standing family commitment to Home Rule, was thought to be sufficiently 'safe' and an ideal candidate to unite both parties. Unfortunately his obvious Scottish Party connections blinded members of the NPS to his abilities to stand as an able candidate who had taken on board the task of representing the nationalist cause in good faith.[57]

The National Party put forward an alternative proposal which was finally agreed. A sub-committee consisting of MacCormick and Muirhead from the National Party, together with MacEwen and McDowall, was formed to attend a meeting with the Ayrshire Nationalist Association and submit a short leet of three candidates: A. D. Gibb, McNicol and Bannerman. The local nationalists were to choose a candidate from the three and this would subsequently be endorsed by the executives of both parties. In spite of the fact that the Scottish Party was represented by two candidates, the NPS man, McNicol, won easily:

> Sir Alexander MacEwen and McDowall spoke very strongly for the adoption of Bannerman. I knew our folks were sound so I got up and made a completely impartial speech saying choose which ever you like and all agree. A vote was taken and by a large majority McNicol was chosen.[58]

However, in spite of the agreement, the Duke of Montrose was not happy with the result, much to the chagrin of MacCormick. They believed that by proposing Bannerman they were attempting to make a genuine compromise and McNicoll's candidature was, they argued, not representative of both parties. However, MacCormick was not impressed by their meanderings:

> Had McDowall on the phone. Duke of M. not satisfied with the choice of candidate. I am getting fed up. They are worse than a lot of fussy women and only is Sir Alexander MacEwen, Gibb and McDowall of any use to us. If they fib again we must go ahead and fight them. Perhaps between Sir A. M. and yourself (Neil Gunn) you could think of something over the week which would avoid impasse. You see, if we can actually get them supporting an out and out nationalist candidate in Kilmarnock then that will be the their most effective way to put an end to them as a separate force.[59]

MacCormick was aided in his plans to secure a joint candidate by the fact that MacEwen and Gibb were becoming impatient with the Scottish Party's lack of realistic proposals. Indeed, they made plain their frustrations with Montrose and gave further indication how disorganised and incoherent their strategy was. MacCormick took their internal disharmony to be a good sign:

> I have learned authoritatively, through a confidential source, that at the Scottish Party Executive yesterday, Dewar Gibb had a pretty serious row with the Duke. I believe that the Duke had been saying something in the usual vein about no separation when Dewar Gibb asked him for heaven's sake to stop all that blarney and get down to hard facts.[60]

Initially, MacCormick believed the solution to the problem was to try and wean those elements in the Scottish Party with whom he felt a political affinity over to the ranks of the NPS. He was convinced that during the negotiations he had shown enough good faith to induce MacEwen and others into believing that the National Party was a mature enough organisation to represent their own political views and aspirations. According to MacCormick:

> The view of all was that breakdown would mean a setback for years if not the end of the National Party ... I still think we can snatch good out of it and use the association to compel Sir A. M. to leave his doubting Thomases behind and lead the worthwhile elements into our own ranks.[61]

While MacCormick was fighting for his political life, he still failed to appreciate that MacEwen was not always acting for the same objectives as he himself sought, but was, first and foremost, furthering his own political priorities which were often inimical to that of the NPS.

The candidature of McNicol was most firmly opposed by Montrose, Sir Daniel Stevenson and Rosslyn Mitchell. Mitchell had indicated that he would leave the Labour Party and help the nationalist cause if the two parties could get their act together and put up an 'outstanding and able candidate'.[62] Not surprisingly, this was used to try and invalidate McNicol's candidature. Further pressure was added by the fact that one of the National Party's most eminent supporters, Lord Dalziel of Kirkcaldy, was prepared to contribute financially on the condition that the two organisations settle their differences.[63] However, the problem facing the National Party, as Archie Lamont pointed out, was that McNicol was a boná fide nationalist and if he came out against a Scottish Party opponent, it would help silence the mounting criticism from within the rank and file that the NPS had turned its back on its original objectives.[64]

As the Scottish Party was not a conventional political organisation, its members were not rigid in their support for their own group. Their flexibility in the political sphere was used to blackmail the National Party with Daniel Stevenson and other prominent members of the SP Executive threatening to support the Free Trade candidate unless the NPS agreed to compromise. The crisis was exacerbated by the fact that the pro-mergerites in both parties had gone so far down the unification trail that a failure to secure a compromise at the Kilmarnock by-election would lead to a real danger of the two organisations disintegrating and with them the Home Rule cause. It soon became apparent that the only real alternative for the mergerites was to produce a suitable candidate from the Scottish Party because it was unlikely that anyone from the NPS would be acceptable. The key to success would be to find someone who could be trusted by the members of the

National Party. The ideal person, in all probability, was MacEwen and although McNicol was himself in favour of this, MacCormick and Muirhead were uneasy about such a solution. However, the impasse was breached by the members of the Kilmarnock NPS who suggested that MacEwen should go forward as the candidate. MacCormick explained how this situation arose:

> ... when Sir Alexander MacEwen was down in Kilmarnock with Muirhead and myself ten days ago, at the time the Kilmarnock Association had adopted McNicol, the Chairman had said, quite off his own bat, that it would be a splendid way out of all the difficulties if Sir A. himself would stand. Sir A. had replied that it was impossible for him to stand...[65]

However, as the situation became more exacerbated and after giving the matter some thought, he decided that he had an obligation to do his utmost to secure a compromise by using his personal standing with both organisations. In many ways MacEwen was uniquely positioned to be an ideal candidate and he was quite aware of this. MacCormick continues the story:

> ...he told me he had been taking everything into consideration and had decided that he would allow his own name to go forward if that was mutually acceptable. I told him that I had no personal objections to him. He did not like the solution and was afraid of the effect on the National Party. He was then undecided, but when the Scottish Party Executive met he seems to have thought that it was the only way to prevent a premature split and the appearance of an independent Liberal and he offered his name accordingly.[66]

Although MacCormick was not exactly pleased with the situation there was little he could do as events had overtaken him. If he wanted co-operation, and he was convinced that they could not survive without it, he more or less had to accept MacEwen's *coup d'état*. MacEwen was the most respected of the Scottish Party members in the eyes of the NPS and he was seen to be the keenest pro-mergerite. However, and this was probably what made MacCormick nervous, no one could ascertain the degree of Scottish party complicity in securing his nomination. In any case, it was the only realistic way out of the impasse that MacCormick had, albeit inadvertently, created for himself.

MacEwen was adopted as the Honorary President of the Kilmarnock branch of the NPS while still retaining his membership of the Scottish Party Executive. A set of proposals was quickly drawn together upon which the joint election campaign would be fought. The National Party was careful to stress that they had not departed from their original objectives (as defined in the restatement of policy in 1933) but, in the interest of maintaining unity, things had to be kept to a minimum of detail. The guiding principle for cooperation was that both parties agreed that a future Scottish Parliament would be the final arbiter on all Scottish affairs:

> As both parties believe in the right of the Scottish people to determine the future status of Scotland, it has been found possible to agree upon a joint candidate going forward with the following aim: The establishment in Scotland of a Parliament which shall be the final authority on all Scottish affairs, including taxation and finance.
>
> Both parties are agreed that the institution of tariff barriers between England and Scotland is undesirable and that Imperial matters, Defence and Foreign Policy should remain matters of joint concern between Scotland and England. There shall only be such future modification or revision of the Act of Union as is necessary to obtain the foregoing objects.[67]

The joint election statement rode roughshod over many difficulties and the speed with which it was concluded, and the consequent lack of consultation with the rank and file, caused a great deal of resentment among several members. The point concerning the 'Act of Union' was considered to be particularly insensitive because this was not part of the NPS's policy. Tom Gibson and his wife, Elmà, both announced that after the election they would be resigning from the Executive. They objected to what they saw as the undue influence of the Scottish Party and pointed out that there was little point in fighting off the Fundamentalist challenge only to hand control of the party to the 'extremists' on the other wing of the national movement:

> I am not going to allow myself to be dictated to by any group of self-appointed dictators as the Scottish group — I refused and fought Grieve's attempt — I did the same with Clann MacColl and Gillies' people and I most decidedly object to the decision of the National Council to permit this latest group: the Scottish Party... My resignation is a definite protest against the silly childishness of the Scottish Party and any recognition of it.[68]

Elmà Gibson echoed the fears of many by protesting that the merger issue was going all the one way and she doubted the sincerity of the motives behind the proposals because of the intransigence of the Scottish Party. In short, the National Party was being used:

> I won't be surprised if you get your man into Westminster. On the same policy you would get other members into Westminster too, but you will not get them out ... You say that we have been making no progress for two years. I say that we have been going back. Don't you think that it is significant that our progress came to an end when our original policy became something to be explained away and not something to be upheld and expounded. I welcomed the hope of unity between the SP and the

NPS and quite recognised the need for concessions on both sides. I was quite prepared to swallow that childish nonsense about the Treaty of Union: but have the SP made any concession whatsoever? They even abandoned their agreement to accept the local candidate. They have simply taken over our organisation and forced their policy on us. God knows what further watering down we will be expected to accept meekly in another six months.[69]

Elmà Gibson's analysis of the situation and her reservations were shared by others in the party, of whom the most important were Robert and Roland Muirhead. The brothers were uneasy about the drift towards moderation and they did as much as they could at the National Council meetings to stall the accommodation process. This antagonism was noted by MacCormick who observed that 'they regard the whole approach to the Scottish Party with regret and are looking for loopholes to escape from it'.[70] In many ways MacCormick was right. However, the number of loopholes available for escape was diminishing rapidly. The opposition within the National Council was weak regarding the agreement to fight a joint election campaign and whatever acquiescence existed was reinforced by the necessity of preserving the fragile unity in the national movement after the manoeuvring which had led them into such a tight corner.

MacEwen's appearance on the scene as a political knight in shining armour was not as entirely fortuitous as it would have perhaps seemed. He was noted for his ambition and was, conveniently, in the right place at the right time. His correspondence with other members of the Scottish Party Executive reveals a hard and businesslike approach to dealings with the NPS and he was never afraid to turn the screws tight to get what he wanted.[71] MacEwen's experience in local government and public life meant that he was the most skilful and able negotiator in the Scottish Party and he was likewise the best informed member concerning the current National Party strategy. Of all the people in the national movement, he, more than anybody, was in the best position to act as a pivot between both organisations. Together with these advantages, the two parties had, for once, found an able candidate who was able to use his experience in political life and his excellent track record in public service to maximum effect. MacEwen campaigned with great energy and was better able to face questions than some of the previous National Party candidates who scored quite badly on this front. His political stature and the novelty effect of a united nationalist movement candidate meant that MacEwen received considerable press coverage and his meetings were well stocked with a variety of speakers from both parties.

The campaign was, in essence, an exercise in cross-party cooperation which, if it was successful, would demonstrate the feasibility of unity. The election was not only a contest for votes but also the test bed to prove the credibility of an united party and as such, it was important that MacEwen achieved a good showing.

The Nationalists started off at a disadvantage by only getting their campaign running three weeks before polling day. They also did not have effective enough organisation on the ground and many parts of the constituency went uncanvassed.[72] However, in spite of these problems, most of those involved believed that things were going well enough to be confident about the prospects for union. During the campaign MacEwen more firmly than ever before advocated a fusion of the two parties:

> Whatever the result of this election, it is already proving an important step in the history of the Nationalist movement. The wisdom of the National and Scottish Parties joining forces is abundantly justified, and, to me, it is almost unthinkable that those who have worked together so loyally and earnestly in this election together should ever be divided until their task is accomplished.[73]

One of the reasons for MacEwen's acceptability as a serious political contender in the election can be explained by his impeccable Liberal credentials, which, more often than not, crept into the campaign, much to the chagrin of some members of the NPS who felt that he was too closely identified with his former British party. A lot of his canvassing was done by the Young Glasgow Liberals and, at the same time, Sir Daniel Stevenson claimed that if MacEwen was returned he would pursue a Liberal policy at Westminster.[74] While this may have gained him some Liberal votes, it did not endear him to those in the National Party who were still suspicious of his motives.

The mergerites, however, turned a blind eye to these minor indiscretions and argued that the fact that the two parties were able to cooperate in an election campaign was evidence of the efficacy of a merger. Walter Murray, the editor of the *Scots Independent*, reviewed the situation:

> The agreement negotiated between the National Party of Scotland and the Scottish Party is for the by-election in the Kilmarnock division only, but in principle it obviously goes much further. If the two self-government parties have been able to find a common platform for the one by-election it is hardly possible for them to remain separate indefinitely, and the basis of cooperation may therefore have to be regarded as preparing the way for ultimate fusion.[75]

For many nationalists it was a welcome change to place the emphasis on unity rather than division and this allowed MacEwen to expound the practical and positive aspects of self-government, instead of fighting a rearguard action against inter-nationalist intrigues. Also, because of his membership of the Scottish Party, the separatist bogey was not so readily raised by the press and in some quarters he was accorded respect for being a non socialist candidate.[76] In any case, it must have come as a welcome relief to the mergerites to find that MacEwen had polled just over 17% of the votes cast, to date the best showing made by a nationalist candidate.[77]

For many in the National Party the result was a vindication of the change in policy towards a more moderate, or as it was preferred to be known, 'common sense' nationalism. On the surface it appeared that by combining forces, the two parties could achieve greater electoral support than either could attain on their own. As the leader in the *Scots Independent* put it:

> The programme adopted by the National Party at the annual conference in May has been triumphantly vindicated on the field of electoral battle and it must now be pursued to its logical conclusion.[78]

However, in spite of their elation, the result was in many ways misleading. MacEwen was undoubtedly the prime beneficiary of the fact that there was no Tory candidate as a result of the electoral pact formed by the National Government. Many Conservative voters would obviously feel easier casting their votes for MacEwen rather than the socialist tainted National Labour candidate. Evidence for this can be found in the press reports of the campaign in which there are several references to Tory supporters applauding his nationalist, but non-separatist, non-socialist philosophy.[79] It may have been this factor which accounted for their good showing rather than the fact that the two nationalist parties had at last combined their efforts. In any case, this was not taken into account at the time by those involved who believed that finally the self-government cause was getting underway.

Yet in order to achieve a unification there would have to be a meaningful compromise from both groups. In essence, the bottom line for this would be a trade-off in which the NPS would concede to moderate their self-government aspirations while the Scottish Party would accept the principle of belonging to only the new nationalist body. Although members of the National Party were prepared to tone down their self-government demands, they were adamant that there could be no commitment to a devolutionist or 'stepping stone' policy.

As far as they were concerned, they had given away as many concessions as they could and that the final arbiter on Scottish affairs would have to be the Scottish Parliament. The new proposals which were put forward among members of the National Party were weak and lacked the detail and structure which had been built into their previous policies. However, such pedantry was not thought to be important because, according to MacCormick:

> There were as many opinions as members of the movement: no constitutional objective was immutable, we were in a position to make big advances by gaining valuable recruits and we ought to take it.[80]

For MacCormick the issue of personalities was more important than policies. The majority of members of the NPS Executive were coming to accept this view, and although many believed that the proposals for the constitution of the new party could have been worded better or differently, the most important thing was that, in spirit, it was acceptable. However, not everybody was happy about the situation and doubts still lingered. This was especially true of those 'grey areas' such as defence, foreign policy and imperial matters, which did not fall into the remit of belonging to Scottish affairs. R. F. Muirhead argued that if the Scottish Party could not accept that, in principle, the final authority on all these issues had to be the Scottish Parliament, then:

> It may be that the NPS will have to choose between giving up the principle in order thereby to include a larger following, or, on the other hand, holding fast to the principle though it may involve slower growth.[81]

However, MacCormick had little time for Muirhead's arguments, neither did the majority of the National Executive. The case was put that when the National Party had stuck to its 'principles', its growth was slow and erratic and had seemed to peak and peter out. According to MacCormick the time was now over for hair-splitting and theoretical argument. He wanted action and claimed that the way for nationalists to solve their problems was by 'putting our faith in our convictions rather than written statements'.[82]

Once the National Executive decided to embark on a policy of fusion with the Scottish Party a select group was formed to pave the way and conduct the official negotiations. This body was called the Reconstruction Committee and was set up in December, 1933. This group operated in conjunction with a similar organisation from the Scottish Party and they were given the remit of hammering out proposals which would form the foundations of any merger.[83] However, as most of the process towards unification was handled by informal talks between key people in both organisations, the Reconstruction Committee was little more than an official rubber stamp. Both committees merely reported back to their respective National Executives what had already been decided by those conducting the informal discussions. However, before any action could be authorised it had to have approval from the National Executive.

The first stumbling block to hit the nationalists was the issue of the proposed objective of the new party and, in many ways, it was simply a re-run of the argument concerning the correct terminology. One group wanted to use the phrase 'the British group of nations', while the other preferred 'the British Empire' when talking about the status of an independent Scotland.[83] The proposed objective which caused the problem went as follows:

> The objective of the Party is self-government for Scotland on a basis which will enable Scotland as a partner in the British Empire with the same status as England to develop its National Life to the fullest advantage.[84]

Many in the NPS preferred their original objective because it did not firmly intertwine Scotland within the context of a form of British government. The more progressive nationalists, such as Archie Lamont, were not in favour of tying the new party to an imperialist system:

> Mr Lamont took exception to the proposed new objective on the grounds that it implied approval of the British Empire as presently constituted with subject as well as free nations. Scottish Nationalists must be prepared to take a wide view and seek to do as they would be done by, with reference to India, for example.[85]

However, he received little support from the majority in the National Executive with most favouring Charles Stewart Black's assertion that 'we should be proud of the British Empire'.[86] This was yet another indication of the National Party's gradual shift towards a more right wing political stance.[87]

Roland Muirhead was also uneasy about redrafting the four-point policy of the NPS because, he argued, the Scottish Party had always engaged in a constant wavering of interpretations to suit their own ends. As time went on he became less convinced of the efficacy of the redrafting of policy which had led to the expulsion of the Fundamentalists. Although Muirhead at the time believed the restatement of policy in May, 1933 was not connected with the Scottish Party, he became more and more convinced that the whole thing had been arranged to suit the accommodationists in both parties. He was soon airing these views and claimed that the restatement of policy was 'drafted with one of our men in touch with the Scottish Party'.[88] He went on to elaborate:

> It was not our own spontaneous idea of a policy. Neither was the new object. To many nationalists the idea of a glorified Empire was not acceptable at all. He knew no reason why the Scottish Party wished to alter the object. If we were all firm on the matter, we might be able to keep our object as before.[89]

Muirhead found it difficult to accept that his party had changed into a more establishment minded organisation and although he blamed the Scottish Party, he could not avoid the conclusion that many senior members of the NPS were just as keen to alter the nationalists' objective. When the issue came to a vote in the National Council, 14 supported the redraft with only the Muirhead brothers and Archie Lamont objecting, preferring instead the old policies and objective.[90] With this major stumbling block removed, the next stage was for each party to pass the following resolutions at their respective annual conferences:

> (1) The establishment of a Parliament in Scotland which shall be the final authority on all Scottish affairs including taxation. (2) Scotland shall share with England the rights and responsibilities they, as mother nations, have jointly created and incurred within the British Empire (3) In a manner representing the will of her people, Scotland should set up jointly with England, machinery to deal with these responsibilities and in particular with such matters as Defence, Foreign Policy and the creation of a customs union. (4) It is believed that these principles can be realized only by an independent political party which has no connection or alliance with an English controlled party.[91]

The resolutions were to form the basis of the new party's political programme and as such were conceived so that:

> ...all the essentials of a self-government policy are contained in the foregoing statement, and it is believed that the achievement of self-government on that basis will enable the Scottish people as partners in the British Empire to be the final arbiters of their own destiny.[92]

Once the resolutions were passed the following subsidiary resolutions were also framed for submission, the first to the Scottish Party and the second to the NPS:

> (A) This Conference of the Scottish Party, following upon the acceptance of resolution I, both by this Conference and by the Conference of the National Party of Scotland, resolves to unite with the name of 'the Scottish National Party'.
> (B) This Conference of the National Party of Scotland, in as much as Resolution I had been passed by both this Conference and by a Conference

of the Scottish Party, hereby resolves to unite with the Scottish Party, and in pursuance of that resolution to amend Clause I of the Constitution to read name: The Scottish National Party.[93]

Once the formalities were over, the new party was finally absolved of the separatist spectre which had dogged the nationalist movement. The SNP was a fundamentally different animal from the National Party in that whereas the NPS had been in favour of something akin to Dominion status, the new party stressed the continuation of a partnership with England which removed that possibility of independence in the international sphere. The argument behind this policy was that it would be wrong for Scotland, as a mother nation of the Empire, to down-grade herself to a 'colonial' status.[94] In previous times, the National Party acknowledged the possibility that they could radically change the nature of the British state; however, there was no such threat from the SNP. The new party stated quite categorically that the proposed Scottish Parliament should have authority with respect to those matters considered to be 'Scottish affairs'. Previously, the NPS had advocated 'national sovereignty' and 'independence within the British group of nations' and many believed that this included the right to self-determination in the fields of foreign policy and defence. Although such ideas were subject to a variety of interpretations, they did not emphatically limit the amount of national sovereignty possible to the Scottish nation in the same way as was being proposed by the SNP. In this way, the new party was more in line with the Home Rule movements of former times in that self-government was firmly placed within the context of the continuation of some form of overall British government. In the last analysis, it has to be said that in terms of fighting for 'national independence' in the normal sense of the word, the creation of the Scottish National Party was undoubtedly a retrogressive step.

All this meant very little to MacCormick who was confident that the proposals would be met with enthusiastic approval from members of both organisations. Furthermore, to pacify any lingering pangs of doubt, he argued that in essence the new party was still adhering to the four principles which were originally embodied in the policies of the National Party:

> It expresses in simple terms a responsible and dignified ambition for our country. When that programme has been carried out, Scotland will be a completely free, self-governing nation, continuing in friendly partnership with England, and fulfilling her responsibilities as a mother nation in the British Empire.[95]

In fact, it would be more accurate to state that the Scottish National Party was adhering to what MacCormick believed were the original objectives of the NPS, in spite of the fact that his ideals were not universally shared by other members. For him, it was simply a matter of clarification and the removal of obstructive ambiguities. The new name for the party was chosen by way of a compromise in that it contained the principal elements of both older titles, but also, it was stressed, maintained a continuity with the past. It was claimed that there was 'no break in the chain first formed in 1928'.[96] In many ways, the creation of the SNP can be seen as the culmination of the moderates' campaign to establish their vision of what was meant by Scottish nationalism. They now had a political organisation which could back up their case, unhindered by the separatist stigma which had hounded the National Party to its grave.

In addition to being shorn of the separatist bogey, it was hoped that the new party would have a broader appeal than the NPS on account of its narrower and minimalist objectives, which, it was believed, would permit people of different shades of ideological opinion to join its ranks. Although the nationalists never specifically mentioned it, the SNP was clearly influenced by the formation of the National Government and the idea, which was growing fashionable throughout Europe, that unity on a 'national' basis could overcome conventional political difficulties.[97] Like many other political groups in Europe which faced an impasse, Scottish nationalists opted for action of any kind, so long as it was dramatic, in the hope that they could break out of the stalemate. The dramatic effect of unification acted as a positive distraction and took members' minds off previous problems and difficulties, although in reality the political scenario had not significantly changed. The propaganda of the SNP reflected this drift towards utopian idealism rather than political realities:

> The Scottish National Party is nevertheless a great political experiment. It differs materially in conception from the British National Party, so called. That was a combination brought about by Party leaders in the panic of a national emergency. No man left his Party... Conservatives, Liberals and Socialists huddled together as lions and hinds are said to do when floods drive them close together on the high ground for safety. When the floods recede, let the hinds look to themselves ... But the Scottish National Party is not a panic emergency party scrambled together temporarily. It is a carefully planned organisation, where the rank and file, as well as the leaders are drawn together by a great spiritual force — the desire to serve their nation. Each must leave his old party, sometimes cutting personal ties of a lifetime, before he becomes an active member of the new party. Loyalty to our nation takes the place of loyalty to party.[98]

In spite of the denials, it is clear from this passage that some of the rhetoric of the National Government had rubbed off on the thinking of the SNP. In order to encompass people of widely differing political ideologies, the Scottish National Party had to abandon most of the social and economic policies of the NPS, which tended towards the left of centre, and replace them with a quasi-utopian brand of nationalism. This philosophy contained little that was specific and veered towards being apolitical in tone. Another important shift in nationalist opinion occurred with the formation of the SNP in that whereas nationalism was regarded primarily as a political strategy by the NPS, it was now believed to be a credible philosophy in itself. Muirhead and Gibson, for example, argued that self-government was the best way to achieve economic and social reforms and for them, a large part of their nationalism was simply a practical means to an end. However, the new party endeavoured to make nationalism an end in itself by appealing to concepts of loyalty to one's nation and that this could solve any type of difficulties.[99]

This political idealism which was afloat in Britain, Europe and the United States at this time, was also present in the SNP's naive attitude to surmounting ideological differences. The Scottish National Party effectively moved back to the Scottish Home Rule Association's dictum that the conventional political divide could be overcome by the unifying force of the demand for self-government. However, the difficulties of adopting such a strategy soon came to the forefront when the party tried to come to terms with the political realities which were now facing them. Even before the SNP was officially launched the 'Reconstruction Committee' which had been set up by both parties to look into social and economic problems, could make little progress because of the widely divergent political beliefs held by individual members.[100] As a result of this there was an early tendency to take a neutralist approach to specific issues which could not be reduced to a simple case of Scottish grievances against an uncaring Britain. When the Scottish National Party entered the political arena, most of its energies had been diverted away from the real issues of the day. This in turn made it difficult for them to take a coherent stance on a whole range of economic and social matters.

The principal reason for the tendency towards a nondescript political stance can be explained by the undue influence exercised by former members of the Scottish Party and their bed-fellows who had belonged to the NPS. In spite of a numerical superiority in the region of ten to one (at least), MacCormick made every effort to ensure that the Scottish Party was given equal representation in the newly formed SNP. At the first annual conference, former Scottish Party members received 45 delegate cards, which was about the same as that issued to the NPS, in spite of the fact that they only had a membership of about 500 compared with the exaggerated roll of over 14,000 claimed by the National Party.[101] The same over-preponderance manifested itself in the selection of office bearers for the SNP. The Duke of Montrose was made President, Sir Alexander MacEwen was given the Chairmanship, and in the other minor offices there was an almost even split between former members of both parties.[102] The same thing happened in the newly formed National Council, to which the former National Party Chairman, Roland Muirhead, was demoted. The mergerites in the NPS were only interested in attaching the personnel of the Scottish Party for prestige purposes and, perhaps most importantly, to give a new sense of leadership and direction. It was to this end that they were given such a prominent part to play in the new party. It is perhaps wrong to describe the merger issue as a fusion of two political parties. For one thing the Scottish Party was never really a political organisation as such. It had a very small membership, and as a body capable of winning votes it had neither the means for conducting electoral campaigns nor none of the conventional party discipline necessary for such undertakings.[103] In essence, the Scottish Party was little more than an élitist pressure group. However, it was precisely for this reason that many in the National Party wanted to take them on board, or to be more accurate, be taken on board by them. MacCormick and a majority of the NPS National Council wanted their prestige, money and guidance because, they believed, it was these vital elements which the national movement needed most, and which on their own, the National Party could not provide. The reality of the merger was that the NPS did not join with another organisation, but rather, accepted a new body of leadership which fused with the old one to produce a distinctive change in nationalist direction. However, it has to be emphasised that the National Party of Scotland had been moving down this road under its own volition for some time and that the creation of the SNP was merely the finishing touch to a long and tortured process.

Historians have generally given the merger of the two parties a negative assessment, principally for the reasons which will be elaborated on in the following chapter. However, they have been equally unkind towards MacCormick without setting his achievement in the proper context. Although the merger ultimately proved to be disastrous for the cause of Scottish nationalism as a whole, it should not be forgotten against what criteria it was set up in. It is far too easy to regard the manoeuvring of MacCormick as inept and flawed; however, the same cannot be said for his overall strategy. Principally, he wanted to convert the Scottish establishment to the cause of Home Rule and, if he had been successful, the nationalists would have found their task much easier, having support from the most important and influential section of Scottish society. For MacCormick, the best way to do this was to tone down policies which frightened them and court those who seemed favourable to the idea. On both these counts he was successful and, more importantly, he had the majority backing of his own party. There was no question of the National Party being dragged screaming and kicking into a merger that it did not want. There were few resignations and few protests with most carrying on as normal.[104] Although this strategy was doomed to failure, few on the ground doubted its wisdom, nor could they see what lay ahead.

NOTES

1. See chapter three for some background material on the internal problems of the NPS.
2. See chapter three and the minute book of the National Executive Council of the NPS, page 8. McIntyre collection, National Library of Scotland (NLS)
3. Minutes of the National Executive Council of the NPS, pp. 25-26. McIntyre collection NLS.
4. Ibid.
5. Ibid.
6. Ibid.
7. T.H. Gibson to R.E. Muirhead, 27th of February, 1933. Gibson Mss, Box 4, File 79.
8. T.H. Gibson to Neil Gunn, 8th of June, 1933. Gunn Mss, Box 15, Dep.207. NLS.
9. Neil Gunn to A.D. Gibb, 28th of March, 1933. Gibb Mss, Box 1, Dep.217. NLS.
10. A.M. MacEwen, *The Thistle and the Rose* (1932). The Duke of Montrose, *Self-Government for Scotland* (1933). G.M.Thomson, *Scotland: That Distressed Area* (1937). A.D.Gibb, *Scotland in Eclipse* (1932)
11. A.M. MacEwen, *The Thistle and the Rose*, page 5.
12. The principal sources are those cited above.
13. See the correspondence between both men in Gibb's papers. Dep. 217 NLS.
14. See their respective Home Rule schemes in the works cited above.
15. G.M. Thomson to George Dott, 19th of July, 1929: "Take my friend Dewar Gibb, for example, he stays in the Conservative Party because he has, after fighting two elections, a chance of a safe seat and he feels, career apart, that he can be of more use to Scotland in Parliament than out of it." Dott Mss Acc. 5927 NLS.
16. He was offered the University seat should he join the NPS in April 1932. C.S. Black to A.D. Gibb, 29th of April, 1932. Box 2, Dep. 217. NLS.

17. Alexander MacEwen was active in the Liberal Party at Edinburgh University and became a member of Inverness Town Council in 1908 and a magistrate two years later. At this time he began to take an interest in social problems and in 1913 he gave evidence before the Royal Commission on Housing in Scotland. From 1925-31 he was Lord Provost of Inverness and was involved with many municipal improvements as well as being Secretary of the Highland Reconstruction Association. In 1931 he became a member of the Scottish Development Council.

18. G.M. Thomsom to G. Dott, 16th of September, 1930. Dott Mss. Acc. 5927. NLS.

19. A.D. Gibb to N.M. Gunn. 4th of January, 1933. Gunn Mss. Box 15, Dep.209. NLS.

20. MacEwen, op.cit. pp. 152-158.

21. MacEwen writing in the *Scots Independent*, May, 1933, Page 104.

22. The Duke of Montrose, op.cit. pp. 4-5.

23. MacEwen, op.cit. p.149.

24. Montrose, op.cit. p.11.

25. See A.D.Gibb, *Scottish Empire* (London 1937)

26. Ibid. pp. 308-315, also *Scotland in Eclipse*, p.187.

27. J.M.MacCormick, "Looking Forward", *Scots Independent*, August, 1933.

28. J.M. MacCormick, *The Flag in the Wind* (1955) p.67.

29. See chapter 6.

30. R.E. Muirhead to A.W. Donaldson, 20th of November, 1933. Muirhead Mss. Acc. 3721 Box 80. NLS.

31. See the correspondence between G.M. Thomson and A.D. Gibb. Box 2. Dep. 217. NLS.

32. G.M. Thomson to A.D. Gibb, 20th of January, 1933 Gibb Mss. Box 2. Dep.217. NLS

32. N.M. Gunn to A.D. Gibb, 28th of July, 1933 Gunn Mss. Box 15. Dep.209. NLS.

33. J.M. MacCormick to N.M. Gunn, 29th of July, 1933 Gunn Mss. Box 15. Dep.209. NLS.

34. Ibid.

35. Ibid.

36. A.M.MacEwen, "The Scottish Party", *Scots Independent*, May, 1933. p.104.

37. A.M. MacEwen to A.D. Gibb re. the Kilmarnock election. (undated) Gunn Mss. Dep. 217. NLS.

38. G.M. Thomson to A.D. Gibb, 26th December, 1932. Gibb Mss. Box 1. Dep. 217. NLS.

39. Ibid.

40. A.M. MacEwen to A.D. Gibb. (undated) Gunn Mss. Dep. 217. NLS.

41. Ibid.

42. Ibid.

43. This will become more apparent in the following pages.

44. *Scots Independent*, April, 1933. Page 87.

45. J.M. MacCormick to T.H. Gibson, 24th of August, 1933. Gibson Mss. Box 1. Acc. 6058. NLS.

46. Ibid.

47. T.H. Gibson to N.M. Gunn, 20th of October, 1933 Gibson Mss. Box 1. Acc. 6058. NLS.

48. Ibid.

49. T.H. Gibson to R.R. MacEwen, 8th of August, 1933. Gunn Mss. Box 15. Dep. 209. NLS.

50. See previous pages.

51. Ibid.

52. Evidence gathered together from the correspondence between Montrose, Gibb and McDowall. Gibb Mss. Dep. 217. NLS.

53. J.M. MacCormick to N.M. Gunn, 29th of September, 1933. Box 15. Dep. 209. NLS.

54. Ibid.

55. Ibid..

56. T.H. Gibson to J.M. MacCormick, 29th of September, 1933. Gunn Mss. Box 15. Dep. 209. NLS.

57. Information gathered from the correspondence of J.M. Bannerman to his son. I am grateful to Dr. J.M.W. Bannerman for access to this material.

58. J.M. MacCormick to N.M. Gunn, 29th of September, 1933. Gunn Mss. Box 15. Dep. 209. NLS.

59. Ibid. 30th of September, 1933. Gunn Mss. Box 15. Dep. 209. NLS.

60. Ibid. 9th of August, 1933 Gunn Mss. Box 15. Dep. 209. NLS.

61. Ibid. 8th of October, 1933 Gunn Mss. Box 15. Dep. 209. NLS.

62. Minute book of the National Executive Council of the NPS page 44. McIntyre collection, NLS.

63. A.D.Gibb, *Scotland Resurgent* (Stirling 1950) page 253.

64. Minute book of the National Executive Council of the NPS, pages 40-44. McIntyre collection, NLS.

65. J.M. MacCormick to T.H. Gibson, 9th of October, 1933. Gibson Mss. Box 1. Acc. 6058. NLS.

66. Ibid.

67. *Scots Independent*, November, 1933. page 5.

68. T.H. Gibson to N.M. Gunn, 20th of October, 1933. Gunn Mss. Box 15. Dep. 209. NLS.

69. Elmà Gibson to N.M. Gunn, 12th of October, 1933. Gunn Mss. Box 15. Dep. 209. NLS.

70. J.M. MacCormick to T.H. Gibson, 21st of February, 1933. Gibson Mss. Box 1. Acc. 6058. NLS.

71. This is based on the correspondence between MacEwen and Gibb in Dep. 217. NLS. Also MacEwen's papers Acc. 6713. NLS.

72. *Scots Independent*, December, 1933. page 25.

73. Ibid. page 17.

74. Minute book of the National Executive Council of the NPS page 50. McIntyre collection, NLS.

5. Walter Murray, "The new phase in Nationalism", *Scots Independent*, November, 1933. page 16.

76. Gathered from press cuttings. Box 71. Acc. 3721. NLS.

77. The results were: National Labour : 12,577 Labour : 9,924 Independent Labour : 7,575 SNP : 6,095
78. *Scots Independent*, December, 1933. page 25.
79. *Glasgow Herald*, 14th of October, 1933.
80. Minute book of the National Executive Council of the NPS page 60.
81. Ibid. page 67.
82. Ibid. pages 51-54.
83. Ibid. page 61.
84. Ibid.
85. Ibid. page 74.
86. Ibid.
87. See the previous chapter for evidence of this.
88. Minute book of the National Executive Council of the NPS page 74.
89. Ibid.
90. Ibid. page 75.
91. J.M.MacCormick, "The next step forward", *Scots Independent*, February, 1933. Page 53.
92. Ibid.
93. Ibid.
94. Ibid.
95. Ibid.
96. *Scots Independent*, May, 1934 page 97.
97. See Richard Griffiths, *Fellow Travellers on the Right* (1980) and any standard European history text book for the phenomenon of nationalism as a panacea for social and economic problems.
98. *Scots Independent*, April, 1934 page 81.
99. For example, see C.S. Black's pamphlet *Scottish Nationalism*.
100. Taken from the Minute book of the N.E.C. of the SNP.
101. Ibid. page 62.
102. *Scots Independent*, May, 1934 page 99.
103. See the previous chapter.
104. See the following chapter.

CHAPTER FIVE

The Wilderness Years (1934 – 1939)

When the Scottish National Party was officially launched on the 7th of April, 1934, the new Chairman, Sir Alexander MacEwen, immediately set the tone for the new organisation. Despite the problems of the merger, most members were confident about the prospect of success for the new party and its ambition to obtain self-government. MacEwen believed that the most damaging factor in the development of the national movement was the inability of nationalists to refrain from sectarianism and internal disputes. The electorate, he argued, could hardly be expected to believe that it would be a good thing for the Scots to rule themselves when the proponents of the self-government cause were forever squabbling with one another. It set a bad precedent and MacEwen was determined that the nationalist proclivity towards factionalism had to come to an end:

> The Home Rule Movement in Scotland has been too often marked by rivalries and jealousies. Let us hope that era is now past and forgotten.[1]

From now on party discipline had to be stressed and adhered to, and members would have to face up to the fact that, in a broad church movement, there would inevitably be political differences between people who held opposing ideological beliefs. However, MacEwen stressed that the attainment of self-government was a principle which they, as a party, held to be more important than any ideological consideration, and, if they all kept this in mind, it would bind them together. He expanded his optimistic view of the future as follows:

> We are entering upon a new stage of cooperative effort. Men and women of the Scottish National Party are still free to retain their own views as to social and economic problems, but they will be prepared to put these aside for the moment until they have achieved their common purpose — the redemption of their native land.[2]

The emphasis was now on teamwork and it was expected that members despite the fact that they came from different shades of the political spectrum, would work together in the national interest. Indeed, the idea that there was a tangible national interest would form one of the mainsprings of the SNP's political philosophy. The party attempted to elevate itself above conventional politics and it was hoped that their unselfish pursuit of the nation's well-being would act as a cohesive force:

> The Scottish National Party, in abandoning sectional interests for national welfare, has harnessed a new force in Scottish politics which will unify all Scots who have the welfare of Scotland at heart.[3]

The idea that nationalism or patriotism could act as a palliative for the social and economic problems of the day was essential to the nationalists' philosophy as they ruled out taking up a definable left or right wing political stance. Over the next few months, the SNP would have to set out in concrete terms what it interpreted the national interest to be and how they could best serve it. However, in the meantime, the party could attack the easy target of British over-centralisation and the lack of attention paid to Scottish affairs. Airing nationalist grievances provided a convenient stopgap and it was also an uncontroversial line of argument which gained approval from all types of members. MacEwen argued that it was the nationalist stirrings which induced the Government to transfer the Scottish Office to Edinburgh and that similar agitation had helped to secure orders for steam locomotives to aid the ailing Scottish economy.[4]

The lack of a properly defined political manifesto was not a primary concern of the leaders of the SNP, who believed that the party was in a healthy condition. Most members were buoyant and in confident mood and the emphasis on teamwork and unity was taken to heart by everyone. Few, if any, expressed concern at a lack of policies because it was expected that they would emerge from the national consensus, or more accurately, the feeling of national consensus, which they had created. This manifested itself in the various articles which were published in the *Scots Independent* in which different authors put forward plans for working within the parameters of the idea of national unity. The majority of the pieces were uncontroversial with most writers concentrating on one particular theme, and in many cases simply putting a new gloss on old issues.[5] What was important, however, was the fact that the contributors flung themselves wholeheartedly into the task of helping to create a national policy. Even those who had resigned in protest at the fusion of the two parties soon returned to the fold and accepted the SNP as the legitimate bearer of the nationalist standard.[6] Previous recriminations and accusations of sell outs were forgotten in the quest to build a new force in Scottish politics. Contrary to what many have believed, there was no drop in membership once the new party had been created and the majority of the old National Party branches remained in a healthy condition with expansion being the order of the day:[7]

> The branches have been showing a steady and increased activity. In spite of fears that the National Party would shed members because of the union, the reverse proved to be the case, for affiliation fees at the time of the conference (April, 1934) were up this year as against last year and almost twice that of two years ago. The Scottish Party also showed no loss because of the fusion.[8]

Throughout the first six months of the life of the SNP, branch activity flourished with an increase in the number of special events and speaking tours which culminated in an autumn campaign designed to be the first *salvos* in a general election contest.[9] Throughout this time, there was a steady increase in the number of new branches formed which, again, is another indicator of a party in expansion.[10] Not only did the creation of new outposts and an increasing membership roll help to boost morale and raise confidence, it helped to provide the necessary funds essential to establish the party as an effective political organisation. Among other things, plans were soon afloat to set up a new weekly newspaper which was a good indication that they expected a significant increase in their support.[11] The new spirit of confidence engendered a mood of generosity among the leadership who helped to pay off previous debts and thus left the Scottish National Party as the best off, in financial terms, of any previous nationalist organisation.[12] This was backed up by a fund-raising campaign throughout the branches which was given a new lease of life by the wind of enthusiasm that was now running through the party.[13] In this venture, they were greatly aided by the influx of personalities from the Scottish Party, whose social standing proved a crowd puller at bazaars and other fund raising activities. The experience and public prominence of former Scottish Party members helped to boost the new party's confidence by giving them what appeared to be added stature and political weight, which were two things that had been previously missing from the nationalist cause. However, perhaps the best piece of evidence about the state of health of the SNP is that in November they appointed their first full-time paid official and organiser, which was taken as a step to cope with the party's increased membership and activity. Contrary to what many historians have hitherto believed, the Scottish National Party, with its buoyant membership, high morale and increased organisational network, was better placed than any of its predecessors to make electoral inroads towards the goal of self-government.[14]

In order for the SNP to enter the electoral fray, it had to face up to the principal questions facing the Scottish and British political scene. Perhaps the most important of these was the economic situation with a world recession causing endemic unemployment and a southward drift of industry away from Scotland. Together with the economic problem, there was also turmoil in international affairs, especially as the rise of the dictators was threatening world peace. In order to be a credible political force the nationalists would have to formulate specific policies to deal head-on with these problems which, in fact, were more like crises. Also, they would have to clarify their position on constitutional matters with regard to the relationship a Scottish Parliament would hold with Westminster and the British Empire.

As was stated earlier, the corner stone of the party's philosophy was one which promoted the 'national interest' and a great deal of rhetoric was employed to cover up their lack of detail. In doing this, the SNP courted a number of obvious difficulties in so far as they risked being associated with the rise of militant nationalism, which was perceived as being the greatest threat to democracy and world peace. Strident nationalism was very unpopular in inter-war Britain and the general public was concerned to maintain peace by internationalism and the idea of collective security as propounded by the League of Nations.[15] Not only did the SNP have to address the problem of world peace as a political party vying for power, they also had to dispel any notions that they were similar in thought or deed to the Nazis, Fascists or militarists in Japan. Indeed, MacCormick was later to ascribe the SNP's lack of fortune in the thirties to the fact that by that time nationalism had become a 'dirty word'.[16] It is of little surprise therefore, to find that one of the party's first actions was to issue a statement clarifying their attitude towards Fascism and the nationalist dictators:

> The Scottish National Party is opposed to Fascism and dictatorship in any shape or form, being fully persuaded that is is repugnant to the ancient Scottish ideal of liberty and repudiates the suggestion, implicit in Fascist policy, that Parliamentary government on democratic lines has proved a failure and maintains that until Scotland has resumed self-government Parliamentary government in Scotland on modern lines has not been tried.[17]

The fundamental problem for the nationalists was that by arguing that 'national policies' in the 'national interest' could solve domestic social and economic problems, they were opening themselves up to comparison with their militant namesakes. This was especially the case as some of their members had made favourable noises about Fascism in the past, and some may even have continued to do so.[18] There was an urgent need for the Scottish National Party to expound their theory of nationalism and differentiate it from the national chauvinism which was now threatening world peace, much to the electorate's alarm.

The starting point for such an elaboration was to emphasis that Scottish nationalism belonged to the same family as those of the small nations of Europe whose ideas were liberal, tolerant and progressive. This was in contrast to the nationalism of the major powers which was strident, aggressive and prone to territorial aggrandisement. As such it was condemned outright:

> If the policies of Hitler and Mussolini and Japan are Nationalism: then Nationalism is indeed a world danger of the first magnitude.[19]

It was argued that small-nation nationalism was a counter force to this new threat because such countries were the most loyal to the League of Nations and the idea of collective security. They were also more committed to the ideal of democracy, it was claimed, and much more prone to maintain good relations with their neighbours:

> The danger to the peace and well being of the world today lies not in the unaggressive Nationalism of the little nations that are comparable to Scotland, but in the sinister policies and grasping Imperialism of the so called powers which are preparing the stage for Armageddon.[20]

Although few people, if any, believed that an independent Scotland could present a military challenge to world peace, Scottish nationalists were keen to show that self-government could provide an escape from war. Even the stalwart arch anti-separatist, the Duke of Montrose, jumped on the anti-war bandwagon, proclaiming that Home Rule would provide an additional safeguard against being drawn into another futile war:

> We hear a great deal about world peace and the growing armaments of other nations and we are told that we are going gradually towards another great war ... How does Scotland stand in this question? It is an appalling situation. We have to remember that in the House of Commons our Scottish members number 74 and are outnumbered by eight to one. If every Scottish member voted against a war, it does not matter a bit. Scotland would be drawn into this bloodshed like a trailer on the back of a car. The day has come when, if we are going to have our men butchered and all we hold dear wrecked in this country, as educated people we have the right to say if Scotland goes to war or not. If we have to face the question of war, and, if the cause is just, Scotland will be there side by side with England and do her bit and more: but if there is any doubt about the righteousness of the cause, Scotland will not go to war as far as the British Isles are concerned. Self-government for Scotland is a stroke for world peace, for the peace of the British Isles and a stroke for the safety of your homes and mine.[21]

Given the importance of international relations at this time, the nationalists could not ignore it, although they were ill equipped to deal with the problem. Montrose was simply cashing in on the concern for world peace and, in the process, was guilty of bending his own party's policy. The SNP was committed only to self-government within the realm of Scottish affairs and this obviously precluded taking an active role in foreign issues. Although there had been talk of an independent Scotland taking a seat as a member of the League of Nations, the matter was never satisfactorily resolved. Indeed, the whole issue of what part the Scottish nation would take within the British Empire had yet to be defined, with most members of the party believing that something akin to Dominion status would be the most acceptable option.[22] In spite of the fact that little of substance had been enshrined in party policy on this subject, there was a consensus that foreign policy would still be carried on within the framework of a British Government. This left the SNP at an obvious disadvantage because there was little that they could contribute towards one of the most important political debates of the decade.

In terms of forming a coherent economic policy, the party was hoping to make more solid progress, especially with regard to dealing with the unemployment problem. Using the framework of the 'national interest' idea, MacEwen, MacCormick and Gibson drew up a short reconstruction policy pamphlet which would serve as a starting point for expanding the party's ideas on social and economic issues. MacEwen and Gibson had formerly been Liberals and their thoughts on economic policy closely resembled those of the economic radicals whose ideas were best represented, in a British context, by the Lloyd George wing of the Liberal Party.[23] The SNP rejected both the official treasury view and, especially after the debacle of the second Labour Government, the utopia of state socialism. Essentially, the nationalists' economic policy operated on three levels. The most basic form was one which acted as a national watch dog and, publicising the imbalance between Scotland and England with regard to the effects of the depression, hoped to raise public indignation. This policy operated in conjunction with a statement of broad intent which outlined, in a basic form only, the party's plans for economic reconstruction. Finally, there were more detailed schemes which were drawn up by individual members purely as options to be considered for approval at a later date.

From the beginning, nationalists argued firmly in favour of government intervention as a means to stimulate economic growth and although there were flaws in the capitalist system, they did not believe that it was fundamentally wrong. What was required, they stated in frequent and various articles, was the need for the Government to fine tune and regulate the economy in order to avoid the usual pitfalls associated with the capitalist system, especially unemployment. In rejecting a class orientated view of economics while, at the same time, not accepting outright the doctrine of *laissez faire*, the nationalists, although propounding something similar to the Liberal Party, were able to produce a distinct economic policy which they hoped would contrast favourably with those of the Tory and Labour parties. Also, the 'middle way' between socialism and full blown capitalism, with its implicit acceptance of social responsibility for all classes, fitted in neatly with the idea of a 'national interest':

> We have no intention of maintaining the privileges of the privileged classes, we equally have no intention of carrying out 'working class' legislation without reference to its effect on the whole community. We do not go in to protect the rate payers' interests, nor to squander public money without thought of the consequences.[24]

Although the programme was short on detail and contained little of substance, it did help to set the tone of future nationalist policies. The basic problem, as the nationalists saw it, was one of under-consumption which inhibited domestic purchasing power. Also, the decline of the traditional industries, they argued, could only be offset by developing new sectors of the economy:

> Idle men, idle land, idle millions in banks, idle drifters in the fishing ports, and idle drifters in the House of Commons, and the last are the cause of all the rest ... We realize the difficulty of re-establishing shipbuilding and our heavy industries, but the development of Scotland along other lines is crying aloud for attention.[25]

The answer to the problem, it was claimed, lay with the actions of central government and the moral responsibility it had to its people. The idea of national unity was crucial in their philosophy for 'national redemption'. Unnecessary conflict and confrontation were to be avoided as the whole community was expected to pull its weight in solving the country's problems:

> The Scottish National Party makes no appeal to class interests, to sectional or sectarian prejudices, or to worn out political creeds. It takes its stand on the urgent necessity for all men and women of goodwill in Scotland to unite in the work of national redemption.[26]

The nationalists wanted to use the estimated 10 to 14 million pounds spent every year on unemployment relief to develop the Scottish economy by starting public works which would improve the economic infrastructure. There was, it was claimed, no contradiction in having 'national enterprise' existing alongside private enterprise. As J. L. Kinloch explained, 'there are certain things which can only be done by a nation and only a nation can do a nation's work.'[27]

The nationalists heartily condemned the National Government's efforts to promote economic development and likewise dismissed the various bodies and agencies which had been set up to help and advise in this venture. The Scottish National Development Council was given a cautious welcome, although it was claimed that it would be impotent because of their refusal to take an active political stance.[28] Sir Alexander MacEwen attacked the Rose Report by which, as the *Scotsman* put it: 'the distressed areas are left with but small expectations'.[29] Rose's proposals did not recommend an active government role for the solution to the south west's endemic economic problems and MacEwen described them as 'timid, trivial and partial'. He went on in a bitter tone:

> It is the greatest piece of mental laziness and moral cowardice ever performed by a Government...Sir Arthur Rose fails completely to grasp the fact that Scotland's depression is a national problem which can only be tackled by a National authority backed up by adequate finance. New and lighter industries in suitable localities, the construction of railway locomotives and carriages in Scotland, state aid for low temperature carbonisation of coal, utilisation of hydroelectric power, the development of aviation, motor car construction, the encouragement of rural industries, afforestation, small holdings, the building of houses, roads, bridges, piers, — these are some of the things a Scottish Government could set on foot.[30]

MacEwen wanted the SNP to adopt a bold and imaginative economic policy and he believed that this was essential for the party's success. Indeed, he attributed the lack of nationalist progress prior to the formation of the Scottish National Party to the fact that there was no coherent and well thought out economic strategy to accompany their claims for self-government:

> In almost every election we have fought, all the candidates have declared themselves Home Rulers of one sort or another, so that while we only promised Scottish independence, each of the others offered independence plus something else. That will be altered at the next election; because the Party is working out a constructive policy for Scotland.[31]

Although this was not strictly true,[32] the SNP set out in general terms their blueprint for economic reconstruction. It was proposed that there should be a scientific survey of Scottish industry, which would show what industries ought to be reorganised and what openings existed for new types of manufacturing. Indeed, Tom Gibson accused the Government of not making available vital information necessary for getting to grips with the roots of Scotland's economic problems.[33] It was also suggested that there should be created an 'industrial bank' which would give assistance, in suitable cases, to new industries or to help with the reorganisation of existing industries. Finally, it was proposed that there should be a 'ruralisation' of industry. Perhaps this was the most significant aspect of nationalist economic policy and the rural and agriculture sector was given a priority above all other sectors. The fixation with the land was a feature the nationalists shared with their European compatriots, who believed that the rural way of life was healthier and better for the national community. Undoubtedly, much of this was a romantic search for a long past golden age before the industrial revolution and the spread of international capitalism and, latterly, socialism. Indeed much of the SNP rural policies were influenced by the activities of nationalist governments abroad:

> Under the Mussolini Law passed in July, 1929, there are now being executed throughout Italy systematic schemes of drainage and irrigation, coupled with construction of roads, aqueducts, schools and other public buildings and farm workers' dwellings. When the land has been made ready by these means it is colonized by the effort of two organisations ... A bold system of planning and reconstruction in contradistinction to the piecemeal offerings reluctantly accorded to Scotland by Westminster.[34]

The Government's refusal to intervene on a large scale in the economy was lambasted by the nationalists who regarded such action as part and parcel of the duties of the elected representatives of the people. They drew inspiration from the economic initiatives that were now taking place in other parts of the world and argued that such policies should be examined and used at home:

> No country is today separating its economic interests from its system of government. In this age of economic planning, politics and economics are inextricably blended. Those who tell us that Parliaments and Governments cannot influence the economic life of the people are hopelessly out of touch with contemporary history. Practically all countries, great and small alike, are experimenting with more or less success in the art of political interference with economic and industrial life. In this matter the days of rigid principle are over, and the era of empiricism has arrived. Great experiments in national economic planning are going on in Russia, Italy, Germany and the United States, besides many other lands, and they are not proving fruitless or ineffective.[35]

Not only was the Government criticised for not stimulating economic development, it was also attacked for doing little in the way of setting up protective legislation for Scottish industry. The 'free market' forces, which were allowed to apply to the Scottish economy were blamed for the southward drift of manufacturing production and the unchecked influence of the City of London was held responsible for putting financial interests before industrial ones.[36] The nationalists wanted to see the creation of safety mechanisms which would protect the economy from being determined by purely financial considerations. For example, Archie Lamont advocated a scheme whereby it would become law that no company could operate in Scotland unless a majority of its shareholders were Scots. The ideas behind this proposal were to minimise the financial influence of London. Economic nationalism and the desire to maximise self-sufficiency were salient parts of the SNP's philosophy:

> Our country is so rich, potentially, that really we stand in no need of outside capital. London government and London head offices, as well as being unnecessary, are actually dangerous ... concentration of Scottish wealth and Scottish natural resources in Scottish hands, is the only way to prevent the closing down of Scottish industry.[37]

The SNP used the Clydesdale Bank's economic report as further evidence to back up their claim for economic nationalism. The report indicated that the trend towards national self-reliance was one that they expected to continue and that this would entail nations relying more and more on their own natural resources in order to undertake the production necessary for their own needs.[38] It was further argued that this process would require skilful planning and industrial reorganisation on a massive scale. All this was fuel to the nationalist fire, and the SNP advocated the full use of natural resources and toyed with the idea of protectionism as a means to provide the cover necessary to build up a newly formed industrial base and a more modern Scottish economy.[39]

However, although industrial regeneration was considered to be important, it was not the economic sector which received the most attention with a plethora of detailed policy options being produced. The nationalist interest in agricultural redevelopment has already been mentioned, and it is this area which provides the best insight into the Scottish National Party's economic and, more importantly, wider political philosophy. The promotion of land resettlement was an issue upon which there was almost universal agreement among party members. The dependency of the shipbuilding industries and other export related works on the fluctuations of world trade led the nationalists to look for economic developments in which they could control events. It was thought that by putting people back to small land holdings, the nationalists could solve the unemployment problem. William Power proposed that it would be possible to settle about 150,000 new cultivators which represented over half a million people, within a few years.[40] However, it was admitted that those settlers would only be able to exist at subsistence level and would have to augment their income by working in rural industries. Tom Gibson was the most vociferous proponent of a 'back to the land' campaign. He believed that the era of large centralised economic units was coming to an end and he based this upon developments in other parts of the world. Henry Ford was quoted to back up his case: 'The real machine age will involve the agriculturisation of industry and the industrialisation of agriculture'.[41] Gibson believed that the current economic trend was to develop new local small-scale industries which would be suited to fully exploit the existing local natural resources and, by using improved transport and cheaply supplied electricity, their produce would be cost effective enough to compete in the market place. Evidences of rural modernisation in France, Sweden and Italy were cited to point the way for the future of the Scottish economy.[42]

Although MacEwen was also interested in rural development, his concern was largely pragmatic and based upon his experience and involvement in the Highlands, where he was a public figure. However, unlike MacEwen, Gibson was more ideologically motivated by the desire to develop a policy for land resettlement. Like many other nationalists in Europe, Gibson had a dislike of the cartelised and over-powerful industrial and financial concerns which could not be subjected to national control and whose interests were dictated by an impersonal and international capitalist system. He was one of many whose faith in the pre-war economic system was shaken to the core by the world recession and the ensuing unemployment problem. Gibson also believed that industrial society tended to destroy national values and identities in contrast to that of rural communities which strengthened a collective sense of community. His tendency towards a corporatist system of economic management was motivated by a belief that the people were being squeezed by the interests of international socialism on the one hand and big-business capitalism on the other. His conviction that the nation had to manage both of these forces in the interests of the population at large led him to make a dangerous statement in favour of some kind of dictatorship:

However much we disagree with part of Hitler's policy and activity we must not allow such disagreement to make us forget that the basis of his economic belief, is, to quote an authority, the destruction of the great industrial and financial state laboriously erected in Germany during the first quarter of this century — the cumbrous, complicated, incredibly artificial state symbolized by the immense horizontal trusts of the late Hugo Stimes. In its place will grow a state of small farmers, craftsmen, professional workers, a pyramid with agriculture at its base.[43]

Although Gibson was an astute commentator on economic affairs, his disillusionment with the free trade capitalist system led him to adopt romantic notions which, in many ways, were backward looking and the tendency towards autarky was symptomatic of economic introspectivism. His remedy for the problems of the Scottish economy was almost quite naive in its simplicity. Gibson argued that over-centralisation, of any kind, was the principal source of economic dislocation:

Build up, however, a strong rural polity around the industries settled in the rural areas, and at once there is provided direct employment — spare time and otherwise — for those in these areas and the unemployed in our cities, provide a market at their door for their products and with the inevitable increase in the aggregate local taxable capacity for a material reduction in the rates payable per unit or per person and advance in social amenities. More and more land would be forced into use and no longer would we hear the cry that small holding or small farming was an uneconomic proposition.[44]

However, such proposals were too abstract and far fetched to be of any practical use as a realistic solution to the contemporary economic malaise. Although it has already been stated, and it had to be emphasised, that the SNP did not adopt specific policies other than those of general intent, such ideas were important in that they flavoured the party's outlook and their political image. There were some realistic and immediately realisable objectives, such as improving the fishing fleet and the extension of the tourist industry. However, by and large, most of what the nationalists advocated was general and non-specific and, more often than not, tended to be rural-centric. In spite of this, few members of the SNP asked the pertinent question as to how such objectives would appeal to one of the most industrialised nations in the world.

Another aspect of policy that the Scottish National Party had to clarify was the constitutional question, particularly with reference to the role that a self-governing Scotland would occupy within the British Empire. All other nationalist policies were ultimately dependent on how much

independence a Scottish Parliament would enjoy to diversify from the
Westminster Government. Also, as the British Empire was considered
vital to economic interests, it was crucial that the SNP cleared up how
their policies would affect Scottish trade. It was with this objective in
mind that the Duke of Montrose proposed a visit to the Irish Free
State, Northern Ireland and the Isle of Man, in order to compare and
draw lessons from their respective forms of self-government.[45] The
purpose of the delegation was to find evidence to refute the common
arguments against the nationalist policies, especially the claim that
Scotland was financially dependent on England and that left to her
own resources she would not be able to maintain the same standard of
living. It was also proposed that they would make enquiries as to how a
Scottish Government would be able to help industry, agriculture and
fisheries.[46] Other things were also to be considered:

> The working of the various constitutions, questions relating to tariffs,
> quotas, etc. financial relations with Great Britain, matters affecting Empire
> and foreign policy, local government, education, unemployment, etc. were
> all examined in so far as they have a bearing on self-government. Above all
> we wished to ascertain whether the possession of self-government provided
> a moral and intellectual stimulus to the peoples concerned.[47]

Each system of government was examined and those points which suited
and backed up the nationalist case were emphasised, especially with
regard to economic development.[48] However, the real crux of the matter
was in proving that self-government in no way implied a threat to the
British Empire and, with this in mind, the case of the Irish Free State
was dismissed:

> In any case the unhappy history of Ireland has no parallel in Scotland and
> Press comments on affairs in Ireland have no bearing on the question of
> Self-government for Scotland.[49]

The SNP were keen to draw fire away from comparisons with the Free
State and were constantly emphasising how relations between the two
nations were improving.[50] The self-government schemes of the Isle of
Man and Northern Ireland were hailed as shining examples of how
Home Rule did not impair loyalty to the Crown:

> The intense loyalty of Northern Ireland and the Isle of Man disposes
> completely of the suggestion that self-government involves any idea of
> separation from the British Commonwealth of Nations or from the Crown
> as a symbol of unity.[51]

The report also highlighted how Ulster businessmen were now converted
to Home Rule because of the administration's efforts to promote their

economic interests.[52] Also, it was shown how self-government led to an improved use of financial resources with each respective parliament paying what they considered a proportionate contribution towards the imperial upkeep.[53]

Having resolved the constitutional question, or so it seemed, and having established a framework for social and economic policies, the leaders of the SNP hoped to improve the party's standing by organising an extensive autumn campaign Increased speaking tours and local branch activity were used to try and stir up public support and bring in new members. In addition to this, the press was courted for publicity and fund raising activities were set afoot to provide the necessary finance for expansion. On the surface then, confidence among party members was high and there were great expectations for prospects in the new year of 1935.

Such hopes were forlorn as cracks soon began to appear in the fragile semblance of unity. As has already been mentioned, the principal *raison d'être* of the SNP was the belief that members could put the interests of the self-government cause above those of normal political ideology. However, the expected cohesion which MacEwen and others hoped for, gradually began to crumble under the weight of trying to reconcile people who held fundamentally opposing views. The first serious split occurred at the end of 1934. The cause of the row was a series of articles which appeared in the *Weekly Herald* written by Kevin McDowall, who was, one of the principal founders of the Scottish Party. Basically, McDowall was a fervent imperialist and advocated full support for the maintenance of the British Empire which, he claimed, was a cause that was more important than obtaining self-government. He allocated for himself the responsibility of trying to convert Conservative supporters to the nationalist cause and the passion of McDowall's commitment was such that many members of the SNP were worried that they were being represented as a right wing party.[54] However, it was his emphasis on the British Empire rather than on self-government which annoyed many nationalists who thought that although members were allowed to hold their own political views, felt that McDowall was causing unnecessary friction and his tactlessness was endangering unity. As a party internal memorandum on the issue explained:

1. On amalgamation it was recognised that there were mere devolutionists and out and out separatists in the new party.
2. In view of this, all those desirous of carrying on in the new party and yet of doing everything possible to forward our cause concentrated on

the non-controversial and left alone points which if discussed could only lead to trouble and which did not call for an immediate solution.[55]

It was claimed that McDowall's strident views on the Empire were both insensitive and impolitic. Also, his constant forays into the press were held responsible for misrepresenting party policy and his aggressive attitude to those who did not agree with him were another point of contention. His discipline was condemned, as was his unconstructive attitude:

> Mr. McDowall, practically alone, has persistently defied this tacit agreement by rather loudly and challengingly proclaiming his loyalty to the Empire as the first point in his creed.[56]

Even those members of the SNP who might have been sympathetic to McDowall's ideas were appalled by his destructive outbursts. The Duke of Montrose went so far as to say that 'the proper place for anyone with his views was the Junior Imperial League'.[57] The trouble arose from the fact that McDowall was adamant in his interpretation of party policy and would not tolerate any deviation from this view. He claimed that there would be no withdrawal of Scottish members from Westminster, who would remain there in order to continue with the running of the British Empire. Although this was not officially enshrined in party policy and was open to debate, what was intolerable was the way in which McDowall castigated those who did not wholly support him as being separatists and supporters of Sinn Fein.[58] Even the Duke of Montrose did not escape his wrath.[59] He even went so far as to accuse leading members of the National Council of breaking with party policy.[60] Although there were many in the party who supported his ideas on Scottish representation at Westminster, what they could not accept was the public airing of nationalist disunity, and accordingly, McDowall was given a thorough dressing down by Montrose.[61]

Throughout the first three months of 1935, the SNP leadership endured a sniping campaign from McDowall and his supporters. The tactics used became increasingly personal and there were constant threats of resignations and secessions. A resolution on imperialism was rejected by the National Council and his attempt to alter the party's constitution on the 9th of March, 1935, likewise failed.[62] Although Sir Daniel Stevenson supported McDowall, his defeat led him and two of his supporters to resign from the Council, including the Treasurer, H. A. Browne. Few people were unhappy to see him go, especially as he had publicly supported a non-rationalist body.[63] In future it was decided that no member should take part in any controversy in the press.[64] The

Duke of Montrose wrote to McDowall: 'I think it is a great misfortune that you spend so much time setting snares of an unfriendly nature'.[65] While the National council concluded:

> The cause of the trouble was that Mr. McDowall had supported another body in the University and at almost every meeting of the Council had raised trouble, while he had also written the most insulting letters to the Duke of Montrose.[66]

However, perhaps the most significant aspect about the McDowall secession was the effect it had on the party's morale and also the fact that it raised suspicions about the former Scottish Party group. Former National Party members increasingly scrutinised their colleagues for sins of weakness and backsliding. For example, it was thought that McDowall intended to take Montrose, MacEwen, Sir Daniel Stevenson and Mrs Burnett-Smith with him.[67] In February, 1935, the Duke was heard to make favourable noises about the Liberal Party which immediately set off alarm bells in the mind of Tom Gibson. It was up to MacCormick to reassure him:

> I did not see the Duke's remarks on Liberals but frankly I am not worried. I know the Duke is sound of head and anything he says which might jar a little is usually out of an excess of zeal.[68]

In addition to the prospect of former Scottish Party members forming ties with other political parties, there was also the problem of a widening of the left-right divide. The Duke of Montrose, for example had made some rather unflattering remarks about hitch hikers whom he had described as hooligans. This was picked up by the *Forward* newspaper, which goaded socialist nationalists such as R. E. Muirhead and J. L. Kinloch: 'Scots workers are not going to desert their own leaders to follow any Duke or other well known political reactionary'.[69] Further problems were caused by the fact that Muirhead had secured for a limited time two columns per week in *Forward* to propound the nationalist cause. The two principal writers were Archie Lamont and Oliver Brown who took a left wing stance on the self-government question which, again, had to tread a careful line between adherence to the tacit agreement on avoiding sensitive issues and expressing a personal opinion.[70] More tension was revealed when R. E. Muirhead felt it incumbent to correct A. D. Gibb's assertion that his former comrades in the Labour Party were marxist.[71] All this was further evidence of a widening gulf between the left and right wings of the SNP.

Not only was there increasing tension between the two opposing ideological bodies within the party, there were also considerable strains

on the question of strategy. Many former members of the NPS felt that
the relegation of conventional politics and the promotion of those
interests which only had a national dimension did not favour their
particular vision of Home Rule. It was believed that the party's present
course had an unnatural bias towards the conservative wing of the
movement. Much of this was purely a question of tactics and where
nationalists expected to gain their electoral support from. Naturally
many former National Party members expected that the reservoir of
nationalist support was to be found among the working classes and
accordingly, they expected the SNP would respond to this fact of
political life. However, the restraints of pursuing a 'national interests'
only policy meant that the SNP had the appearance of a cautious and
conservative organisation and made little direct appeal to those sections
of society which were the greatest areas of potential support. Under
the guise of promoting the national interest Kevin McDowall
concentrated his fire on trying to convert former conservative voters,
and the effect this had on the image of the party worried many, including
John MacCormick, who expressed his concerns to MacEwen as early
as the Summer of 1934:

> I wonder whether we are in a sense growing too respectable and too
> cautious. Are we not more and more shaping our policy in such a way as
> to try and appeal to what I might call the Conservative voter. For example,
> McDowall's recent contributions to the press. I would not for a moment
> wish to criticize McDowall. He is a great worker and quite entitled to try
> and win over the Tories. But on the face of it, should not our great
> endeavour as a Party be, to win over that mass of working and crofting
> classes ... On the one hand the Tory Party is strong and united as it ever
> was and more than likely to go back into power. On the other hand, both
> the Liberal and Labour Parties are in very low water.[72]

However, MacCormick was not the only person who began to feel that
the SNP was uncomfortable in its self-imposed restraints.

Neil Gunn echoed MacCormick's views to MacEwen and argued
that the party had to make itself more appealing to their potential
supporters. Although he agreed with the idea of propounding policies
in the national interest, he believed that a more vigorous and direct
strategy was required and that there was little point in trying not to
offend Conservative supporters. He claimed that the SNP had to
promote the interests of those people who were likely to support the
nationalist cause at the expense of those who would not:

> Can we not boldly prepare something for the Autumn Campaign; a charter
> for the Liberties, setting forth in constructive terms the kind of economic
> and social revolution we wish to achieve in Scotland? We need to get more

idealism, more passion into the movement and it is along such lines that it can be done. It is certain that we are not going to capture the big industrialists and those who follow them. Then why not forget them when shaping our policy? We need not go cautiously for fear of offending them, for our very existence offends them anyway.[73]

Gunn wanted the party to clarify and expound directly the nationalist attitude to the possibility of another war and in his view this meant pacifism. He also argued that the Scottish National Party ought to take the side of the smallholder against that of the landowner and that the rights of tenants had to be improved. Gunn's leftward trend continued by advocating the nationalisation of key industries such as electricity and rail transport. Also, he stated that there ought to be more democracy in the system of government.[74] Although such policies might prove to be popular with certain sections of society, they would not be accepted by many key people in the SNP. For example, the Duke of Montrose would not agree with Gunn's proposals for land reform, nor would any former members of the Scottish Party countenance the prospect of nationalisation. In the interest of keeping the peace, such arguments never reached the negotiation stage and the party ploughed on with the advocacy of the 'national interest' idea.

Further pressure was brought to bear on the left when the National Executive of the National Council decided to bring out a new official publication in addition to the *Scots Independent*. The leadership's commitment to the former NPS newspaper had begun to wane, and in January 1935, publication ceased for a while. Many members of the National Executive believed that stricter control over official party publications was required and that the best way to achieve this was to set up a new journal with the appropriate safeguards built in from the outset.[75] Although the *Scots Independent* did not openly criticise the leadership nor the strategy that was being followed, it did sail close to the wind on several occasions with articles propounding the relief of unemployment by taxation and withdrawal from the British Empire.[76] As the *SI* had been in the hands of radicals since 1926, many former members of the Scottish Party were naturally suspicious of its motives. The new journal, the *Scottish Standard,* was weighted heavily in favour of former Scottish Party members with three out of the four directors coming from that stable.[77]

Although this widening gulf is evident with the knowledge of hindsight, at the time such divisions were not considered important and the party went ahead with preparations for the forthcoming general election. By the Spring of 1935 it was proposed that 10 seats would be contested with the appropriate candidates selected and in place.[78] The party chose to fight mainly in constituencies which had already been fought and where experience had been gained. The leadership believed that the best chances for the Scottish National party were in Ross-shire, Inverness-shire, and the Western Isles where political opportunism, branch strength and the land reform programme combined to give them a fighting possibility of winning. However, although the leadership was prepared to contest parliamentary seats, they were not willing to enter into municipal elections, much to the chagrin of several members on the left.[79]

What internal stability and electoral credibility the Scottish National Party had built up since its inception, was shaken to its core in May 1935, when the President, the Duke of Montrose, announced his intention to resign his Conservative whip in the House of Lords and join the Liberal party. Although he intended to remain with the SNP, his decision shocked many members. In the first place, few people were even aware that Montrose held the Tory whip because it was believed that the party constitution outlawed membership of any other political party.[80] At a previous National Executive meeting the issue had been raised and it had been decided that dual membership would not be tolerated.[81] Initially, Montrose proposed in a letter to the *Glasgow Herald* in May that the SNP and the Liberal Party ought to merge into one body.[82] The Duke took his step without any prior consultation and his decision was a unilateral one which took everyone by surprise. Coming on top of the McDowall secession, the effect on the party looked as if it would be calamitous and Neil Gunn thought that it was imperative that Montrose's decision ought to be kept secret until after the General Election:

> All I should like to indicate what I feel would be the result on the fortunes of our Party of the taking of any decisive or disruptive steps by one at once so eminent in our Party... There is no doubt that if before the impending General Election your Grace publicly joined with the Liberal Party, the effect on the SNP would be near disastrous. I am just back from a fortnight in the Irish Free State where I was questioned on the recent break up of the SNP. This was a reference to the McDowall secession. In short, the idea has got through that we are disintegrating through repeated internal disruptions and if you were now made to appear in the press publicly to sever your connection... with the SNP the effect on the fortunes of those who continue to fight in the nationalist ranks would be one of bewildering depression.[83]

Evidently Montrose had either become disillusioned with the party, or no longer had any faith in its abilities to bring about self-government on its own, as his diminishing attendance at National Executive meetings tends to suggest.[84] He claimed that his principal reason for wishing to join the Liberals in the House of Lords was that he would be able to use his influence within that party to much better effect rather than acting as a solitary SNP peer.[85] He also argued that he could not represent the nationalists in the Upper Chamber because there was not a realistic SNP policy upon which he could base his actions.[86] Montrose either did not know that his party had formulated a limited programme, or he chose to ignore it. In any case, the impression he gave of being totally out of touch with the party of which he was President was an extremely bad advertisement and embarrassment for the SNP.

On the issue of being a member of another political organisation, Montrose set the party a bad example and indeed, his ignorance of what the SNP strategy was designed to achieve was appalling. He acted as if the long drawn out and difficult negotiations which had led to the creation of the SNP had never taken place. On this issue, the President managed to ride roughshod over most of the inbuilt safety devices that former members of the National Party had insisted upon before the new party was formed.[87] For Montrose, there was never any suggestion that he could not belong to another political organisation and he went so far as to claim that he had never hidden his membership of the Conservative Party.[88] It became obvious that he did not believe the SNP was a proper political party as such:

> The suggestion that I should act as a solitary SNP peer in the House of Lords without any general policy is quite unpractical in politics and would do no good whatsoever. I do not see that to remain Conservative and also a bearer of the SNP is any better than to become a Liberal and be an office bearer in the SNP In either case, a clash of interests is likely to arise at election times, but it would be more consistent to be a member of the old party which supports Home Rule than the one who opposes it.[89]

Montrose could not see any harm in members of the SNP belonging to other political organisations, so long as they did not oppose Home Rule. The Duke had a radically different interpretation of nationalist strategy when compared to others in the party. As far as he was concerned, the whole idea behind the SNP's policy on unity meant that, in a party political context, members were expected to drop issues concerning conventional politics:

> I am under the impression that we have agreed to submerge our opinions on other principles, until such times as there was a Scots Parliament ...

> You must recollect that the Scottish National Party has no other policy on their platform but Home Rule. It is entirely different from any other Party. But we individually have, no doubt, an interest in other things besides Home Rule and from time to time we may wish to promote them. We cannot do so through the Scottish National Party — it has no general policy, and therefore it is necessary to do it through other channels or parties. Do you think that people should really be silent on tariff questions, financial questions, constitutional or socialist questions, defence, foreign policy etc?[90]

The demoralising effect of the party's President not accepting its own policies must have been considerable. Also, at the same time, it became apparent that the popular novelist Anne S. Swan (Mrs Burnett-Smith), who was one of the SNP's better known catches, was still an active member of the Liberal Party.[91] Those former members of the NPS who believed that such actions were incompatible with party policy now faced the difficult dilemma of deciding how best to discipline those who would not give an exclusive commitment to the SNP.

A major problem facing those who wanted to resolve the question of dual membership was the fact that events had largely overtaken them and there was no time to organise a coherent response. The annual conference took place within a week of Montrose's decision and the resolutions submitted were clumsily put together. It was proposed that members of the SNP should not be allowed to join other parties, but this was defeated. In the end, it was left to John MacCormick to cobble together a compromise resolution which allowed dual membership provided that SNP office bearers did not take an active part in the work of an English controlled party.[92] The very vagueness of the statement effectively allowed things to carry on as they were and did nothing to put pressure on those in other parties to leave. With one eye on the forthcoming general election, the leadership was anxious to prevent any splits or disunity which might affect the party's electoral performance. Muirhead and MacCormick favoured a softly, softly approach to the problem and did not believe that draconian measures would work. They wanted to gently nudge the offenders back on to the correct path. As Muirhead explained:

> It was made clear that members of the SNP were expected to take the same view as the old NPS regarding membership of English controlled parties ... Personally I do not think it is desirable to expel any member who does not immediately conform to the NPS practice ... It is extremely unfortunate and hurtful to our Party that several of our prominent members have not yet left their old parties. We must just continue to show those members that they are expected to give their whole interest and attention to the SNP.[93]

In many ways, the biggest barrier to party unity was MacEwen's original stress on abandoning conventional politics in favour of an umbrella organisation which was committed above all to obtaining self-government. The failure to concentrate on economic and social policies and establish some form of coherence with regard to overall strategy and party identity left gaps, in which divisions and misunderstandings were allowed to develop and grow. On the eve of the General Election of 1935 the SNP had become more of a movement, rather than a political party. An irreversible decline had begun.

Despite some guarded optimism, most members of the party were not confident about their prospects for success. The toll of the McDowall secession, Montrose's and others' involvement with the Liberal Party, and a steady diminution of commitment in general, meant that the nationalists were in no fit state to fight a general election. The number of seats to be fought was cut to seven as a result of inadequate finances and candidates, and although many members worked enthusiastically and hard, there was an air of despondency running throughout the campaign.[94]

The leadership did not expect the party to do well; however, when the results became known, it was clear that the nationalist movement had suffered its greatest setback since entering electoral politics.[95] The SNP had contested five out of seven seats already and in each of them the party's performance had declined significantly.[96] Only in Inverness and the Western Isles, where MacCormick and MacEwen were the respective candidates, did the SNP put in, by their standards, a decent performance which in any case was only 16.1% and 28.1% of the votes polled.[97]

A number of reasons can be advanced to explain why the Scottish National Party did so badly in the General Election of 1935. The principal weakness of the party was that their policies were inadequate to deal with the demands of the electorate. Perhaps the two most significant issues in the election were the international situation and the problems of the economy, and in both of these areas, the nationalists were especially weak. In the international question, the SNP had little to offer in constructive terms to deal with the problem of heightening tension. As the party policy stated clearly that foreign affairs were to be handled by the Westminster Parliament, the SNP could not realistically offer an independent course on foreign policy and could not detach the Scottish nation from the British course in the international scene. In any case, the nationalist candidates on their election manifestoes supported the British government's action on Abyssinia.[98] It is hard to believe that people could realistically be expected to vote for a party which, apart from only putting up seven candidates, could not bring any pressure to bear on the course of foreign policy.

On the economic front, the Scottish National Party did propound a number of policies which were, by and large, constructive. On the election manifestoes it was proposed that there would be national control of credit, transport and power and that industry ought to be decentralised, together with a policy of land reform.[99] However, as it was apparent to members of the party that such proposals did not command universal support among nationalists, it was obvious to the electorate that sincerity and total commitment were lacking. Given that many of the SNP's policies were of a leftward persuasion, the fact that many of the party's leaders projected a right wing image could not have helped their electoral credibility. This was not made any easier by the constant portrayals of the SNP as a Tory organisation by the Labour Party.[100] Perhaps an even greater weakness was to be found in the fact that the nationalists hardly concentrated on the problems of the traditional heavy industries and this could not have endeared them to the working classes in the urban seats. It is significant that the nationalists did best in Inverness and the Western Isles where the party's programmes of land reform, rural development and promotion of the fishing industry were undoubtedly appealing to the local electorate.

However, the SNP was not only handicapped by its policies and their relevance to the electorate; there were also significant organisational problems. There is evidence to suggest that many in the party did not believe in the efficacy of contesting elections and that this was a source of difficulty in raising finance.[101] Also, many constituencies were without a proper organisation, and coordination with headquarters was poor.[102] There was a failure by the National Council to plan a coherent election strategy and there was even evidence of confusion among candidates, especially concerning Elma Gibson who was supposed to have been replaced by a less experienced nominee.[103] In many constituencies there were insufficient workers and local branches had not made their presence felt among the community. Again, it is significant that in Inverness and the Western Isles, local branches were active and had thoroughly canvassed their respective areas.[104] Indeed, it was those factors concerning organisation that the party leadership put the blame on for their poor showing, and as such, they were targeted for improvement in 1936.[105]

For many, the election failure could only be attributed to the fact that the SNP needed a more attractive and coherent set of policies which would have to be actively promoted by all members of the party. Others, meanwhile, believed that it was necessary to reassess current strategy, even if it meant renouncing contesting elections and instead cooperating with other political parties. In any case, the one thing all nationalists agreed upon was that the SNP had, in one way or another, to modify its approach in its quest for self-government. All this was done amidst an increasing atmosphere of despondency and a collapsing of morale. On the 7th of February, 1936, Sir Alexander MacEwen offered his resignation as Party Chairman after a critical article appeared in the January *Scots Independent*.[106] It was argued that MacEwen's residence in Inverness was a considerable handicap in his dealings with organisation. Also, there was tacit criticism of the leadership for not pursuing a bold enough policy. Tom Gibson was aware that the collapse of morale had affected MacEwen quite badly and it was reported that he was considering rejoining the Liberal Party. Muirhead, who had always been suspicious of MacEwen's Liberal tendencies,[107] was convinced that he was intent upon approaching his former party:

> I also noted in the press recently that Sir Alexander MacEwen was considering whether or not he would go forward as a Liberal Home Ruler ... from a conversation with Sir Daniel Stevenson I think the report in question was correct. Sir Daniel phoned me at the works today and pressed me for an agreement that Sir Alexander should go forward on the joint ticket...I further gathered from Sir Daniel that he intends to support the candidate of an independent Liberal unless the SNP agrees to Sir Alexander going forward as a Liberal Home Ruler.[108]

The prospect of cooperation with the Liberal Party was one which had existed since the party was formed. Montrose's decision to take the Liberal whip was probably aided by the fact that such tendencies abounded in the SNP. Indeed, the party organiser, J. B. Webster, was formerly the full-time organiser of the Liberal Party, which, together with a large number of former Liberals amongst the nationalist ranks, made comparisons between the two parties obvious. On his election manifesto MacEwen stated bluntly that he was a Liberal and J. M. MacCormick was especially attracted to this party. As early as February, 1935, he was toying with the idea of flirting with the Liberals:

> I do not think that it would do any harm to make our faith especially attractive to Liberals just now. They are nearest to us in many respects and more important, are without real leadership of their own.[109]

MacCormick's intention was undoubtedly to steal the Home Rule mantle from the Liberal party and establish the SNP as the sole bearer of the self-government standard. Rumours were also circulating in the party that MacCormick was planning to form some type of radical movement which would affiliate to the SNP.[110] The idea behind this proposal was to provide those of a more radical persuasion with a platform for their ideas. However, many in the party were opposed to a process of further disintegration and MacCormick was forced to drop this plan in the meantime.

The shock of electoral defeat and an apparent reversal of the SNP's fortunes, compelled Sir Alexander MacEwen to reassess the party's strategy, especially with regard to cooperation with other parties:

> It seems to me that we should reconsider whether we should revise our attitude towards members of other parties ... There was a disposition on the part of some to adopt a too exclusive attitude, and to frown on those who feel that they can reconcile the promotion of self-government with allegiance to other political parties. If we are to attract to our ranks the latent sympathy of which I have spoken, we must drop this attitude of exclusiveness.[111]

However, others in the SNP held a completely different point of view and were determined that the party ought to stick to its present course. The failure of the leadership to enter the SNP into the Ross and Cromarty by-election was lambasted by this wing of the party, who were doubly suspicious following MacEwen's pronouncement and the rumours of him toying with the idea of going forward as an independent Home Ruler.[112] The official reasons for the SNP's decision not to stand were that after the general election, the party did not have enough time to organise a campaign and also, that in such a large constituency, the logistics were not within their capacity. Under a banner heading of 'How not to do it', the *Scots Independent* accused the leadership of a failure of nerve and determination and demanded that nationalists ought to contest all by-elections.[113] All in all, it was hardly an auspicious start to the new year of 1936.

Roland Muirhead's decision to fund the *Scots Independent* through the auspices of the Scottish Secretariat opened up a valuable channel for those who were disgruntled with the direction the party appeared to be following. For many, the blame rested fairly and squarely on the shoulders of those who had shifted nationalist strategy away from that of the NPS towards that of the Scottish Party. The reason for low morale, it was claimed, lay with the shift towards moderation:

> The tampering with the wording of the object and policy which began in 1932 and culminated at the fusion of the National Party of Scotland with the Scottish Party, must be held as responsible for the weakening of the

enthusiasm of its members... results of this were the resignation from the Party of a number of hard working and enthusiastic Scottish Nationalists, the expulsion of others and the incoming into the SNP of some very moderate Nationalists. But more damaging to the Party was its act in putting at its head a member of the Scottish nobility, that relic of the past, an action distasteful to the democracy of Scotland.[114]

The *Scots Independent* also sought to move the SNP over to a much more radical and left of centre standpoint, and was adamant that it was only from this position that the party would be able to attain electoral success. In short, the Labour Party was the hunting ground in which the nationalists would find the most accessible game:

> Those who engineered the fusion of the NPS and the SP surely could not have recognised that if the Party was to grow, it must look to do so from Labour voters, since Unionists and Liberals (what is left of them) are afraid of Home Rule as they see quite clearly that if Scotland gets self-government she will have a radical and Labour Government, and they hate the idea of Socialism in power.[115]

The original idea of relegating conventional politics in favour of a broad church movement committed to Home Rule was becoming forgotten as the SNP began to divide among a left wing body, which was more strident in the degree of self-government it wanted, and a right wing or centrist group, which made more moderate demands. Also, these sections clashed over the form of strategy the party ought to follow with the left putting forward the case for contesting elections, while the right began to stress more and more the necessity of cooperation with other parties. By the beginning of 1936, both groups had their respective mouthpieces which increasingly began to disparage each other's point of view.[116]

However, not everything was gloomy in the nationalist camp. The opportunity of a Scottish Universities by-election provided the SNP candidate, Dewar Gibb, with the chance to redeem the party's electoral credibility. For this contest the nationalists were much better prepared and organised, while Gibb proved to be an able candidate and ran a vigorous campaign. Of great importance was the fact that all sections of the SNP enthusiastically supported him. His principal opponent was Ramsay MacDonald, the National Government's candidate, and Gibb came behind him in second place, polling over 9,000 votes, 31% of the total votes cast.[117] Although the nationalist obviously benefited from MacDonald's unpopularity and the reluctance of Tories to vote for a former Labour Prime Minister, the result was very respectable and did much to raise party morale and, despite Gibb's right wing tendencies, he was momentarily the left's hero.[118] This achievement was believed to vindicate the strategy of contesting elections. However, not everybody was convinced.

Immediately after the 1935 General Election, the right began to put forward an alternative method of obtaining self-government which stressed a cross-party and, to some extent, an apolitical approach to the problem. In December 1935 the *Scottish Standard* outlined a set of proposals which, it was argued, should found the basis of the Home Rule movement. Attention ought to be paid to propaganda and membership of the SNP be opened to all those who believed in the cause of self-government. Also, it was suggested that the party bring together eminent economists, clergymen and people from the business world, together with leaders of other political parties in order to work out schemes which would show how Home Rule would work in practice. Finally, it was proposed that the cross-party movement press for a plebiscite on the self-government issue.[119] However, Gibb's result in the Universities in late January 1936, temporarily put the brakes on this argument, and it was decided that some seats would be worth fighting, but not all of them.

The Scottish National Party contested the Dumbarton by election in March, 1936 and did extremely poorly, securing a mere 6.8% of the poll.[120] The campaign was badly organised and the party failed to achieve any momentum, while the Labour party secured a considerable success. This failure came at a bad time for the SNP and wiped out the small degree of confidence which Gibb's result at the Universities had built up. Both sides of the divide in the party intensified their campaigns to move the organisation towards their particular direction and morale was low when members met for their annual conference in May 1936. A whole battery of opposing resolutions was put forward and the end result was an uneasy compromise, which both sides interpreted as a victory. On the issue of membership, it was announced that those who belonged to other political parties could remain on the understanding that they did not hold office. Also, the objective of the party was shortened and simplified to 'Self-government for Scotland', with all other subsidiary clauses concerning the Empire and Commonwealth removed. The idea behind this was to remove all frippery and there was a forlorn hope that somehow this would prevent disputes if it was not there. Needless to say there were a multiplicity of interpretations. Some believed that it meant self-government in the fullest possible sense, while others argued that it was a broadening of the party's parameters to include anybody with an interest in achieving some form of Home

Rule. A resolution concerning cooperation with other parties was held over until a special conference in October.[121]

Many were unsatisfied with the results, including Tom Gibson who demanded a purge of all those who belonged to other parties.[122] On the whole the radical wing seemed to do best, although their account of events was more pessimistic than that given by the *Scottish Standard*.[123] Montrose and MacEwen gave up their positions and were replaced by Muirhead as President and Gibb as Chairman. Although Gibb was on the right of the party, he did not believe in cooperating with other organisations in contrast to his former allies.[124] However, his assessment of the SNP's fortunes was far from optimistic:

> The Party seems to be slowly disintegrating. Montrose is joining the Liberal Party. MacEwen is resigning from his post as Chairman and I have had to take it on. MacCormick is (together with Oliver Brown) evidently wanting to form a Socialist Radical group, with what relationship to the Party I know not. Resolution after resolution was on the paper indicating a desire for the conservation of our strength for the fighting of proper elections to the exclusion of mad adventures like the last Dumbartonshire election. A good period of regeneration and reorganisation was plainly the wish of the Party.[125]

The nationalist movement was riven with suspicion and although everyone agreed that recuperation and reorganisation were necessary, a number of protagonists were keen to put the SNP on a different direction. As far as the *Scots Independent* was concerned, the divisions which were now splitting the party were irreversible:

> Many delegates stated that fighting elections was a waste of money. We take an entirely opposite view ... this lack of progress and even the tendency to decrease... is fully accounted by the fusion of the National and Scottish parties. When a right wing organisation is fused with a left wing organisation the whole body suffers a set back.[126]

For this section of the party, there could be no question of compromise and they were furious at the decision not to contest the Springburn by election.[127] For the radicals, the constituency seemed ideal because of its working class nature and its easy access to SNP activists. Many believed that a left wing nationalist campaign would prove electorally popular and would not accept the official explanation that there was not enough time to organise.[128] For some, it smacked of a right wing conspiracy. For others, such as Tom Gibson and the Duke of Montrose, the alternate tendencies of the left and right proved to be too much and both resigned in protest.[129]

The special conference of October 1936 paved the way for the leadership to open up negotiations with other parties in order to obtain cross party cooperation on the Home Rule issue. The architect of this plan was John MacCormick who had never really relinquished his pet idea of a Scottish Convention.[130] He believed that fighting elections was not proving successful and would take far too long to achieve any worthwhile results. MacCormick wanted nationalists to get under the skin of the establishment and pursue every possible avenue which could further the aims of the self-government cause. Accordingly, he started to set up negotiations with the Liberal Party because he believed that they would be most susceptible to his ideas.[131] The confusion which existed in the party at this time allowed MacCormick a freer hand than would normally have been the case. Even some of those who would not have previously approved of such a scheme, such as Neil Gunn, accepted the proposal out of desperation that the SNP had to somehow get itself out of the morass in which it now found itself. However, Gunn still had doubts about MacCormick's strategy:

> The inherent danger in your plan is a subtle dissipation of national energies and a transference of a personal loyalty to another Party ... It might be possible, as you suggest, to work within the Liberal Party ... what is now before the Party challenges in a fundamental way the past tactics of the Party.[132]

However, irrespective of whatever strategy the SNP followed, many, including such diverse personalities as MacEwen, Gunn and Lamont, believed that the party had to put forward a coherent economic policy, and it was the absence of this factor which accounted for their poor electoral performance.

Gunn believed that the SNP's electoral strategy could not be judged properly and that any attempts at cross-party cooperation might be pre-emptive in view of the fact that, if they could put forward an attractive economic programme, the electoral success which they had striven for, might not prove so elusive. He argued that it was the lack of such a policy which had crippled the SNP at the polls:

> In short we are driven back on the old question of an economic programme ... and I am convinced that any patchwork programme — partly socialist, partly Tory etc., such as we now have formed up — it is not of the slightest use... It seems to me, it logically forces on to us one of the two alternatives; either the Party adopts one of the existing economic faiths such as socialism or liberalism and goes all out on it on a national basis or it follows the suggestion of your (MacCormick's) memorandum and acts through all the other parties, remaining itself, the rallying ground and inspiration of the self-government movement.[133]

For Gunn the SNP had to form an economic policy, or effectively cease to exist as a normal political party. The left of the party used the *Scots Independent* to voice their claims for a left of centre strategy and advocated social reform and extensive nationalisation.[134] Alexander MacEwen used the *Scottish Standard* to put forward his proposals for reconstruction and enlisted the assistance of prominent economists to analyse the problems of the Scottish economy and suggest remedial measures.[135] However, most of these projects were constructed within the parameters of the British nation and seldom took into account the role of a Scottish Parliament. Many of the measures put forward were taken on board by the SNP, although the reality of the situation was little different from before. The principal problem concerning the nationalist economic programme was not so much its content, but the degree of seriousness with which the party took it.[136] Also, the SNP still had little to offer in realistic terms with regard to Scottish industry as it then stood. Within the party there were two strands of economic thought. On the one hand, there was the left wing of the movement which advocated policies dependent on Scotland having more or less total economic freedom. The right wing, meanwhile, argued that expert and cross-party opinion was vital in formulating solutions to the problems of the Scottish economy as it then existed and were, more often than not, unrelated to the question of self-government.

By the beginning of 1937, the divisions between the left and right of the party had largely become meaningless as the SNP became more firmly a left of centre political organisation. Most of the prominent former members of the Scottish Party had either left the party or had ceased to play an important role in its organisation. [137] Also, the ease with which socialistically inclined policies were adopted is further evidence of the decline of the right, although some, such as A. D. Gibb and Robert Hurd, remained.[138] The main concern of the SNP was now the question of electoral strategy, and whether or not to cooperate with other political organisations. This debate had taken place for several years and, by and large, the dispute did tend to revolve around the left and right wings of the party. However, the diminution of the right meant that such compartmentalisation was no longer possible by 1937, especially as individuals such as Oliver Brown and A. D. Gibb took contrary positions from their normal ideological bedfellows.[139] Perhaps John MacCormick best represented the position in which the SNP now found itself. It was a radical left of centre political organisation, but committed to cooperating with other political parties and this, inevitably, meant that the seriousness with which it took its policies was not quite what it should have been.

The party began the year by questioning its current strategy and the initial optimism which pervaded the nationalist ranks at its inception had more or less vanished. The leadership began to advocate policies which more resembled those of a pressure group rather than those of a serious political party. In the search for an alternative strategy which would capture the success which had for so long eluded them, the party put proposals forward which were a hotchpotch of different measures, often with little coherence and little thought. Confidence was at a low ebb, according to D. H. McNeil, who stated that the SNP could not make up its mind concerning the correct strategy to take and that the party did not have the professionalism of other political organisations necessary to compete against them. The solution, McNeil believed, was to adopt a broader approach which allowed nationalists the opportunity to pursue their preferred avenue for success:

> To my mind, active nationalism must now proceed by sections, some fighting die hard elections, others forming self-government wings within the Liberal, Labour, and Tory Parties. What part is the SNP to play in the future?... To my mind it cannot take complete charge of the movement so long as it maintains its present constitution.[140]

This was more or less a tacit admission that the SNP had given up hope for winning a substantial number of seats at elections. Other tactics were taken on board including the setting up of a Convention for Scottish Self-Government,[141] and informal talks with other Home Rule bodies such as the ones which existed within the Labour and Liberal parties.[142] Petitions were sent to the Scottish Universities calling for a report into the problems of the Scottish economy and attempts were made to establish a self-government forum among Scottish MPs.[143]

However, this line of argument did not hold much water with a substantial section of the party which gathered around the *Scots Independent*. This body wanted to maintain the normal functions associated with a conventional political party including contesting elections and propounding a specific set of policies. It was believed that the SNP's election prospects would improve on account of their vigorously propounded economic policy. Archie Lamont was one person who believed that this was the correct way forward:

> The SNP has recently made great advances in policies. Already we have economic formulae calculated to break the back of large capitalism and ensure individual liberty by means of the small ownership of land and the national control of transport and banks.[144]

Lamont argued that the party would improve its popularity if it took up a strong stand against involvement in war. Consequently, he put forward the case that nationalists ought to oppose conscription and any involvement with the war effort until the Scots had a Parliament. The SNP echoed the popular concerns about the rising international tension and adopted Lamont's proposals concerning war at their annual conference in May 1937. This was done without any difficulty and even Andrew Dewar Gibb acquiesced in this decision.[145]

In June, the party had an opportunity to test how its policies would go down with the electorate with the announcement of a by-election in Glasgow's Hillhead constituency. As the leadership had decided only to contest seats in which it was perceived that the SNP would do well, Hillhead seemed an ideal target. It had a large middle-class element which MacCormick hoped to impress and it also encompassed Glasgow University which had previously proved friendly to the nationalists' claims. However, the campaign got off to a bad start with the candidate, MacCormick, stressing aspects of the sectarian divide rather than concentrating on the SNP's economic and social policies and their attitude to war. He argued that section 18 of the Education Act which provided for separate Catholic schools ought to be abolished and that no benefit should be paid to the unemployed Irish labourers who had not been in residence in Scotland for a certain number of years.[146] Although such proposals won approval from Andrew Dewar Gibb, they caused great resentment among many members of the party who believed that such tactics were divisive. Archie Lamont was most critical:

> I cannot agree to the tactic of appealing to a popular prejudice against a class who is attracted to Scotland under capitalism, to become our poorest wage slaves.[147]

He further argued that if there were to be immigration controls then they ought to be equally applied to the English, who, Lamont believed, were a greater threat to Scottish society than the Irish.

The campaign was apparently well run, although MacCormick failed to attract many people to his meetings, and the local population showed little enthusiasm for the nationalist cause. The result was a poor one, with the SNP coming in last place, securing only 9% of the votes cast.[148] The failure to secure even a modest showing meant that the leadership, and especially MacCormick, devoted more effort into achieving greater cooperation with other parties. He was apparently unconcerned that members had been leaving in protest at this manoeuvre and believed that there were no alternatives to the present course of action. He outlined his thoughts on the matter to that far from sympathetic body, the *Scots Independent*. First of all, he dealt with the defections:

> We recognise that their only fault is their failure to accommodate themselves to the necessities of working in harness with others. But their defections have been marked by neither a real loss of strength by the Party nor by the establishment of any better or more effective instrument for the achievement of our common ends.[149]

However, the loose discipline of the Scottish National Party meant that many of the most ardent opponents of MacCormick's policy did not leave, but stayed on, fighting through the columns of the *Scots Independent* a campaign of attrition. The majority of those who had resigned, like Tom Gibson, had done so because they believed that the SNP had ceased to function as an effective political organisation.

MacCormick believed that it was possible for the party to exist as a separate entity while cooperating with other parties. He was impervious to the dangers of the SNP being swallowed up by the other more powerful organisations and failed to see how such actions might render the party superfluous, as the larger established bodies could take the lead in the Home Rule cause:

> Only as an independent force can the Party take advantage of every opportunity to advance its aims. This does not mean that the Party can never enter into arrangements with other organisations. I can foresee that our growing strength will make it desirable for other bodies to angle for our support and cooperation. As an independent body there is no reason why we should not strike a bargain advantageous to ourselves if such a prediction comes true. I think it quite possible that the time will come when all progressive parties in Scotland will seek to cooperate with each other and there are good grounds why the Scottish National Party, grown stronger in the meantime, should benefit by such a move.[150]

MacCormick's strategy was based on unguarded optimism and there was no evidence to back up his claims. Indeed, the party's performance in recent by-elections tended to suggest that there was little chance of the nationalists making any sort of political impact. The negotiations which had been undertaken with the Liberal Party had borne little fruit, the only outcome of which was to put forward a joint candidate in the Glasgow University Rectorial election.[151] Also, the Labour Party was in no hurry to push things forward with a Scottish National Convention.[152] MacCormick now went back, publicly, on the party's previous strategy and concluded that only in a few selected seats would it be worth putting up a candidate. The SNP only had to show that their cause was popular for the other political parties to join in with the Home Rule cause. According to MacCormick:

> When the Party was founded most of us believed it would be necessary to win a majority of seats in Scotland before we could make our demands. I now feel that we were wrong and after winning at least a handful of seats we may at last begin to achieve our objective.[153]

The opposition to such a strategy came principally from two directions. On the one hand A. D. Gibb rejected such cooperation, largely because of his political convictions and, on the other hand, there was a group which largely resembled the Fundamentalists in the old NPS. Gibb argued that the party had to maintain unity and that alliances were dangerous in that the SNP could be taken over, after all, 'It is the National Party and no other which has put the question of self-government into prominence'.[154] Also, Gibb was ideologically opposed to the Liberal and Labour Parties and feared that involvement of these bodies could lead to a socialist Scotland, something which he did not approve of. He argued firmly that the concept of popular nationalism should take precedence over all other concerns.

By the end of 1937 there was a clearly defined group within the SNP which was ideologically committed to the left, convinced of the efficacy of contesting elections and, perhaps most important, argued the case for an independent Scotland with no strings attached to Westminster. Many of the Fundamentalists who were expelled from the NPS were back in the ranks of the Scottish National Party. Arthur Donaldson, Angus Clark and others were writing in the *Scots Independent* demanding independence in 'the fullest sense of the word' and based their vision of the future on the Scandinavian model, rather than as a partner in the British Empire. Indeed, a considerable degree of hostility towards the Empire surfaced. According to Angus Clark:

> Nationalists should never forget that the ills from which our country suffers come from the English Empire. The saddest pages in our history were not only made possible, but inevitable by the foolish and pathetic devotion of our people to Britishism and Imperialism.[155]

Other nationalists such as Robert Muirhead believed that empires were a thing of the past, while Arthur Donaldson argued that, in the event of war, the British Empire would not last.[156] The idea that Scotsmen should go to war to defend the imperial tendencies of the British state was one that was especially repugnant to this group. Indeed, as early as March 1938, plans were being made in opposition to the possible introduction of conscription. Arthur Donaldson was prominent in this movement. He wrote to Muirhead:

> The intent of this letter is to ask you if you know of any preparations being made to organise Scottish opposition to compulsory service under present conditions. My idea would be the formation of a new organisation... and the preparation of a covenant pledging all its signatories to refuse to submit to compulsory service, military, industrial or otherwise.[157]

However, there were also other indicators pointing to the existence of a more militant brand of Scottish nationalism.

In January 1938, the growing division within the ranks of the SNP was highlighted in the Scottish Universities by-election, where A. D. Gibb was the nationalist candidate. Almost immediately Archie Lamont announced in *Forward* that he would not be supporting the Party Chairman and instead urged people to vote for the Labour Party.[158] The reasons for Lamont's actions were obvious enough. He claimed that Gibb was really a devolutionist and that his ideas and political convictions were repugnant to the Scottish people.[159] Lamont was able to do this, safe in the knowledge that there was unlikely to be any disciplinary action taken against him as the party's structure and coherence had almost ceased to exist. In spite of this, Muirhead was furious.[160] Party discipline was now becoming a major problem especially in view of the fact that just two months previously Oliver Brown was openly campaigning for the Labour Party at Greenock.[161] However, given the gulf in ideological convictions which existed within the SNP and the differences of view concerning electoral strategy, there was little anyone could do to hold it together. In many respects the party simply drifted apart with both sides of the divide on the issue of cross-party cooperation, effectively going it alone on their respective projects. The Universities by-election only became acrimonious because Gibb and the Fundamentalists, although agreeing on strategy, were poles apart concerning ideology. In any case, the result was a bad one with Gibb only able to secure 18% of the vote, coming bottom of the poll.[162]

While MacCormick and his wing of the party pursued the formation of the Scottish National Convention, the remainder of the SNP fought to establish ideological superiority. Essentially Gibb was massively outnumbered; however, he still held the chairmanship and was respected by MacCormick and his friends who intervened to ensure that his position was secure.[163] Gibb was also, to some extent, protected by R. E. Muirhead, who kept out some of the more severe criticisms from the *Scots Independent*.[164] However, there was nothing he could do to stop the adoption of left centre policies which, in any case, both Muirhead and MacCormick supported, much to the chagrin of Gibb, especially the decision to support the anti-Fascist League. The leftward movement of the party was something he wanted to stop but was powerless to prevent, although much of this was only his imagination and was not universally shared with other moderates. Also, Gibb was a latent supporter of Fascism which was a fact he kept quite secret from others in the SNP. Early in 1939, he wrote to MacCormick and informed him of his intention to resign from the party if certain demands were not met. These included an overhaul of the SNP's organisation and MacCormick's position as the Honorary Secretary to be properly defined. Also, and most importantly, he demanded that the *Scots Independent* be purged of its left wing bias and instructed to cease criticisms of the leadership.[165] Throughout 1938, the intensity of the attacks on the party's direction increased, and previous attempts to bring it under control were firmly rejected:

> Prof. Gibb should understand in a paper like the *Scots Independent* where all sides have freedom, never meant the worsting of the truth. I [Archie Lamont] have dealt with Gibb's prejudices in the past and I shall deal with them in the future, when and how I choose.[166]

Also, the *Scots Independent* was opening up its columns to all sorts of people whom Gibb described as undesirable, among whom was Hugh MacDiarmid (C. M. Grieve) who was now putting forward the Communist Party's line on the Home Rule question.[167]

Gibb detested communism and socialism and could not rest easy with the thought of the SNP cooperating with the anti-Fascist League which was widely perceived as being an organisation of the far left:

> I hate communism with all my heart and, despite the uninformed outcry against Fascism, I can see it as the world's greatest danger. In Scotland more than in England, hatred of Hitler is the order of the day. The communist rats, recognising in him the single force which has their measure and can deal with them, are all for moderation and for an alliance with the other so called forces of the left against what they please to call the fascist menace.[168]

For Gibb, the enemy was not Fascism, but Communism, and the fact that the SNP was in an alliance with the CP appalled him. All the more so because he was favourably disposed towards Hitler and Mussolini:

> I have every respect for Hitler and Mussolini and intense admiration for them in almost every way ... My own view on Hitler's Jewish policy, after

discussing it with German supporters of the regime, is that much right is on his side... I agree that communism is too largely Jewish in origin and development.[169]

In addition to anti-Catholicism, Gibb had acquired a taste for anti-semitism, and should his views have become public, the damage done to the SNP would have been inestimable. However, such pronouncements remained private.

Initially, Muirhead was reluctant to give in to such pressures concerning the *Scots Independent* and, consequently, Gibb offered his resignation on March 2nd, 1939. His official reasons for wanting to leave were that he no longer felt any loyalty to the other office bearers in the SNP and the fact that the party was moving too far to the left:

> Any pretence that the Party is not overwhelmingly socialist must now be abandoned ... it has become intolerable for me to be constantly confronted with articles in the *SI* which I find myself in absolute disagreement with ... The Party has a curiously contradictory determination not to do anything which would wound the feelings of the Irish Roman Catholics.[170]

Also, the reply from Gibbs confidant reveals that the circles in which he was now moving were far from healthy, if indeed, sane:

> The Party's manifesto which appeared in the *SI* recently appeared to be convincing evidence of the ascendancy within the Party's council of a reckless and subversive element that was prepared to sacrifice Scotland's interests for the sake of International Jewry and the doctrines of the Jewish ideology.[171]

However, Muirhead was anxious to prevent another schism and the resulting bad publicity that would follow the resignation of the party's Chairman and reluctantly agreed to bring the *Scots Independent* under the direct control of the leadership.[172] As a result of this compromise, Gibb held over his resignation and agreed to remain on as Chairman for the time being. In any case, Muirhead, although in sympathy with much of what was written in his journal, was worried about its increasing tendency towards extremism. The *Scots Independent* had given support to the IRA and allowed Wendy Wood access to its pages. As a result of this, it was decided to withdraw it from sale at the annual conference.[173] Although the SNP took over the journal in the late spring of 1939 it was only an uneasy peace that ensued, and the criticisms, though modified, still flowed. However, with the approach of war, attention was drawn away from this dispute which seemed trivial compared with what was happening elsewhere in the world.

In January 1939, the creation of a Scottish National Convention was announced, which was the result of two years of negotiations carried out by John MacCormick on behalf of the SNP. It was hoped that this organisation would be able to find a solution to the impasse which the self-government movement now found itself in. In many ways the Convention was a success for MacCormick, because he was able to secure genuine cross-party cooperation and hopes were high, especially as the Labour Party was once again showing interest in Home Rule.[174] The attention paid to securing cross-party cooperation meant that there was a diminution in interest in contesting elections. In the summer of 1938 it was decided that the party would contest no more than five constituencies.[175] Also, branches which requested a sitting candidate were refused.[176] The principal problem with the Convention was that it was slow in getting off the ground and was only able to pass draft resolutions in late September, by which time war had been declared and the project had to be abandoned. Obviously the exigencies of wartime would put a brake on future progress. However, by this time, attention in the party had moved away from the question of endorsing cooperation or going it alone, and revolved around the issue of involvement in the war. Unlike the previous dispute, in which members could back the Convention, while still supporting the principle of contesting elections, or vice versa, the problem with the war was that it was a case of being for or against, and there was no halfway house. At the annual conference of 1939, the SNP backed down over the question of non-involvement and, reluctantly, agreed to support the war effort.[177] It was this issue which was to dominate the Scottish National Party for the next three years.

NOTES

1. Sir Alexander MacEwen, the *Scots Independent*, May, 1934, page 99.
2. Ibid.
3. The *Scots Independent*, April, 1934, page 81.
4. The *Scots Independent*, May, 1934, page 99.
5. See the previous chapter, especially the economic ideas of Tom Gibson.
6. George Dott, Tom Gibson and William Thomson had all left the NPS in protest at the Union. However, their contributions to the *Scots Independent* soon began to appear again. Both Thomson and Gibson were appointed to the National Council of the SNP.
7. This is not the view of previous historians of the National movement. H.J.Hanham, *Scottish Nationalism*, pages 163-169. J.Brand, *The National Movement in Scotland*, pages 228-236.
8. The *Scots Independent*, May, 1934, page 97.
9. Ibid.

10. Branch activity in the columns of the *Scots Independent*.

11. Minutes of the National Council of the SNP, 7th of September, 1934, page 63.

12. Minutes of the National Council of the SNP, 4th of May, 1934, page 53.

13. *Scots Independent*, October, 1934, page 178.

14. The assessment offered here is different from that of Hanham and Brand.

15. For the political impact of pacifism and the idea of collective security see Martin Ceadel, 'Interpreting East Fulham', in C.P.Cook and J.A.Ramsden (eds), *By elections in British Politics* (London 1973).

16. MacCormick, *Flag in the Wind*, page 88.

17. Minutes of the National Council of the SNP. 1st of June, 1934, page 90.

18. See C.M.Grieve's comments on the subject in chapter two, also A.D.Gibb's comments on pages 41-42.

19. *Scots Independent*, April, 1934, page 87.

20. Ibid.

21. Quoted from a speech made at Stirling, 23rd of June, 1934. *Scots Independent*, August 1934 pages 153-154.

22. See chapters 3 and 4

23. See Robert Skidelsky, *Politicians and the Slump : The Labour Government of 1929-31* (1967) for the economic policies of the Liberal party.

24. J.L.Kinloch, The *Scots Independent*, May, 1934 page 104.

25. *Scots Independent*, June, 1934, page 113.

26. *Scots Independent*, July, 1934, page 135.

27. *Scots Independent*, May, 1934, page 104.

28. *Scots Independent*, May, 1934, page 106.

29. *Scotsman*, 14th of November, 1934.

30. *Scots Independent*, December, 1934, page 213.

31. *Scots Independent*, August, 1934, page 145.

32. See chapter three on the policies of the National Party of Scotland.

33. *Scots Independent*, March, 1934, page 80.

34. *Scots Independent*, February, 1934, page 56.

35. *Scots Independent*, May, 1934,page 106.

36. *Scots Independent*, February, 1934, page 56.

37. *Scots Independent*, April, 1934, page 86.

38. Reprinted with comments in *Scots Independent*, April, 1934, page 88.

39. Party programme reprinted in *Scots Independent*, July, 1934, page 135.

40. *Scots Independent*, February, 1934, page 56.

41. *Scots Independent*, May, 1934, page 102.

42. Ibid.

43. Ibid.

44. Ibid.

45. Minute book of the National Council of the SNP. 1st of June, 1934. page 90.

46. Self-Government in Practice: A Report of a Delegation appointed by the Scottish National Party to visit Northern Ireland, the Irish Free State and the Isle of Man to study certain aspects of self-government, SNP pamphlet pages 1-2.

47. Ibid. page 2.
48. Ibid. pages 28-29.
49. *Scots Independent*, September, 1934, page 170.
50. Minute book of the National Council of the SNP, 8th of December, 1934, page 109.
51. *Scots Independent*, September, 1934, page 170.
52. *Scots Independent*, September, 1934, page 169-170.
53. Ibid.
54. See previous pages.
55. R.E. Muirhead to A.D. Gibb, 1st of February, 1935, Muirhead Mss, Box 11, Acc. 3721. NLS.
56. Ibid.
57. J.M. MacCormick to T.H. Gibson, 10th of December, 1934, Gibson Mss, Acc. 6058, file 5, NLS.
58. R.E. Muirhead to A.D. Gibb, 1st of February, 1935, Muirhead Mss, Box 11, Acc. 3721. NLS.
59. Minute Book of the National Council of the SNP, April, 1935, page 125.
60. Ibid.
61. J.M. MacCormick to T.H. Gibson, 10th of December, 1934, Gibson Mss, file 5, Box 1, Acc. 6058. NLS.
62. Minute Book of the National Council of the SNP, 9th of March, 1935, page 79.
63. Ibid.
64. op.cit. page 80.
65. Duke of Montrose to K. McDowall, 5th of March, 1935, Gibb Mss, Box 2, Dep. 217. NLS.
66. Minute Book of the National Council of the SNP, April, 1935, pages 124-125.
67. J. MacDonald to T.H. Gibson, 13th of March, 1935, Gibson Mss, file 5, Box 1, Acc. 6058, NLS.
68. J.M. MacCormick to T.H. Gibson, 7th of February, 1935, Gibson Mss, file 5, Box 1, Acc. 6058, NLS.
69. Forward, January, 1935.
70. R.E. Muirhead to A.D. Gibb, 3rd of March 1935, Muirhead Mss, Box 11, Acc. 3721, NLS.
71. R.E. Muirhead to A.D. Gibb, 7th of November, 1936, Muirhead Mss, Box 11, Acc. 3721, NLS.
72. J.M. MacCormick to Sir A.M. MacEwen, 5th of August, 1934, Gunn Mss, Box 15, Dep.209.
73. Neil M. Gunn to Sir A.M. MacEwen, 7th of August, 1934, Gunn Mss, Box 15, Dep. 209.
74. Ibid.
75. Minute Book of the National Council of the SNP, 4th of January, 1935.
76. For example the articles by Archie Lamont, July 1934, page 133 and R.E. Muirhead, October, 1934 page 183.
77. Minute Book of the National Council of the SNP, 3rd of November, 1934, page 107.

78. Ibid.

79. Ibid. 7th of September, 1934 page 96.

80. See the previous chapter.

81. Minutes of the National Council of the SNP, 8th of December, 1934 page 109. Montrose was present at this meeting.

82. *Glasgow Herald*, 4th of May, 1935.

83. Neil M. Gunn to Montrose, 10th of July, 1935, Gunn Mss, Box 15, Dep. 209, NLS.

84. Taken from the minute book of the National Council of the SNP. Monthly attendance records.

85. Montrose to Gunn, 15th of July, 1935, Gunn Mss, Box 15, Dep. 209, NLS.

86. Montrose to MacEwen, 15th of July, 1935, Gunn Mss, Box 15, Dep. 209, NLS.

87. See the previous chapter.

88. Montrose to Elma Gibson, 15th of May, 1935, Gibson Mss, file 5, Acc. 6058, NLS.

89. Montrose to MacEwen, 15th of July, 1935, Gunn Mss, Box 15, Dep. 209, NLS.

90. Montrose to Elma Gibson, 15th of May, 1935, Gibson Mss, file 5, Acc. 6058. NLS.

91. This was raised at the National Council meetings but only her past involvement with the Liberal Party was stressed in the Scots Independent.

92. Report of the Annual Conference, 1935, Young Mss, Box 44, Acc. 6419.

93. R.E. Muirhead to Elma Gibson, 10th of June, 1935, Gibson Mss, file 5, Box 1, Acc. 6058, NLS.

94. The columns of the Scots Independent did not make much of the campaign partly because the election was sprung on them, and also because resources were scarce.

95. The results were: Greenock 3.3% Kilmarnock 6.2% Dumbarton 7.8% E.Renfrewshire 10.4% W.Renfrewshire 11.3% Inverness 16.1% Western Isles 28.1%

96. See the previous two chapters for earlier election results.

97. These two seats were the ones in which the Party expected to do best in. Gunn to MacCormick, Gunn Mss, probably early September, Box 15, Dep. 209, NLS.

98. It headlined MacEwen's manifesto for the Western Isles. A copy is available in the Gunn Mss, Box 15, Dep, 209. NLS.

99. Ibid.

100. Especially in *Forward*.

101. Reports of draft resolutions in the minute book of the National Council of the SNP, January 1935-May, 1935.

102. Reports on organisations in the minute book of the National Council of the SNP, January, 1935.

103. Minute Book of the National Council of the SNP, October, 1934.

104. Neil Gunn to MacCormick, September 1934, Gunn Mss, Box 15, Dep.209, NLS.

105. Report on organisation in the minute book of the National Council of the SNP, January, 1935.

106. Minute book of the National Council of the SNP, 2nd of January, 1936, page 77.

107. See the previous chapter.

108. R.E. Muirhead to T.H. Gibson 7th of February, 1935, Gibson Mss, Box 1, file 5, Acc. 6058, NLS.

109. J.M. MacCormick to T.H. Gibson, 7th of February, 1935, Gibson Mss, Box 1, file 5, Acc. 6058, NLS.

110. A.D. Gibb to Elma Gibson, 12th of May, 1936, Box 1, file 5, Gibson Mss, Acc. 6058, NLS.

111. Sir Alexander MacEwen, Scottish Standard, January, 1936, page 6.

112. This view was clearly expressed in Scots Independent, February, 1936, page 1. 'Although the failure of the SNP in putting forward a candidate for Ross and Cromarty seems a blunder of the first magnitude. Immediately...Nat. Labour, Unionist and Labour parties became active, but for days there was no apparent move by the SNP latterly there appeared in an English controlled newspaper news to the effect that Sir Alexander MacEwen of the SNP has been asked to appear to stand as an independent Liberal and he agreed to consider the prospect. It would now appear that the officials at headquarters had in fact thrown away this splendid opportunity...and had instead confined themselves to an attempt at wire pulling with a section of the Liberal Party in order that the Chairman should not stand as a Scottish Nationalist candidate but as a Liberal Home Ruler.'

113. Scots Independent, February, 1936, page 2.

114. Ibid.

115. Ibid.

116. For example, the Scottish Standard frequently the 'failure of the Scottish Socialists' and 'the Record of the Socialists in Scotland'. While the Scots Independent attacked more the Liberal and Tory parties.

117. The results were: National Labour (MacDonald) 56.5% SNP (Gibb) 31.1% Labour 12.4% Source F.W.S. Craig, British Parliamentary by-elections 1833-1987.

118. See Scots Independent, February, 1936.

119. Scottish Standard, December, 1935.

120. The results were Labour 48.1% Conservative 45.7% SNP 6.2%

121. Report of the Annual Conference of the SNP 1936, Young Mss, Box 44, Acc. 6419.

122. Tom Gibson, letter to *Scots Independent*, September, 1936, page 7.

123. *Scots Independent* June, 1936, the *Scottish Standard* changed now to 'Outlook', June, 1936.

124. Gibb gave an outline of his attitude in *Scots Independent*, December, 1937, page 3.

125. A.D. Gibb to Elma Gibson, 12th of May, 1936, file 5 Box 1, Gibson Mss, Acc. 6058, NLS.

126. *Scots Independent*, June, 1936, page 2.

127. *Scots Independent*, September, 1937.

129. Minute book of the National Council of the SNP 13th of November, 1936, page 192.

130. See chapter three.

131. J.M. MacCormick to T.H. Gibson, 7th of February, 1935, Gibson Mss, file 5, Box 1, Acc. 6058, NLS. Also the relevant chapter in *Flag in the Wind*.

132. Neil M. Gunn to MacCormick, 2nd of July, 1936, Gunn Mss, Box 15, Dep. 209. NLS.

133. Ibid.

134. These arguments were put forward by Archie Lamont and Oliver Brown.

135. Particularly J.A.Bowie: see his *The Future of Scotland* (London 1939)

136. In essence, what was now being proposed was just the same as the ideas put forward earlier on, see pages 7-15. The Party had put most of these policies on the 1935 Election Manifesto.

137. Sir Daniel Stevenson, Sir Robert Patrick Wright, A. Ernest Glen, J.Sinclair, J.Bannerman, Harold Alexander, and Mrs Burnett Smith, were all former members of the Scottish Party who had been elected to the National Council in 1934, but were no longer taking an active part. In addition to this, Montrose, McDowall and Harold A. Browne had also left. By 1937, A.D. Gibb, Robert Hurd and Sir Alexander MacEwen were the only original members of the Scottish Party left in the National Council. Taken from the Minute Book of the National Council of the SNP.

138. Other members of the Scottish Party obviously filtered through the ranks but their contributions to Party policy were almost non existent.

139. Gibb did not believe in cross-party cooperation while Brown did and kept in touch with the Labour Party.

140. D.H. McNeil, *Scots Independent*, April, 1937, page 3.

141. See the following chapter for the Scottish National Convention.

142. During the Summer of 1937 talks began with MacCormick and the Liberal Party (see Flag in the Wind, pages 89-93) Also, MacEwen began talks with his former Party and the London Labour Self Government Committee was also approached. Reports of these meetings occur regularly in the Minute Book of the National Council of the SNP.

143. Minute Book of the National Council of the SNP 5th of March, 1937 page 209.

144. *Scots Independent*, June, 1937 page 3.

145. Report of the Annual Conference of 1937, Young Mss, Box 44, Acc. 6419 NLS.

146. *Scots Independent*, July, 1937 page 3.

147. Ibid.

148. The results were: Conservative 60.2% Labour 29.7% SNP 9.0% source Craig op.cit.

149. *Scots Independent*, October, 1937.

150. Ibid.

151. Minute Book of the National Council of the SNP, 5th of March, 1937 page 210.

152. See following chapter.

153. *Scots Independent*, October, 1937.

154. A.D. Gibb in Scots Independent, December, 1937 page 3.

155. *Scots Independent*, January, 1938 page 6.

156. *Scots Independent*, April, 1938 page 11.

157. A.W. Donaldson to R.E. Muirhead, 17th of March, 1938, Muirhead Mss, Box 5, Acc. 3721. NLS.

158. R.E. Muirhead writing to the editor of Forward 17th of October, 1938. Muirhead Mss, Box 5, Acc. 3721, NLS.

159. Lamont in the *Forward*, September, 1938.

160. R.E. Muirhead in the *Forward*, October, 1938.

161. Report in the Minute Book of the National Council of the SNP, January 1938, also *Scots Independent*, December, 1937.

162. The results were: National Government 48.8% Independent 19.5% SNP 18.2% source Craig, op.cit.

163. Report in the Minute Book of the National Council of the SNP, February, 1938.

164. Muirhead to Donaldson, 17th of October, 1938, Muirhead Mss, Box 5, Acc. 3721. NLS.

165. Memo in Gibb papers, Box 2, Dep. 217 NLS.

166. *Scots Independent*, September, 1938, page 6.

167. The best exposition of Grieve's 'The Red Scotland Thesis: Forward to the John MacLean Line' is to be found in the *Voice of Scotland*, June-August 1938. Grieve wrote the headlining story in Scots Independent, March, 1939.

168. A.D. Gibb to Rugg-Gunn, March, 1939, Gibb Mss, Box 2, Dep. 217, NLS.

169. Ibid.

170. Letter of resignation March, 2nd, Gibb Mss, Box 2, Dep. 217. NLS.

171. Rugg-Gunn to A.D. Gibb, 28th of February, 1939, Gibb Mss, Box 2, Dep. 217. NLS.

172. Minute Book of the National Council of the SNP. 14th of April, 1939, page 313. Young Mss.

173. Report in the Minute Book of the National Council of the SNP, February, 1939.

174. Especially Tom Johnston, see the following chapter.

175. Minute Book of the National Council of the SNP, May, 1938.

176. Ibid.

177. Report of the Annual Conference 1939, Young Mss, Box 44, 6419, NLS. The opt-out clause read as follows 'conscript and all other forces are only to be used for the defence of Britain or to fulfil the moral obligations involved in a real system of collective security'.

CHAPTER SIX

The SNP During the War, 1939 –1945

When war broke out in September, 1939, the SNP had already begun to display all the hallmarks of a political organisation which was fundamentally divided and lacked any sense of a positive direction.[1] For several years, the party had built up a continuing mountain of problems, none of which appeared to be anywhere near to being soluble. Amongst the most pressing of these were an uninspiring leadership, poor discipline, low morale, declining branch activity, increasing financial pressures, and last but not least, the stigma of being nothing more than an inconsequential fringe group in Scottish politics.[2] As if this was not all bad enough, the impact of war compounded the situation by forcing the leadership to face up to a particularly difficult dilemma and formulate a wartime strategy which would prevent the nationalists from splitting into hostile and opposing factions. In many ways, the SNP had created a façade of unity which had been founded on little more than a unanimous condemnation of the foreign policy of Neville Chamberlain. Now that the war had finally arrived, the party had to take on board the fact that for three years their members had, in theory at least, pledged themselves to refuse to serve with any of the Crown forces until the Government acceded to their demands for self-government.[3] This policy of anti-conscription, which many in the conservative wing of the organisation were uneasy about, had come home to roost with a vengeance[4]. The leadership was totally unprepared, and their resolution to back the 1937 Conference decision began to waver as they considered the ramifications of not only refusing to offer full compliance in the war effort, but also endorsing a campaign which would be widely interpreted as being unpatriotic and a hindrance in the armed struggle. The confusion and procrastination was exacerbated by the nationalist penchant for adopting contradictory and ambiguous resolutions whose primary function was to appease the various factions and maximise the semblance of unity. It was in keeping with this tradition that, while still pledging opposition to the introduction of conscription, the party passed a motion at their annual conference in May 1939, which supported 'measures for Scotland to play a full part in the defence of the country'.[5] Furthermore it was agreed that compulsory enrolment in the armed forces would be tolerated, provided that the Government gave a commitment to the effect that 'conscript and all other forces are only to be used for the defence of Britain or to fulfil the moral obligations involved in a real system of collective security'.

Where the SNP stood on the question of participation in the war effort, and, more importantly, the issue of whether or not nationalists would do military service, nobody, not even the leadership, knew. In the first few weeks which followed the outbreak of the Second World War, the party vacillated in all directions, desperately seeking a strategy which would free them from the contradictions of their previous policies.

Within the hierarchy the clique which had gathered around MacCormick and William Power, the journalist and former editor of the *Scots Observer*, took the decision to give a qualified public declaration in support of the war effort.[7] This was done without any formal consultation with the other members of the National Council and was based on the pretext that it was their duty to defend the Scottish nation from the possible threat of German aggression.[8] MacCormick effectively staged a *coup d'état* which by-passed the section of the SNP which advocated a more militant stance against involvement in the war, much to their extreme annoyance.[9] In any case, the argument was put to them that, whether they liked it or not, they were now at war and the realities of the situation left them with no alternative course of action. MacCormick claimed that to refuse to give a commitment to the war effort would lower the party's already limited public esteem and, more importantly, it was their duty to aid the interests of national security in order to defend their liberty and democracy.[10] Also, the leadership was acutely aware that should the SNP embark on a policy of non-cooperation, it would open them up to the charge of treasonable activities and the full onslaught of a government clampdown.[11] Furthermore, given the volatile nature of public opinion, MacCormick was anxious not to be wrong footed into marching the SNP along a route which went against the popular mood of the nation. In public, the leadership emphasised that the principle behind the decision to go to war was right, although in private many harboured serious doubts:

> Scotland and the Scottish people are in ever present danger of attack from without. We see no alternative to resolute defence. Our country must be protected with all the means at our disposal ... we are unflinching in our determination to assist with all means in our power towards the defeat of Nazi Germany.[12]

The public face of the party, the *Scots Independent*, was edited by John MacDonald who was militantly pro-war, and from the outset, the official nationalist periodical put forward the message that the rank and file should endeavour to protect their country from invasion. Also, it was claimed that they had a moral obligation to help defend the freedom of their fellow small European nations:

> The SNP maintains its attitude of last month, and being prepared to support a war which is fought for the liberties of small nations, wishes to be assured that these are the Government's objectives, and therefore, wishes the Government to publish its war aims.[13]

In keeping with a policy of cautious acquiescence, the party offered its services for civil defence purposes and agreed to give full cooperation to the Ministry of Information.[14] Also, members were actively encouraged to apply for posts in wartime administration and the facilities of the SNP offices were offered to Tom Johnston, the Scottish Regional Commissioner.[15] On the surface it appeared as if the nationalists were prepared to throw their lot in with the struggle against Nazi Germany, although behind the scenes the reality was quite different.

In spite of the fact that the party had officially come out in support of the war, most members of the hierarchy were uneasy about the situation and were still trying to ascertain the direction in which public opinion was moving. As part of the policy of keeping a foot in both camps, it was emphasised that they would not unconditionally follow the lead of the Chamberlain Government. There was an initial consensus among the leadership that war could still be avoided and many were convinced that a peaceful settlement could yet be reached.[16] This line of argument was most fervently pushed by the Chairman, Andrew Dewar Gibb, who for the next two years was to spend a considerable amount of time denouncing the Government for grossly mishandling the international situation.[17] Others displayed much more ambiguous tendencies, such as John MacCormick, who, while still supporting the mobilisation for war, attended peace rallies as a principal speaker and called for an end to hostilities and an immediate armistice.[18] Other prominent members of the National Council, such as R. E. Muirhead and J. L. Kinloch, stuck fast to their ILP tradition and argued that the nationalists ought to take the lead in establishing an anti-war movement, which, they believed, would attract popular support.[19]

In spite of these misgivings and political meanderings, the thorny question of conscription and whether party members ought to refuse to do National Service still remained, as the Government had no intentions of meeting the SNP's demands to instigate self-government. In a desperate attempt to prevent the party from carrying out its threatened anti-conscription resolution, MacCormick twice wrote to the Scottish Secretary of State, John Colville, in an effort to obtain Government assurances that they 'recognise the right of all small nations in Europe, including Scotland, to self-determination'.[20] However, such pleas fell on deaf ears and no reply was received, and with this went any hope of an easy opt-out. On the 7th of October, the National Council overwhelmingly voted to support any young nationalist who refused to be conscripted on political grounds, and indeed, McCormick offered his legal services to defend them.[21]

Given the fact that the SNP was supporting the war on a point of principle and was participating in the measures for civil defence, while, at the same time, rapidly moving towards an anti-conscription policy, many members felt that there was an urgent need to clarify the party's attitude to wartime activity.[22] Confusion was rife among the rank and file, who felt that the leadership's directives were both contradictory and misleading. The anti-conscriptionists claimed that their case, and official policy for that matter too, was being adversely affected by the fact that the Government had been given a bond of loyalty to help in the war effort.[23] Others argued that the hierarchy ought to encourage nationalists to refuse National Service and instigate a more vigorous campaign of opposition.[24] However, MacCormick refused to issue a statement elaborating on the SNP's attitude to the war, believing that the time was not yet right for such a move. Indeed, the first official communiqué to the local branches from Headquarters following the outbreak of war contains no mention of the anti-conscription issue, and the party was set the rather unimaginative goal of political survival as the top priority.[25] As was mentioned earlier, MacCormick was anxious to avoid being pressurised into taking any steps which might prove to be politically inexpedient. Accordingly, the SNP embarked on a seemingly ambiguous policy which took just enough steps to keep both the pro-war and the anti-war factions in check, while MacCormick mapped out the lie of the political landscape ahead.[26] However, by keeping the organisation in a deliberate state of limbo, the leadership bought enough time to dissipate any powerful surges of militant pacifism which may have been spreading through the ranks.

Although MacCormick was sympathetic to the claims of individual conscientious objectors, he would not countenance any effort to organise an anti-conscription campaign as this was a form of action which he believed to be, in both a moral and political sense, fundamentally wrong and irresponsible.[27] Some, such as Douglas Young, the Chairman of the Aberdeen branch, and Arthur Donaldson, leader of the Scottish

Neutrality League, which had now changed its name to the United Scotland Movement, were becoming more strident in their demands for a high profile plan of opposition to the introduction of conscription, and called on members to carry out official party policy.[28] However, MacCormick and Gibb skilfully manipulated the National Council meetings in such a way as to deny their opponents the necessary forum from which they could launch their intended campaign.[29] Also, the *Scots Independent* began to make strenuous efforts to dampen down anti-conscription enthusiasm and the membership was repeatedly warned of the dangers of taking precipitous action:

> In the interests of Scotland we have to save what can be saved of her. It would be possible for nationalists, no doubt, to run their heads into the noose, and get themselves thrown into prison or put before a firing squad. In that way many would be cut off and the movement disrupted. But would that be of much avail after the war, when the time comes again to resume, as nearly as possible, where we left off? Surely not ... Praise peace then, and help on its coming. Keep together in your organisation. In serving the defence of your country, keep together in your units-as far as possible.[30]

Instead of jumping headlong into militant pacifism, the rank and file were urged to keep calm and concentrate on the rather mundane task of maintaining the SNP as a functioning political organisation.

From the outset of war, political survival was deemed to be the National Party's first and most important priority. With having only a short and rather turbulent history behind them, and having few or no elected members serving in any tier of government, the SNP was especially vulnerable and susceptible to wartime disruptions. Also, by concentrating on a purely administrative strategy, MacCormick was able to divert attention away from the more militant forms of activity which were being bandied about. In order to keep the party's fragile organisation intact, members were urged to try and obtain administrative jobs or work connected with civil defence, rather than join the armed forces. It was proposed that propaganda efforts would still be carried out and that branch activity should continue as near as was possible in the circumstances. [31] The hierarchy was aware that they did not have the financial reserves or the grass roots stability of the other political parties and unless concerted action was taken, there was a very real danger that their own organisation would be swept away in the ensuing chaos of a society at war.[32] The issue of conscription was a factor which was responsible for a massive destabilisation of the SNP and MacCormick tried to defuse the situation by limiting nationalist ambitions until after the war, by which time, he claimed, the opportunities would be greater. In the meantime, it was argued, the rank and file should content themselves with the preparatory work necessary for the peacetime reconstruction:

> We must preserve the Party. The Council's policy in these times is guided by the belief that at the end of war, a great opportunity will be afforded to Scottish nationalists. It is therefore vitally important that the Party carry on its work in the meantime, increase its influence on Scottish opinion, and prepare itself with the full consciousness of the responsibilities which may yet fall on it.[33]

In many ways MacCormick's strategy was a success. He was able to hold off the anti-conscription challenge until December, when a special conference was called to debate future policy. By that time the mood of the SNP, certainly the National Council, had come to accept that there was no alternative to fighting Hitler and that any attempts to organise a mass anti-conscription campaign would be both futile and damaging to the nationalist cause. In any case, the deliberate stalling and the leadership's refusal to give a clear line of action, meant that those members who had been called up in the meantime would have to act according to their own conscience and judgement, rather than rely on any notions of official party policy. The vast majority offered no resistance and by the end of the year there had only been one reported case of a nationalist refusing to be conscripted. [34] More than anything else, the fact that there appeared to be no popular rank and file support, although it can be said that few members were likely to stand up on their own, emerged as the most significant factor in preventing the SNP from adopting any serious notions of an anti-conscription campaign. With the number of people backing their case rapidly declining, those who advocated non involvement in the war effort found that their position had dramatically weakened.

On the 12th of December, MacCormick finally bowed to the pressure of party activists and a special conference was held in order to debate proposals for future strategy and, in particular, the motion from Douglas Young's Aberdeen branch that 'The SNP should not observe the political truce, should not cooperate with the Government, and should assert the right of Scotsmen to refuse military service to a non-Scottish government'.[35] However, a grim mood of realism had spread throughout the party and few had serious doubts as to the outcome. Most members were aware that the war in Europe was being fought for ideals with which they totally concurred, and that such ideals, for the meantime, were more important than the furthering of party political interests.

Neil Gunn captured the prevailing fatalism with which the recourse to arms was gradually becoming accepted as inevitable:

> I should imagine that the great majority of members believe in prosecuting the war, and the [National] Council's position is accordingly a difficult one, particularly as opinion is even divided there. I think myself it is very necessary to keep the Party in being and the effect of any step should be considered accordingly. Take these Aberdeen resolutions, for example, do they emanate from a large body of opinion, or a very small one? ... The position therefore, to me, is that we must press as strongly as possible and by all means to realize our aims, but not in such a manner as to disassociate, implicity or explicitly, from such forces as may be fighting to retain individual expression of opinion ... this very freedom is, as I say, implicit in the Scottish tradition ... I am aware that many members may think that this is an Imperialist war all round. I have, I may emphatically say, a great deal of sympathy with that view. But the fact does remain — and we have to face it that here (in contradistinction to some other countries) we can press publicly for our aims, that we can express our opinions about the Westminster Government.[36]

In many ways the argument boiled down to a question of priorities and most members, however reluctantly, were forced to accept that the preservation of democracy was more important than the transient principle of refusing to serve a British Government in wartime. Also, although many were sympathetic towards the aims of the anti-conscription movement, they were unwilling to support any action which would seriously threaten the fragile unity of the party.[37] The Aberdeen motion was defeated, as was a more extreme one from Bridge of Weir which called for an even greater campaign of opposition to the war.[38]

However, by way of a compromise and motivated by the prevalent need to maintain unity, it was agreed that moral support would be forthcoming to those who refused to be conscripted on account of their political beliefs:

> The Party, while recognising the majority of the Scottish people have acquiesced in conscription as a necessity in the present emergency, nevertheless considers, and will strongly urge, that the definition of conscientious objections should be enlarged to include objections based on profound political convictions.[39]

This resolution helped to patch over differences and, more importantly, provided Young and Donaldson with the necessary loophole through which they still continued their anti-conscription activities. However, in spite of this sizeable maverick element, the majority of the SNP decided that they ought to accept the war as an unavoidable fact of life which would undoubtedly hamper their progress. In the meantime, it was agreed that their energies would be put to most profitable use by conducting themselves responsibly and preparing the ground for the peacetime effort.

By the beginning of 1940, the party was formulating the outline of a coherent policy regarding involvement in the war effort. Increasingly the leadership put pressure on the anti-conscriptionists to abandon their campaign. No matter how unpleasant nationalists found the situation it was stressed that opposition to the war was of no avail:

> An opposition which should confine itself to legal methods would be ignored. Any other would be silently and easily suppressed. This is not Ireland or India. The movement is ten years old not a hundred.[40]

Apart from the practical difficulties which would result from initiating an anti-conscription campaign, the leadership hammered home the message that the war was being fought for justifiable reasons. The official policy of 'acquiescence' in the war effort was deemed to be correct because it was claimed to be in keeping with nationalist philosophy:

> . . . 'acquiescence' is good because the war is just. If a body of men held fast by freedom, it is surely this Party. What more natural than that it should range itself behind those who are seeking to establish freedom in Europe? Were Scotland free, she should have inevitably taken part in this war.[41]

In spite of the new official, bellicose attitude, the SNP continued to exhibit dichotomies within its strategy, as efforts were still being made to have military tribunals accept the legitimacy of nationalist objections to military service. While petitions were being sent to Government officials and MPs on the issue of anti-conscriptionists, the party was urging members to take an enthusiastic and active interest in the war-effort. The rank and file were to maintain a vigilant eye on Scottish wartime administration and report to headquarters any incidents which worked to the detriment of Scottish interests. [42] However, it may be said that the primary function of such a ploy was, first and foremost, to involve nationalists in the war effort and draw the sting from those who advocated a total abstention from England's war.[43] The *Scots Independent* toned up its commitment to the struggle against Hitler and the leadership decided that the newspaper ought to be made more attractive to the general public, even if this meant that it would no longer reflect the popular opinions of the SNP membership.[44] Such a move was not popular with many ordinary activists who believed that they were being left out of the decision-making process which, in turn, only helped to contribute to a growing feeling of disenchantment with the party's direction and lack of coherence.[45]

Although there was a consensus that the SNP should continue to exist as an independent political organisation, there was still confusion as to the exact role the party would play in the politics of wartime Scotland. The leadership was unable to decide whether or not to contest any elections which might occur or to observe the wartime political truce, in spite of the fact that they had not been invited to sign it. The pro-war faction argued the case that to contest by-elections would go against the spirit of supporting the war effort and that the self-government cause would be better served by concentrating on propaganda and other aspects of pressure politics.[46] However, such a policy was dangerously inactive and held no attraction for the bulk of the membership who were increasingly expressing their frustrations to the organising secretary, J. M. McNicol.[47] By the time of an announcement of a by-election at Argyll in April, 1940, the issue had not been satisfactorily resolved and various sections of the movement were each pursuing their own preferred policy option. MacCormick was still endeavouring to get the National Convention off the ground, which had to be postponed indefinitely as a result of the outbreak of war. The principal idea behind this strategy was to broaden the party's contacts and form a Scottish Council of Action which would be composed of various prominent people. MacCormick sought, and obtained, permission to open up informal talks with other political parties and influential organisations with a view to laying down the framework for a united front on the self-government issue.[48] As part of this process, discussions were held with the Liberal Party to see if they would be willing to allow J. M. Bannerman to contest the Argyll seat on behalf of the SNP, and in doing so, avoid breaking the electoral truce.[49] However, the negotiations were soon to break down, as the Liberals believed that such a strategy was a trifle risky and were worried about being so closely identified with extremist elements in the nationalist movement.[50]

Once again opportunism proved to be the determining factor in shaping SNP policy and MacCormick was reluctant to pass up on the chances that the by-election in Argyll seemed to afford the party. Given the fact that the constituency was a Tory seat at a time of rising discontent with the Government, he believed that it presented them with an ideal situation in which they could capitalise on Chamberlain's unpopularity. Also, by registering the discontent with the present course of the war's direction, the party was able to convince itself that it was doing no more than its patriotic duty in demanding a more effective course of action.[51] Indeed, the clamour for a Tory defeat was such that the editor of *Forward*, Emrys Hughes, wrote to Muirhead suggesting that Oliver Brown, a former member of the Labour Party, stand as an official nationalist candidate.[52] However, the leadership opted for William Power, principally because he was fiercely anti-fascist and a strong proponent of the war effort, rather than Brown, who was a leading activist in various peace campaigns.[53] In any case, Power fitted in with MacCormick's strategy of presenting the SNP as a patriotic contributor in the struggle to defeat Hitler, and during the campaign, strenuous efforts were made to play down the party's involvement in pacifist activities.[54] In the end, MacCormick's strategy paid off dividends with their candidate polling over 7,000 votes against the Conservative's 12,000, which was quite easily the best nationalist electoral performance to date.[55]

Rather than be taken as evidence of a nationalist upswing, the result was determined by a number of fortuitous events which combined to give the SNP an excellent fighting chance. In the first place, Power, as the principal opposition candidate, was able to pick up the Liberal and Labour vote, as well as cashing in on the Government's unpopularity. Also, the Tory Party machine had been adversely affected by the wartime call-up and the SNP was able to hold a significantly greater number of public meetings than their rivals.[56] Indeed, it was expected that Power would have done even better had it not been for the fact that the German invasion of Denmark and Norway had taken place 24 hours before polling day, which produced a patriotic swing to the Government.[57] The result helped him to stem the rising tide of ordinary members' discontents and helped to boost party morale. However, perhaps the most significant factor in the campaign was the aggressive attitude displayed towards the Conservative Party which was singled out for special treatment on account of its hostility towards self-government:

> Who is not against us is for us. There is but one party in Scotland avowedly anti-national militantly pro union. We must sweep that Party out of power in our constituencies. We must take the lead, we must rally all the enemies of the reaction, we must achieve that unity of radical thought and purpose which of itself alone will end the reign of Toryism in Scotland.[58]

This was part and parcel of MacCormick's evolving strategy for the National Convention and was designed to solicit sympathy from the Liberal and Labour parties. However, it has to be stressed that the Argyll by-election was a one-off decision and was not, as some members believed, a major policy initiative. In any case, the issue was further clouded by the outbreak of German hostilities and the ensuing British political crisis which absorbed most of the party's internal debate.

The ending of the 'Phoney war' led to a greater nationalist commitment to involvement in the war effort and provided the *Scots Independent* with all the justification needed to vindicate the current pro-war stance: 'with the brutal invasion of Denmark and Norway, the veil is finally stripped from the face of Nazi Germany'.[59] More pleas were issued to the rank and file to join in with civil defence and be on the lookout for fifth columnists and enemy infiltrators. At the annual conference of May 1940, members who belonged to pacifist organisations such as the United Scotland Movement were expelled for engaging in covert actions which both imperilled the war effort and brought the SNP into disrepute:

> The Council resolved that membership of the United Scotland Movement — or of any body holding similar aims — is incompatible with membership of the SNP, and the office bearers of the Party are hereby authorised to refuse to recognise as a member of the Party any person who is known to them to be a member of such bodies.[60]

The foremost victim of this purge was Arthur Donaldson who, with Muirhead's secret support, was the principal strategist of the anti-conscription campaign.[61] The leadership condemned the Movement publicly and, according to one source, informed the authorities of its activities.[62] In keeping with the surge towards a greater commitment to the war effort, the conference took the extreme measure of drawing up plans to form a provisional Scottish government in the event of communications being cut with England. The main idea behind this was that they would continue the struggle against Germany.[63]

However, a more immediate target for the party's criticism was the Chamberlain Government and their handling of the military campaign:

> The Council of the Scottish National Party, having considered the great danger in which the successful German invasion of Norway has placed Scotland, and being convinced that the present Government is unfit to undertake the defence of this country, hereby calls upon the people of Scotland to bring pressure to bear on their members of Parliament to secure the resignation of the present Government and demand the appointment of an effective Secretary of State for Scotland who will be a member of the war cabinet.[64]

In many ways, the nationalists were merely mirroring the wider attitudes of society and when the Churchill Coalition was sworn in, the SNP, in a wave of patriotic enthusiasm, gave them an almost unqualified statement of support:

The Council of the Scottish National Party affirms its intention to support the war effort of the Government and its determination to protect Scotland from inequitable treatment which is not genuinely necessitated by the war effort.[65]

This keenness to help the Churchill Coalition extended so far as not to contest elections which might prove embarrassing for the Prime Minister. However, many members felt that this was going too far, and MacCormick believed that they could still make political capital by fighting elections on the issues of 'Scottish nationalism and the elementary principles of democracy'.[66] Dewar Gibb and the pro-war militants put forward the case that to fight elections during the current emergency would hinder the war effort and 'would not impress the enemy with the homogeneity of the people of this country'.[67] The announcement of a by election at Montrose in the Summer of 1940, brought these tensions out into the open and the National Council was, more or less, evenly split over the issue. In the end, it was argued that the present time was not an opportune moment to contest elections as it would distract people from their civil defence duties and such action would not be deemed patriotic by the electorate. However, the most important factor in determining the decision was the realisation that the party did not have the requisite resources to mount an effective campaign.[68] With a significant section of the hierarchy opposed to the idea of contesting elections, both for political and practical reasons, the cross-party convention seemed to be the best avenue for furthering the self-government cause.

In September 1940, John Taylor, the Scottish Secretary of the Labour Party, published an article in which he outlined proposals for Home Rule after the war.[69] MacCormick responded warmly to these favourable utterings and formally put forward the case that self-government would be best served by the setting up of a united Scottish Front.[70] The principal driving force behind this idea was a continuation of the anti-Conservative theme which had been used during the Argyll by-election. MacCormick's position in the SNP had been strengthened by the resignation of Dewar Gibb, who found the anti-Tory stance too much to stomach, and his replacement by the more pliable William Power as Chairman.[71] Gibb had been the stalwart opponent of the Convention idea and his removal greatly facilitated the party's willingness to enter into cross-party negotiations.[72] MacCormick was keen to capitalise on the Scottish grievances which appeared to exist within the Labour movement and he was confident that they would soon be able to enlist STUC support. As he explained: 'they [Scottish workers] were almost ripe for a movement of secession from the English Trade Unions, and the discontent at present manifested among the rank and file would soon be reflected in the Executive'.[73] However, MacCormick, in seeking Labour support, was primarily motivated by expediency and opportunism, and not any ideological considerations, although such trappings were used to make the idea more palatable.[74]

Points of contact were soon established in order to set up negotiations which would formulate proposals for the setting up of a convention which would debate and put forward plans on self-government and post-war reconstruction. The organisation was described in the following terms:

> Scotsmen and Scotswomen preparing for the attack on post war problems ... composed of representatives from Scottish industrial, political and cultural bodies throughout Scotland, so that there may be in being a purely Scottish representative body which can and will act in Scottish interests.[75]

The principal SNP demand concerning the Convention was that it would also press for a plebiscite on the self-government question once the war was over. Again this was in keeping with MacCormick's philosophy of trying to find the quickest and least painful way of establishing Home Rule, and it also had the benefit of circumventing the direct use of political parties by making the issue the primary concern of a specific popular ballot. It was hoped that the other political organisations would support this proposal and it was made known that the SNP would refrain from contesting elections against official candidates who were prepared to commit themselves to the plebiscite idea.[76]

By the beginning of 1941, MacCormick was able to report that his negotiations with Lady Glen-Coats had been successful and that the proposals for a plebiscite would soon be discussed by the Liberal Party Executive.[77] Also, John Taylor had intimated that the Scottish Labour Party would, in principle, support the nationalists' plans and that they would ensure that they would suffer little in the way of interference from their London headquarters.[78] It was agreed that the next step ought to be the setting up of a special meeting to which all of the parties would each send three representatives who would plan and frame the proposals for post-war reconstruction and the plebiscite on self-government. However, a by-election was in the offing at Dumbartonshire and this, more than any other factor, coloured the attitudes of the participants involved in the cross-party talks.

The Liberal Party was the least affected by the ensuing by-election as they would be unable to contest the seat on account of the electoral pact. Also, because of their limited number of Scottish MPs, they had little to fear from the nationalist threat to challenge constituencies which fell vacant. However, they were keen to ally nationalist support to their cause and, for sound practical reasons, had no wish to offend them. Many former members of the SNP had found their way back to the Liberal fold, which not only helped to strengthen the long-standing commitment to Home Rule, but also acted as an incentive to maintain self-government sympathies in order to wean potential recruits away from the single issue, and to date, hopelessly unsuccessful, National Party.[79] MacCormick had always shown a special dispensation towards the Liberal Party and such attentions had not gone unnoticed with many on both sides of the divide claiming that there was little in the way of policy to differentiate between them.[80]

However, both the Labour Party and the SNP had a lot to gain or lose in the Dumbartonshire by-election. Few in the Labour Party, which was defending the seat, needed reminding that it was a National Party intervention in 1932 which kept Tom Johnston from Parliament and John Taylor was candidly admitting that a similar challenge could present them with problems.[81] Also, it was the first major test for MacCormick's united front strategy and a failure at this early stage would have cost him dearly. Although it is difficult to say exactly how seriously the Labour Party took the SNP proposals, there was a growing rumbling of nationalist sentiment emanating from many quarters.[82] However, in the end of the day, pragmatism was probably the guiding principle as a policy of cautious appeasement was a small price to pay for the removal of a potentially troublesome electoral challenge.

MacCormick was convinced that the opportunities afforded by the wartime truce could be made to work in his party's favour and he was determined to use this form of political blackmail to wring concessions from the Labour Party. Concrete assurances were demanded and anything less would not do:

> The Council of the Scottish National Party in considering its attitude to the Dumbartonshire election, had before it a friendly reply from the Labour Party in response to recent approaches. It was decided, however, to seek further assurances before a final decision should be reached.[83]

In order to drive the message home, the nationalists went ahead with the selection of Robin MacEwen, Sir Alexander's son, as their candidate, and went through the motions of preparing for an electoral campaign.[84] MacCormick's ruse worked and the Labour Party was forced to call a meeting at which they gave the necessary assurances that they were prepared to support the SNP's proposals for a plebiscite and cross-party cooperation on the issue of post-war reconstruction.[85] The nationalists grabbed their opportunity with relish and, after John Taylor had stated quite emphatically that MacEwen's challenge would present them with problems, one of the Labour delegation, Bailie McKinlay, was humiliatingly dressed down and made to publicly recant on his earlier statement that Home Rule was 'nothing more than a political obstruction at the present time'.[86] Also, a further factor in the nationalists' receptivity to the idea of cooperation with the Labour Party was the appointment of Tom Johnston to the post of Secretary of State for Scotland on the 9th of February 1941. A lot was expected from Johnston whose arrival at the Scottish Office was greeted with a marked degree of enthusiasm.[87] Furthermore, it was hoped that the conciliatory gesture not to contest Dumbartonshire would rekindle his former Home Rule fervour and add momentum to the movement for cross-party campaign for a plebiscite:[88]

> The nationalist decision for or against contesting Dumbartonshire hinged entirely on the attitude of the Labour Party towards Scottish self-government in general and the proposed post-war plebiscite in particular... After satisfactory assurances were obtained from the Labour Party, R. R. MacEwen stood down ... It is hoped that Dumbartonshire foreshadows a development in policy which may yet enable Socialists, Liberals and Nationalists to make common cause for a Scottish Parliament, and to collaborate in securing a plebiscite at the end of the war.[89]

Over the next year, MacCormick was to direct all his energy into establishing a Home Rule united front in which the SNP was expected to play a pivotal role.

The principal reason behind the adoption of this strategy was the belief that, with the political constraints imposed by the war, it was the only feasible option open to the party. The massive disruptions which occurred in wartime society decimated normal branch activity and with every other month that passed, there was at least one resignation from a member who was involved with some part of the organisational structure.[90] In any case, the opportunities for making any kind of electoral impact were likely to remain few and far between and, as the war dragged on, the SNP's resources became more and more stretched, leaving only a few constituencies in which they could mount a credible campaign.[91] MacCormick and the leadership were highly sensitive to the fact that to take unfair advantage of the electoral truce would open them up to all sorts of attacks of hindering the war effort. Bearing this in mind, they set to work in formulating a strategy which would somehow legitimise electoral interventions. It was hoped that by securing the tacit approval of the Liberal and Labour parties, and by stressing a nationalist commitment to the war effort, the SNP would be able to challenge any vacant Conservative seats by virtue of the Tory Party's hostility to Home Rule and their prewar record on appeasement and unemployment.[92] In any case, a cross-party approach to the self-government issue had for a long time been MacCormick's preferred option, especially as he had recently come to believe that the National Party was not strong enough to initiate political reform by itself.[93] He was further strengthened in this conviction by the way in which Thomas Johnston took a similar 'above party politics' approach to the administration of wartime Scotland.[94] The Secretary of State had set in motion a series of consultative committees and assorted quangos which were designed to look into the effects of war effort on the Scottish economy and some also had the remit of outlining proposals for post-war reconstruction. These bodies operated according to the devolutionist principle and took a Scoto-centric view of contemporary problems which, as many historians have pointed out, almost resulted in *de facto* Home Rule under Johnston's leadership.[95] MacCormick's priority was to make sure that the nationalists were not left out of the consensus-orientated decision making process which was developing at the Scottish Office. However, more than any other factor, Johnston's handling of the Scottish political scene was to prove to be MacCormick's undoing.

While having much to recommend in the nationalist strategy, especially in the way in which it tried to bring the SNP into the mainstream of the Scottish political establishment, there were also a number of inherent dangers. In the first place, neither the Liberal nor Labour parties could openly acknowledge the existence of an informal electoral pact, which meant that the key element of MacCormick's policy would have to operate on a covert level. Success was ultimately dependent on individual *ad hoc* negotiations which would have to be conducted before each by-election. Such a strategy, existing without any formal guarantees, was bound to be fraught with difficulties, especially as it could be overturned on the whim of their theoretical allies. The nationalist plan contained two of MacCormick's perennial weaknesses; political naiveté and a willingness to conclude bargains without obtaining corresponding promises from the opposition.[96] Also, the SNP greatly exaggerated its own sense of political importance by believing that their threat of an electoral challenge could influence the Labour and Liberal attitudes towards Home Rule and the plebiscite.

To say that optimism was a necessary ingredient in their strategy is perhaps an understatement.

Furthermore, such a convoluted policy, with its intricacies and secret negotiations, was hardly likely to appeal to a membership which was being kept in the dark and impatient with the lack of dynamic and positive leadership. What was wanted was action and such manoeuvres tended to militate against involving the rank and file in normal party political activity. (see below) Also, MacCormick had to overcome the doubts of several prominent members who carried out activities which were not conducive to the success of his strategy. R. E. Muirhead, through the auspices of the Scottish Secretariat, published anti-war pamphlets and made known his hostility to cooperating with British parties. [97] Former Chairman, Andrew Dewar Gibb, opposed the anti-Conservative bias of the current strategy and gave vent to his frustrations in several articles.[98] This meant that MacCormick's plans were not pursued with a total commitment which, in turn, damaged its credibility and spread an aura of confusion among ordinary members. It is hardly surprising, therefore, that the movement for the establishment of a 'united front' took on the appearance of being the work of an individual crusader, rather than the goal of a political organisation.[99]

At first the signs looked healthy and the favourable noises which emanated from the Labour Party helped to boost confidence. In July 1941 Thomas Johnston gave heavy indications that he was prepared to support devolution after the furore which followed the curtailment of the debate on Scottish affairs in the House of Commons.[100] Such vocal demonstrations in favour of self-government by the Labour Party helped to keep in check MacCormick's opponents within the SNP, and even hardliners such as R. E. Muirhead were temporarily won over and praised the way Johnston had raised Scottish grievances at Westminster.[101] The official publication of labour's proposals for post-war reconstruction received a cautious welcome from MacCormick who, although holding minor reservations, was quite confident that there existed enough common ground between the progressive parties to justify the setting up of a united front:

> There is now an apparent measure of agreement between the Liberal Party, the Labour Party and the Scottish National Party that it by no means should be impossible to devise a scheme acceptable to all three.[102]

MacCormick wanted assurances from Labour that their plans for nationalisation of key economic assets would not mean total centralised control from London. Also, he wanted a more emphatic commitment to the setting up of a separate Scottish Parliament which was democratically accountable, rather than what appeared to be being proposed, the enlargement of the Scottish Grand Committee.[103] MacCormick circulated the SNP idea of a federal system of government in the hope that it would find adherents within the Labour Party who would push to have it taken on board as official policy. Although nothing came from this attempt, the mood was still favourable towards the idea of self-government and MacCormick believed that all the signs were looking good.[104] In November, Johnston gave a pledge that there would be more meetings of Scottish MPs in Edinburgh and in December, the Scottish Council of the Labour Party passed by 71 votes to 35 the following motion:

> Whatever the exact powers of our new legislature, we are mostly agreed that a Scottish Parliament elected by the Scottish people would be the best instrument for the efficient government of this country.[105]

Although there was considerable opposition to this movement, mainly from Patrick Dollan and Emanuel Shinwell,[106] it appeared to many that Labour was experiencing a Home Rule revival. MacCormick believed that the tide of events was turning his way towards the creation of a Scottish united front. However, in his enthusiasm, he had grown impervious to the mounting discontent which was rapidly building up within his own party.

Throughout 1941 and well into 1942, the ramifications of MacCormick's policy created a number of distinct tensions concerning the direction in which he was trying to move the SNP. The area of greatest trouble arose from the question of support for nationalist conscientious objectors and the apparent contradictions of the party pleading on their behalf while promoting a more aggressive commitment to the war effort. Although the hierarchy had discouraged members from refusing to enlist, there were a number of nationalist prisoners which, MacCormick believed, gave the movement a bad press.[107] However, the anti-conscription issue placed him in a cleft stick, because, on the one hand, the SNP was tarnished with an unpatriotic image of being against the war effort, yet MacCormick was reluctant to disown the militant wing for fear of a backlash against his policy.[108] The only feasible option open to him was to use every means at his disposal to distance the leadership from the maverick elements. An example of this distancing happened in May 1941, after police raids on the homes of anti-conscription activists, when the party issued a statement that none of those arrested were members of the SNP.[109] The incident was

played down and they refused to denounce the searching of Roland
Muirhead's office for fear of the bad publicity which might ensue.[110]
Also, MacCormick was unwilling to press for the release of Arthur
Donaldson who was held under section 18B of the defence regulations,
and it was left to Muirhead to petition, as an individual, Tom Johnston
to have him freed from custody.[111]

This incident led to the first clear lines of demarcation in the ensuing
split which was to affect the SNP in the early summer of 1942. In May,
Muirhead set up the Nationalist Mutual Aid Committee as an
organisation designed to provide financial support to conscientious
objectors and encourage them to oppose military service.[112] Also, in
the same month following the police raids, the Donaldson Defence
Committee was formed to campaign for the release of the foremost
nationalist anti-conscriptionist. The issue of anti-war involvement
provided a focal point for disgruntled party activists who wanted a more
vigorous defence of Scottish interests and a lessening of contacts with
other political parties.[113] This 'ginger group' was incensed by a *Scots
Independent* editorial written by MacCormick's ally, J. M. MacDonald,
which criticised the activities of Douglas Young who was refusing to be
conscripted on the grounds that the enforcement of compulsory national
service in Scotland was a violation of the Treaty of Union.[114] Young
caused the leadership considerable difficulties because his objections
were not based on pacifist principles, but on the avowedly nationalist
dictum that the Scottish war effort should be conducted by a Scottish
government and that Scottish soldiers should fight in a separate army.[115]
Although such arguments were dismissed as naive and impractical, they
commanded a lot of respect among the rank and file, who were
impressed by Young's courage in tackling the British authorities head-
on.[116] Such a hardline stance was more in keeping with the kind of
positive action which was being demanded by many elements within
the party. The resultant press coverage which ensued from the
controversy gave the SNP more publicity than they had hitherto received
and it also helped to steal the limelight from the leadership's more
respectable approach to politics. Much to MacCormick's chagrin,
Young's action was becoming synonymous with the national movement
in the public's mind, as well as making his own efforts at establishing
cross-party cooperation more difficult. However, although he regarded
the whole incident as an embarrassment, there was little he could do to
have Young disciplined or expelled on account of his growing popularity
among ordinary members.[117] By the beginning of 1942, the divisions
within the SNP were becoming wider and more bitter.

The leadership's advocacy of a total commitment to the war effort had caused chaos in many local branches with the Aberdeen one, largely spurred on by Douglas Young and Oliver Brown, disaffiliating from the party sometime in the middle of 1941.[118] Furthermore, the Falkirk branch decided to suspend all activities during the war because, they believed, there seemed no point to their existence.[119] By 1942, it was apparent that the hierarchy was losing its grip on the control of the local organisations and this was exploited by the 'ginger group' whose appeals for a more active policy found a ready audience. For this body, attention focused on aspects of the war effort itself, and they demanded more dynamic action concerning Scottish grievances, such as the transfer of conscripted female labour south, the Government's failure to place new industry in Scotland, the drafting of soldiers into English regiments and the treatment of conscientious objectors. For Muirhead, McIntyre and others, these issues were considered to be the focal point of nationalist strategy and were believed to be of greater importance than MacCormick's efforts to set up a united front. Although the leadership accepted the validity of these grievances and regularly passed comment on them, they were not the main emphasis of the current nationalist strategy.[120] Instead, attention was concentrated primarily on post-war reconstruction and, largely for fear of upsetting Johnston, little was done to capitalise on the perceived injustices which were being committed for the sake of the war effort. Although the party made token gestures of protest, neither the Secretary of State, nor his government, were accorded the blame.[121]

However, perhaps the greatest failing with MacCormick's strategy was the almost total disregard for the well-being of the ordinary members, and by 1942 there was a constant stream of complaints from local branches regarding the apparent lack of initiative emanating from Party headquarters.[122] In spite of the appointment of Robert McIntyre as the Organising Secretary, and his concerted efforts to form new branches while still trying to maintain the morale of the existing ones, there was little he could do to convince the rank and file that the present course of the SNP was effective.[123] MacCormick refused to bow to the pressure for a more direct and controversial political strategy, and made matters worse for himself by accusing the local branches of being too dependent on the headquarters and lacking in drive.[124] Other complaints concentrated on the lack of democracy within the party and the hierarchy's reluctance to listen to the ideas or advice of anyone who did not belong to the ruling clique.[125] Morale was at rock bottom and McIntyre's monthly reports to the National

Council were a dismal catalogue of continual decline with only the new branches, which were set up largely at his instigation, showing any signs of progress.[126]

The leadership's credibility with the rank and file suffered a severe blow in December 1941, when it transpired that the SNP would not be able to contest the by-election in Edinburgh Central against an official Tory candidate. Poor finances, inadequate resources and a collapsed morale were cited as the principal reasons for not making a challenge, although it was candidly admitted that the hierarchy had been deficient in forming the necessary organisation.[127] The radical wing of the party blamed the leadership entirely for this state of affairs, and it also left a considerable question mark as to the feasibility of MacCormick's strategy. Other factors were soon to knock the current policy for six. Labour interest in the united front began to peter out as Johnston presented an alternative to self-government in the form of his 'strong man in the cabinet'.[128] The Secretary of State's ability to secure economic and political power direct from London and his capacity to deal with the most pressing of Scottish grievances, relegated the idea of Home Rule from many Labour activists' priorities.[129] Also, Johnston's tendency to govern by consensus and utilise the services of many senior Scottish Tories, went square in the face of MacCormick's objective of forming an anti-Conservative front. In spite of the apparent Labour commitment to devolution by the end of 1941, the ensuing months witnessed a dramatic cooling off, and contacts with the SNP were more or less severed. MacCormick's strategy to take the nationalist movement into the Scottish political establishment was floundering as Johnston's forums on post-war reconstruction had been set up without any SNP input and the party's proposal for a plebiscite appeared to have died on its feet. With the leadership's credibility at an all-time low, both within the membership and without, the announcement of a by-election at Cathcart, and the hope that they could repeat the success of the 1940 Argyll campaign, presented MacCormick with a final opportunity to vindicate his strategy.

The nationalist campaign in Cathcart and Douglas Young's trial for refusing to be conscripted, occurred at the same time during April 1942, and brought the extent of the SNP's divisions into the full glare of publicity. Indeed, one could be forgiven for thinking that there existed two separate parties. The by election also tested MacCormick's strategy to the full and highlighted all its inadequacies. The candidate, William Whyte, was one of the most vociferous of the pro-war proponents and from the outset, the tone of the campaign was apologetic:

Far from being insistent upon any extreme point of view, I was prepared
to cooperate with any member of any party who was prepared to consistently
advocate large measures of Scottish reform, and who would recognise the
individual character of Scotland's potential contribution to the war effort.
Unfortunately, it would appear that the discipline of the Tory Party machine
had precluded that possibility.[130]

Whyte pressed forward the anti-Conservative stance in the hope that
he would pick up the Liberal and Labour vote. However, he was careful
not to incur any accusations of damaging the war effort and stressed his
patriotic loyalty:

I believe that the present emergency government led by Winston Churchill
and Sir Stafford Cripps is an essential to victory. I therefore pledge myself
to give general support to such a government...I should state that I have
the utmost confidence in Mr. Thomas Johnston and will endeavour to
give him every support.[131]

Above all, it is Whyte's commitment to the war effort which emerges as
the principal message of the nationalist campaign, and although there
were calls for an end to the moving of conscripted female labour south,
greater democratic control and the setting up of new industries, these
were very much minor points. Even the call for Home Rule was watered
down to the setting up of a British Federation, and there was no mention
of nationalist conscientious objectors.[132] Finally, to cap it all, Whyte
chose not to stand under the SNP banner, preferring instead to be
labelled an independent.

The campaign was a disastrous failure, and unlike Argyll, where the
SNP was guaranteed a monopoly of the opposition vote, in Cathcart
there were other more experienced and able candidates challenging
the Conservative.[133] Whyte's pro-war stance alienated many party
activists, which left the local organisation with inadequate resources
and unable to mount an effective campaign.[134] Also, the publicity from
Douglas Young's trial overshadowed all other nationalist propaganda
and presented the SNP in a totally different light from what was trying
to be projected in Cathcart by MacCormick and the leadership.
Undoubtedly this must have confused whatever potential support existed
and may have been a major factor in Whyte achieving one of the worst
electoral showings made by a nationalist candidate up until that time.
In the end, the efforts to present the party as being a loyal supporter of
the war effort and a bastion of respectability had resulted in their man
coming in fourth position, having only secured a mere 5.5% of the
vote.[135] With this failure, the current strategy was left in tatters, especially
when it is contrasted with Young's performance in court, in which the

defendant made a passionate and unapologetic plea for a much more radical nationalist case. Although Young was found guilty, it was regarded by many as a moral victory and it was taken to signal the start of a more aggressive campaign.[136] With the annual conference coming up in May, the divisions between the moderate and radical wings had become so great that compromise was impossible. Indeed, some, like William Whyte, were baying for blood.[137]

The issue which was to spark off the 1942 split was the choice of Party Chairman. MacCormick and the leadership were in favour of continuing with William Power, while the radicals presented a challenge in the shape of Douglas Young. Previous historians of the national movement have identified most of the key features which took part in the power struggle, and Jack Brand has placed particular emphasis on the growing disenchantment with MacCormick and his tendency to treat the SNP as if it were his own personal organisation.[138] Professor Hanham, likewise, believes the issue of personalities to be an important factor in the ensuing split, although his main stress is on the division between those who favoured a cross-party approach to obtaining self-government and those who wanted the party to be independent of all other organisations.[139] In essence, both writers are correct in their respective analyses, although some of the more complex and subtle factors have been lost in the simplification of the story.

While, with the benefit of hindsight, it may appear as if a split was inevitable in 1942, it was only the militantly pro-war faction which was intent upon disruption.[140] The majority of the membership, MacCormick included, was agreed that there would have to be a major revision of strategy, and this would tend to favour the radical wing's demands.[141] The old policy was admitted to be a failure and MacCormick accepted that the Convention would have to be set up without interfering with the normal political activities of the SNP. Indeed, this was the major reason behind his decision to resign as Party Secretary, as it would allow him more time to further his efforts in the cross-party movement.[142] However, this does not mean that he had lost interest in the SNP, nor that he had ceased to believe it to be the principal catalyst in the drive for home rule. Although MacCormick had argued that home rule could only be realised by the combined efforts of the nationalists, liberals, and socialists, the National Party was an essential part of his plan because, not only did it provide him with a power base from which to operate, but also it acted as a stimulant in making other political organisations take the self-government issue seriously. Indeed, throughout the war, he had been the most vociferous advocate of contesting elections within the leadership.[143] Also, the accusations that he had been conducting secret negotiations with other parties has been emphasised too heavily by Brand and Hanham.[144] All the meetings MacCormick conducted to set up the 'united front' were reported regularly in the *Scots Independent*, and although members were suspicious about this, they were not as underhand as his endeavours with the Scottish Party at the time of the formation of the SNP.[145] While certain sections to the movement could not be appeased, especially Dewar Gibb, Whyte and other pro-war militants who wanted the anti-conscriptionists expelled, they were a very distinct minority whose prominence depended heavily on the support of the moderates.[146] However, the most significant factor in the split was MacCormick's sense of rejection and his shouldering of the cumulative blame for the leadership.

After a noisy debate, although no worse than many previous occasions, Young defeated Power by 33 votes to 29. A number of factors can explain the result, and the vote should not be taken as evidence of a deeply divided organisation torn in half between two radically opposing opinions.[147] In the first place, neither candidate would have been the ideal choice for a majority of delegates. Power was too old, lacked charisma and seemed to represent the lethargy and lack of direction associated with the leadership's policy. However, many would have voted for him, largely to avoid endorsing Young's militancy, although they would be determined to have the party's direction changed by passing motions on strategy. In other words, the narrowness of Power's defeat does not imply that almost half of the delegates were satisfied with the SNP's previous direction. The association of an individual chairman with a particular set of policies was not a strong facet of the National Party, as the adoption of many socialist objectives under the Chair of Andrew Dewar Gibb, who was himself a right winger and opposed to these motions, amply illustrates.[148] Similarly, it cannot be said that the votes for Young were a total endorsement for his line of action.

A further complicating factor in interpreting the split was that although Young was opposed to conscription, he was not of the same political stable as his most prominent supporters, namely McIntyre, Muirhead, Donaldson and Lamont. This body, which Hanham has labelled as the fundamentalist wing, differed from the present policy in that they argued that the party ought to avoid contact with other organisations and seek to win political power by contesting elections. Also, their definition of self-government meant sovereign independence, and they rejected any notions of federalism or devolution which was being mooted in various forms by the leadership. However, Young concurred with neither of these concepts to the same extent as his supporters, as can be gauged from his previous statements and subsequent actions.[149] Had it not been for his anti-conscriptionist stance, there would have been little to differentiate him from MacCormick.[150]

However, the reason for his choice as the radical candidate was twofold. Firstly, he stood for direct action, and this quality was what was felt to be most lacking in the party. Without a more concerted and assertive policy, it was believed that the SNP would suffer perpetual political impotence, and Young was the most ideal embodiment of strident, aggressive and unapologetic Scottish nationalism. Secondly, his undoubted charisma and personality contrasted favourably with the blandness of the current leadership. Also, it was believed that a successful challenge from a convicted anti-conscriptionist would render a complete defeat to the moderate and conservative elements within the party. Furthermore, it would open up the way to enforce more grass-roots democracy on the organisation, which in turn, it was believed, would facilitate a more direct and positive strategy. As McIntyre explained to the conference:

> ...in his contacts with the branches he had often met with dissatisfaction at the Party's lack of direction. For him the question was whether the branches were to play a full part and the Party to be a broad democratic organisation or not.[151]

However, and it has to be emphasised, the radicals thought that their strategy would be imposed without splitting the SNP.[152]

In spite of this desire, MacCormick could not stomach such a shattering defeat, and it went utterly in the face of his deep conviction that Scottish nationalism would have to make itself more acceptable to the political establishment. It would appear that on the spur of the moment he decided to secede, taking the election of Young to be a personal insult against him.[153] When MacCormick left he took about half the conference delegates with him, although the split was not as dramatic as this would seem to imply. For one, many of those who left were soon to return when it became apparent that the party was not going to make such a dramatic shift in direction as the victory of an anti-conscriptionist seemed to herald.[154] MacCormick added fuel to the fire by claiming that the SNP was now an anti-war organisation which was firmly in the hands of republicans.[155] However, the most conclusive evidence that the split was not as serious as historians have made out, is to be found in the small numbers of those who were to found the basis for the National Convention. It took MacCormick over a year to raise 1,000 members, which was perhaps only a third to a quarter of the strength of the SNP.[156] Also, it has to be borne in mind that many supporters of the Convention were also paid-up members of the National Party, and it was with the latter organisation that their loyalties, first and foremost, lay.[157] However, the development of MacCormick's Convention lies outwith the scope of this book.

Professor Hanham has interpreted the split of 1942 as being the result of disagreements over strategy, and there is little here to dispute this. He correctly identifies the MacCormickites' desire to turn the SNP into a more pressure-group orientated organisation, similar to the SHRA, although, as was mentioned earlier, he fails to take account of the duality of the leadership's strategy in using conventional electoral politics with the attempt to create a cross-party movement.[158] The failure of the hierarchy's strategy created a vacuum which the radicals were able to breach by using the rank-and-file discontentment about the lack of direction, although it was the specific issue of the election of an anti-conscriptionist as Chairman which split the party. However, MacCormick's secession meant that the SNP could develop as a normal political organisation unimpeded by the need to take account of emphasising loyalty to the war effort and free from the constraints of trying to strike bargains with other parties.

One of the first effects of the election of Douglas Young as Chairman was to increase the party's public profile. Although it was widely reported that the nationalists had adopted an anti-war policy, they had merely reverted back to the 1939 conference decision. The principle of the war against Hitler was still accepted as being valid, yet Young had now changed the emphasis. 'The Party as a whole supported the war effort and so did he [Young] in his own fashion. But Scotland could only be defended by a Scottish government and a Scottish army and that is what he stood for'.[159] The new leadership had to spend a considerable amount of time convincing members that the SNP had not altered its policy concerning the war but had merely shifted the emphasis. In June 1942 McIntyre wrote to Neil Gunn stating emphatically that the split was not due to any change of policy with regard to the war and that a National Council resolution to that effect had been passed.[160] As far as Young was concerned the damage had been done deliberately:

> The ejected droves have spread a mantle of lies that the Party is anti-war and that I am anti-war...for your [Neil Gunn] information I have never been anti-war...The overwhelming majority of branches, delegates, and members have stayed with the Party, and some who originally left with the

caucus under a misapprehension have returned. Also, some former members have returned.[161]

The SNP now wholeheartedly supported those who refused to be conscripted, and Young regarded such action as simply defending Scottish rights and freedoms. Others, such as R. E. Muirhead and Arthur Donaldson, believed that there ought to be a more vigorous policy of anti-conscription and they were heartened by the emulation of Young's example by other young nationalists.[162] One C. M. Grieve received such encouragement from Muirhead:

> It is certainly encouraging that quite a number of young Scots are standing against the English bureaucrats. I believe that many more would have been with us in this protest but for a weakness which developed in the SNP after the war had broken out...no encouragement was given to younger men to stand out against conscription. A considerable minority of the Party objected to any modification of the original resolution [the 1937 decision to oppose conscription], but they were out-voted. I explain this to you as I think that had it not been for the Party weakening on the anti-conscription question, a larger number of young nationalists would have stood out against conscription.[163]

Whereas the issue had previously been a point of embarrassment, it had now been taken on board as part and parcel of nationalist strategy.

MacCormick's secession removed another obstacle in the development of a more radical nationalist strategy in that the SNP was no longer under the constraint of trying to appease political opponents in the attempt to secure cross-party cooperation. It meant that the party could be more openly critical of the wartime administration of Scotland and, in particular, Tom Johnston, as well as continuing the assault on the Labour Party which had been left in abeyance for several years.[164] One of the first actions of the new leadership was to 'deplore the deporting of female labour to England, demand the Ministry of Labour and Supply in Scotland be put under the control of the Secretary of State and condemn the growing displacement of Scottish by English Labour in Scotland'.[165] From now on the *Scots Independent* would focus on these issues and highlight the existence of Scottish grievances. A good example of this was the agitation against making conscripted women travel south to take part in the production of armaments. The *Scots Independent* attacked the deportations as being harmful to family life, as well as recounting stories of bad living conditions and the strain imposed on young women forced to live in an alien environment.[166] Johnston and the Scottish Office were likewise condemned for doing little to stop this, and the nationalist campaign was able to solicit support from many different quarters.[167]

Whereas the Tories had been the principal target of the SNP prior to the split in 1942, Labour became, once again, the main focus of attention and was attacked because it was believed that their Home Rule commitment was spurious, and also because it was from their supporters that the nationalists sought to capitalise on Scottish grievances. Muirhead was the most vociferous proponent of the argument that it was in the best interests of socialism to support the National Party, and he was not at all impressed by Johnston's promises on post-war reconstruction:

> No doubt the setting up of such committees and advisory councils may be quite satisfying to the Quislings and capitalist imperialists in Scotland as well as the bureaucrats in London...what the ordinary man cannot understand is why the present day followers of Keir Hardie have allowed themselves to be diddled by those Scots and English capitalists and imperialists who are quite pleased when Scottish socialists call for international socialism knowing full well that so long as Scots citizens allow themselves to be fobbed off with an ideal slogan, instead of insisting on the first practical step towards the ideal state, namely self-government, all will be well for capitalist imperialism. So long as Scots Labour men allow themselves to be side tracked by the slogan of a socialist Britain, instead of a self-governing Scotland, there will be little prospect of a Scottish cooperative commonwealth.[168]

As has been mentioned earlier, the Labour Party's interest in Home Rule began to wane during 1942, and although they pressed ahead with proposals on post-war reconstruction, it was becoming less clear as to whether or not self-government would be part and parcel of their aims. Muirhead tried to ascertain Johnston's personal views on the subject, believing that a firm answer of yes or no would give the nationalists something to sink their teeth into. It was believed that the failure to give a firm commitment to Home Rule by the Labour Party could be exploited by the SNP, which would be able to use the ready catalogue of Scottish grievances at hand to back up their case. Muirhead believed that any post-war reconstruction without self-government would be doomed to failure and he communicated these fears to Johnston:

> I have noted with interest the plans which you have been preparing in order that at the close of the war, Scotland might quickly secure reconstruction of her national life. But with the experience of the management of Scottish affairs from London after the last war, I feel strongly that it is quite fatuous to expect these carefully thought out plans of

reconstruction to come to fruition unless Scotland first gets self-government in all its fullness. If, as I earnestly hope, the personal efforts of Mr Douglas Young will ultimately lead to Scotland securing its freedom from the stranglehold of England, all may yet be well.[169]

Johnston's reply is interesting from the point of view of what he does not say. There is no emphatic commitment to Home Rule, although the sentiment is there, which, according to his biographer, is indicative of his 'fervent patriotism directed at practibilities and the milking of opportunities'.[170] However, in view of public opinion's hostility to some of the more damning features of London control, Johnston had to be careful not to dismiss self-government, as his reply to Muirhead in August 1942, reveals:

> I respect your opinion, but I intend to make an effort to keep our country meanwhile on the map and to do my utmost — and within the limits imposed by the circumstances in which we find ourselves — to persuade Scots and English alike that it is desirable we should be allowed to work out our own problems in our own way.[171]

The growing ambiguity of the Labour Party's attitude towards Home Rule was noted and exploited by the SNP, and Johnston's utterings on the subject may have been motivated as much by political expediency as by patriotism.[172]

However, perhaps the most important aspect of the party's development following the split of 1942 was the rebuilding of the SNP into a modern functioning political organisation. Most of this work was carried out by the new Secretary, Robert McIntyre, whose organisational abilities had been well proven in student politics and in the setting up of new branches during the war.[173] McIntyre was different from previous nationalist leaders in that he had a much greater appreciation of the necessity of having a vital and well organised membership. Also, he was a realist and a pragmatist, and was undaunted by the prospect of fighting a long struggle, believing that the SNP should concentrate on attaining steady and constant progress, even if it was at a very slow rate.[174] McIntyre was a disciplinarian and had decided that the party's tendency towards factionalism had to come to an end. From now on, the SNP would project its aims and would under no circumstances modify its approach for the sake of short term expediencies. The emphasis was placed firmly on the necessity of converting the public to the nationalist point of view.[175] However, central to this strategy was the need to build a coherent political identity which would reinforce the rank and file's commitment to the party.

Politically, the leadership was more homogeneous than at any other time in its history. The nucleus of the policy formulation body, McIntyre, Donaldson, Wilkie, Lamont, and Walkinshaw, were all to the left of the political spectrum; they all believed that self-government meant the same amount of independence as was enjoyed by the Commonwealth dominion nations, and, perhaps most importantly, they were all committed to the efficacy of contesting elections.[176] As was mentioned earlier, Douglas Young was the odd man out, although he proved to be of little hindrance on account of the fact that he was to spend most of his time in gaol when the major developments were taking place.[177] Throughout the latter half of 1942 and up until the annual conference in May 1943, the party took the first tentative steps towards forming its own economic policy, propounded mainly in a series of articles written by Colin Walkinshaw for the *Scots Independent*. These moves were important because it helped to give the SNP a sense of a distinct political identity, and the left of centre proposals for nationalisation of key industries and other pre-war nationalist economic themes provided members with the opportunity to contrast their own objectives against those of the Labour Party.[178] However, the issue of contesting elections proved to be a tough nut for McIntyre to crack. A residue of apathy existed about challenging other parties, largely because this was perceived to be an area in which the nationalists had always come off badly, and also because the SNP had not a sufficiently strong sense of political identity.[179] McIntyre was well aware of these difficulties and it was decided not to contest the Midlothian by-election in February 1943. His reasons for not pushing the issue were all sound. In the first place it was recognised that there was not a consensus on the subject and in keeping with McIntyre's commitment to democracy, there had been no opportunity for a meaningful debate nor a proper test of rank and file opinion. In any case, resources were still depleted and an unsuccessful campaign which achieved a poor result would not do morale any good, nor would it help the party come to a reasoned judgement on the issue.[180] However, McIntyre was confident that, with time, the membership would come round to his opinion. Also, the fact that the SNP was making progress in other areas helped to reinforce the cautious, but steady approach.

The annual conference of 1943 was judged by many to be the most successful nationalist gathering for a long time.[181] McIntyre's vision of a vital and functioning political party was visibly taking shape and vindicated his efforts at building up the organisational structure of the SNP. Branch membership was up by 60%, the largest single increase within one year in the party's history; many new local outlets had been set up and the sales of the *Scots Independent* had gone up by 13%.[182] Furthermore, steps were taken to formulate a more coherent objective and the following resolution was passed:

> The restoration of Scottish national sovereignty by the establishment of a democratic Scottish government, whose authority will be limited only by such agreements as will be freely entered into with other nations in order to further international cooperation and world peace.[183]

The SNP finally eschewed itself of any notions of devolution or federalism and this more hardline approach to self-government helped further to create a distinct nationalist political identity. This trend was also reinforced by the adoption of a motion which prohibited National and branch office bearers from belonging to any other party.[184] Discipline was tightened up and all aspects of policy were to be printed in the *Scots Independent* for the benefit of the rank and file. Perhaps the most striking feature about the conference was the degree of unanimity with which the decisions were reached. There is little evidence of division and the resolutions on the objective and the exclusion of other members from different parties were the ones which produced the greatest degree of harmony.[185] Even Tom Gibson was tempted into rejoining the party.[186] However, McIntyre and Donaldson did not get everything their own way as the conference was unable to come to a concrete decision about contesting elections. This was not a result of differences over strategy, but simply a reflection of the lack of confidence in the SNP's political abilities. Members were still wary of committing valuable resources to a policy which had brought much grief in the past. Also, the influence of the Chairman, Douglas Young, was crucial in halting an emphatic endorsement of an electoral strategy, as he still believed that pressure could be brought to bear on the Labour Party in order to induce them to enact Home Rule legislation.[187] Rather than risk opening old wounds, McIntyre concentrated on building up the SNP's political identity which, he believed, once it was strong enough, would take on board the strategy of contesting elections as part of this process.[188]

However, within a very short time, McIntyre was to get his way with the announcement of a by-election in Kirkcaldy in December 1943. The Party had continued to grow stronger in the latter half of the year and the news that Oliver Brown's Scottish Socialist Party would affiliate to the SNP helped to boost confidence.[189] Furthermore, one of the principal barriers to the adoption of a full-blown electoral strategy, Douglas Young, had been persuaded by McIntyre and Donaldson to stand as an official nationalist candidate. The Kirkcaldy campaign proved to be the litmus test for the new initiatives concerning policy and organisation. Donaldson was the election agent and planned the SNP strategy with precision and careful thought. He was also remarkably successful in managing to control and discipline Young, whose character and personality were quite unsuited to conventional party politics.[190] The election marked a turning point in nationalist strategy because it was being fought against a Labour candidate and finally put any aspirations of a cross-party campaign on the self-government issue beyond the pale. The SNP also exhibited a greater degree of professionalism than they had hitherto displayed and Donaldson organised a steady stream of volunteers to canvass the constituency. They took advantage of the Labour Party's inability to choose a suitable candidate and set to work in getting an early start to their campaign.[191] McIntyre's efforts in building up the party's organisational structure paid off handsomely and the SNP electioneering machine was, by all accounts, in better shape than their opponents'.[192]

Young's manifesto was also of crucial importance in determining the outcome of events. The party campaigned on a number of specific issues which unequivocally differentiated them from the Labour Party. The nationalists chose to place the question of the drift south of conscripted women workers and the unfair allocation of new industries at the top of their agenda, and this helped to solicit a great deal of sympathy from the electorate.[193] They also emphasised the Labour Party's guilt in this process by pointing out that the wartime administration was largely planned and executed by socialist members of the Cabinet.[194] Young further highlighted the difference between the Labour Party and the avowedly left of centre SNP by attacking Johnston's pet scheme for the hydro-electrification of the Highlands. The socialist credentials of their opponents were brought into question:

> This [the hydro-electrification scheme for the Highlands] promises 10,000 navvying jobs for 10 years to the survivors of the 51st Highland division, and guarantees £30,000,000 to a few big monopolists to exploit our water resources for their profit.[195]

The leftward character of the National Party was emphasised by a call for the immediate nationalisation of the war industries, including mines and railways, which were to be placed under the control of a democratic Scottish government. Also, Young called for the implementation of a number of social policies, such as the building of public housing, improvements in health provisions and universal education, and the guarantee of full employment.[196] However, the most dramatic difference in the strategy of the SNP was their more aggressive attitude towards the attainment of self-government. The nationalist message was direct and unambiguous, as well as being presented with a degree of forthrightness and confidence which had been absent in previous campaigns. Young demanded that there be:

> ...an immediate general election on a Scottish basis for a Scottish parliament to run a Scottish war effort and post-war reconstruction, having the powers of the Parliaments of New Zealand, Canada and other members of the Commonwealth.[197]

The campaign was an unqualified success from almost every aspect. The organisation had never been in better shape and the members on the ground worked with a great deal of enthusiasm and dedication. Furthermore, the new nationalist attitude and ideas were canvassed with a missionary zeal and confidence, and, most important of all, the result seemed to vindicate the new direction and strategy. The Labour candidate, T. F. Hubbard, polled 8,268 votes against Young's respectable total of 6,621, while the Christian Socialist was pushed into third place.[199] Unlike the Argyll by-election, the SNP was now aggressively advocating socialistic policies which precluded them from picking up the Liberal and Tory vote, and judging from the press reports of the campaign, it would appear that the nationalist championship of Scottish grievances allowed them to tap into a valuable mine of support and sympathy.[200] The result helped to further boost confidence and it also brought the rank and file more firmly behind McIntyre and Donaldson's new approach.

The greater internal coherence and the growing sense of having a distinct and separate political identity was further strengthened at the annual conference of May 1944, when it was decided that they would be 'prepared to accept legislative responsibility for Scottish reconstruction after Scotland shall have [sic] achieved self-government'.[201] This was of great significance as it meant that the party was taking a much longer term of view of its political career. Being a single issue organisation had always been a handicap for the nationalist movement which could seldom muster unity of commitment around social and economic policies on account of the variety of different shades of political opinion that existed within its ranks. However, the SNP was now formulating distinct policies on a whole range of issues and — unlike previous times — was going to stick to them. This, in turn, would help to reinforce their political identity. McIntyre and Donaldson put forward the case that the party would have to offer the electorate realistic political options and that they would have to convince the public that they were serious about their policies. Great care and attention would have to go into formulating these ideas which, McIntyre argued, would have to be precise and accurate if the SNP was going to be taken seriously as a credible force in Scottish politics.[202] Most members agreed with this point of view and the task was taken on in earnest by the appropriate committees.

Other factors can be pointed out to show that that party was becoming more vibrant and healthy. After Kirkcaldy, it was decided that the electoral arena would be the means by which they would seek to attain political power. The levitation of the policy of contesting elections to the central pillar of nationalist strategy was emphatic, and it was agreed that nationalist candidates would stand at local government level, as well as in parliamentary constituencies.[203] Considerable progress was made on the organisational level with yet another rise in the membership and an overall improvement in the financial position.[204] On the propaganda front the Scottish Secretariat was printing a steady stream of SNP pamphlets which were widely circulated and the *Scots Independent* was attracting new readers. Indeed, the editor, Arthur Donaldson, was able to report to the annual conference that the journal had achieved its best ever sales in the previous year.[205] Internal harmony remained intact and a vast majority of the conference delegates backed the new direction. Also, the infusion of new and younger members to the National Council helped to strengthen the resolution to remain on the present course of action, and after May 1944 there were few members of the MacCormick era SNP left in the leadership.[206] The extent to which the McIntyre line had been taken on board can be illustrated by the fact that preparations were soon under way to formulate an electoral strategy for the forthcoming general election which was expected some time in 1945.[207] By the middle of 1944, the modern Scottish National Party had clearly begun to take shape.

As had been mentioned earlier, one of the most important developments in the history of the post-1942 SNP was the evolution of a distinctive nationalist political identity which would help to reinforce the commitment to contesting elections and the belief that self-government meant independence from Westminster in the total sense of the word. Without this identity the party would be in danger of splintering into conventional left/right ideological differences. After 1942 most of the right of centre members left with MacCormick and the few who remained were heavily outnumbered.[208] Never before had the party been composed of people who could all be placed within a fairly narrow band of the political spectrum, and this made the task of moulding or developing a political identity much easier, as the vast majority of the SNP held the same ideological values which were to be found firmly rooted in the left of centre. The adoption of vague policies which were strewn with ambiguities was no longer a facet of nationalist politics as there was now no need to fear upsetting Liberals and Conservatives.[209] Unhindered by having to walk a political tight-rope, Robert McIntyre set to work in formulating the blueprint for future strategy and a coherent party philosophy.

In 1944 McIntyre published these ideas in a pamphlet entitled *Some Principles for Scottish Reconstruction*, and although many of these policies had existed before within the national movement, they were now brought together with a remarkable degree of clarity and coherence.[210] In the mid 1930s the party had tried to formulate a middle way between socialism and capitalism, but this was more often than not a jumbling of individual opinions drawn from both the right and left wings of the movement, and was not an alternative in any real sense to the policies of either the Tory or Labour parties.[211] The reason why McIntyre's philosophy appealed to the membership was that it was a statement of genuine belief, and not, as had happened in the past, an uneasy compromise between two opposing factions. Although belonging to the left of centre stable, the SNP moved in a different direction from conventional British socialist thought by placing heavy emphasis on the community and the rights of individuals rather than centralised planning and control. McIntyre distrusted large organisations from either the state or from business and believed that such developments were harmful to both the nation and the individual:

> Is it to be the happy hunting ground for big business and unscrupulous monopolies? Is it to be a bureaucratic state in which we are labelled and controlled from the crèche to the crematorium in the name of all but for the good of none?[212]

Democracy fulfilled a central role in this philosophy and McIntyre was determined that the SNP should be directed by pragmatism rather than ideology: 'Every Scot must have an effective voice in government and must be sufficiently independent, from an economic point of view, to exercise his democratic rights in freedom, without fear of the state, the combine or laird'.[213] Planning was important, but so was an input from the community and McIntyre's consensual approach to social and economic policies meant that the party did not engage in the dogmatic pursuit of championing one class against another. Housing was considered to be the major post-war priority and a demand for the building of half a million houses was made. McIntyre also pressed for the nationalisation of natural monopolies, the development of new light industries and agriculture, the setting-up of a central Scottish bank and the removal of all power and wealth 'in the hands of alien government, international finance and private monopolies'.[214] Although he failed to utilise fine detail, as was expressed in the precise economic tracts produced by Gibson and Donaldson, and likewise failed to give specific instructions as to how these objectives could be achieved, McIntyre was able to produce the first manifesto which was held together by an underlying coherent set of principles and was also unmistakably their own.

The mixture of social responsibility and the rights of the individual was to become the hallmark of future nationalist philosophy and proved to be the ideal weapon to challenge the centralising tendencies of the wartime administration.[215] Furthermore, it was different from what was on offer from the other parties and not only helped to distinguish them in the public's eye, but helped to reinforce their own sense of political identity. Whereas Scottish interests were often over-ruled or not taken into account by British establishments, the SNP was able to use McIntyre's philosophy as the rationale to justify their action in highlighting local grievances. For example, the public was warned of the dangers of the Labour Party's proposals for nationalisation as, it was claimed, this would mean effective de-nationalisation because Scottish control of key industries would be moved to London.[216] However, perhaps McIntyre's greatest achievement was the way in which he could bring many of the key elements of nationalist thought together into the one broad statement and express them simply and coherently in such a manner as to win more or less wholesale approval from his party.

As the SNP entered into the final year of the war it had begun to speak with one voice. By February 1945, there were already candidates in place to fight the expected general election and all efforts were concentrated on building up resources for the campaign.[217] However, the party was given the opportunity to test its new-found confidence and ability with the announcement of a by election in Motherwell. Again this was a Labour seat, and the leadership quickly mobilised volunteers to assist the candidate, McIntyre, in his efforts to prove that contesting elections was the most emphatic way to further the nationalist cause. Once more the SNP campaigning machine was to show that it was more than equal to the task with the activists engaged in canvassing and distributing propaganda and leaflets.[218] However, the choice of candidate proved to be a crucial factor. As Christopher Harvie has recently pointed out, McIntyre had respectable radical credentials to his name which would not have distanced him too much from Labour voters.[219] Also, unlike Kirkcaldy, where Douglas Young stood, there was no stigma attached to the SNP candidate on account of strident anti-conscriptionist activities, and McIntyre's espousal of the rights of individuals and his warnings against over-centralised bureaucratic control would have made him preferable to his Labour opponent among many Liberals and Tories. A further quality in his favour was his quiet personality, which was unlikely to give offence, and his reputation as a medical man.[220] The combination of a radical party fronted by a man of considerable respectability paid great dividends and the nationalists were able to win their first ever parliamentary seat, capturing over 50% of the total votes cast.[221]

The result was a great personal triumph for McIntyre, and it more than amply vindicated the party's strategy and direction. Although he was only to hold his seat for several months before losing it at the 1945 General Election, the effect of a nationalist MP sitting in the House of Commons was to be of great significance for the development of the SNP. First and foremost, it dealt a blow to those, especially in the Covenant movement, who believed that contesting elections was a waste of time. Secondly, it gave the party greater access to a wider platform, and McIntyre's first action at Westminster, when he refused to be sponsored by two other MPs on account of the fact that he claimed this was a purely English tradition, gave the SNP greater media coverage than at any other time in its history.[222] Also, he used the opportunities to put forward the nationalist case in Parliamentary debates and made two notable speeches on Health and Education.[223] Having a sitting MP within the ranks helped to boost confidence and lent political credibility to the party.

In many ways Robert McIntyre's election on the 12th of April 1945, marks the beginning of the modern Scottish National Party as we know it today. Although there would still be difficulties and disputes in the future, they were never as serious as the ones which had dogged the movement up until 1942. Also, the fundamentals of SNP strategy and identity had been firmly established. The objective of independence, in the sense that a self-governing Scotland would not have any limitations placed on its sovereignty, was firmly enshrined. The adoption of an electoral policy was to be the means by which the nationalists' political aims would be achieved. The exclusion of members from other parties was well under way to being established, and perhaps most important of all, members of the SNP had developed their own distinctive political identity. The extent to which these factors had gelled together can be gauged from the fact that in the aftermath of the 1945 General Election at which the party made only a minimal showing,[224] there were no disruptions or recriminations. Instead, members remained resolved that their direction was the correct one and enshrined it in an official constitution in 1947.[225]

NOTES

1. See the previous chapter for details.
2. Ibid.
3. The official resolution reads as follows: 'This Conference declares that the Scottish National Party is strongly opposed to the manpower of Scotland being used to defend an Empire in the government of which she has no voice, and in all male members of the Scottish National Party of military age hereby pledge themselves to refuse to serve in any section of the Crown Forces until the programme of the Scottish National Party has been fulfilled.' *Scots Independent*, June, 1937.
4. The leading opponents of this policy were Andrew Dewar Gibb, J.M. MacDonald, William Whyte and D.R. Dewar. The latter debated the issue with Douglas Young in the columns of *Scots Independent* in February, 1941, while Power published articles in support of the war in the *Glasgow Herald*.
5. *Scots Independent*, June, 1939.
6. Ibid.
7. *Scots Independent*, October, 1939. p.3.
8. Minute Book of the National Council, 7th of October, 1939. pp. 348-352.
9. R.E. Muirhead to A.W. Donaldson, 24th of October, 1939. Donaldson Mss. Acc. 6038, Box 1, NLS.
10. Minute Book of the National Council, 4th of November, 1939. p.354.
11. A.D. Gibb to J.M. MacCormick, 16th of October, 1939. Gibb Mss. NLS.
12. *Scots Independent*, October, 1939. p.3.
13. Minute Book of the National Council, 7th of October, 1939. p.346.
14. Ibid. 1st of September, 1939. p.341.
15. Ibid. 7th of October, 1939. p.351.
16. Based on the discussions held in the National Council meetings.
17. *Scots Independent*, October, 1939. p.1.
18. This is not mentioned in the *Scots Independent* but is referred to in two letters. A.W. Donaldson to R.E. Muirhead, 20th of September, 1939. Donaldson Mss. Box 1, NLS. Also, Douglas Young to Neil M. Gunn, 7th of June, 1942. Gunn Mss. NLS.
19. Minute Book of the National Council, 7th of October, 1939. p.345.
20. Ibid. p.346.
21. Ibid.

22. Minute Book of the National Council, 4th of November, 1939. p.354. Edinburgh, Paisley, Stirling, Knightswood, Yoker and Bridge of Weir branches had all requested a special conference on the war.

23. This point was made by Robert Hurd. Minute Book of the National Council, 7th of October, 1939. p.346.

24. This line of argument was firmly pushed by Douglas Young, who wrote to Muirhead, MacCormick and Hurd advocating a more stringent anti-conscriptionist policy. Young Mss. NLS.

25. Manifesto issued by MacCormick to all branches, 19th of September, 1939. Gunn Mss. NLS.

26. J.M. MacCormick to Neil M. Gunn, 21st of September, 1939. Gunn Mss. NLS.

27. Ibid.

28. Based on the number of resolutions put forward to the National Council contained in the minute book.

29. Information based on the Minute Book of the National Council. Also, Gibb to MacCormick, 10th of November, 1939. Gibb Mss. Box 4, NLS.

30. *Scots Independent*, October, 1939. p.1.

31. Manifesto issued to all branches by MacCormick, 19th of September, 1939. Gunn Mss. NLS.

32. A.D. Gibb to R.R. Dewar, 19th of November, 1939. Gibb Mss. NLS.

33. *Scots Independent*, October, 1939. p.3.

34. Ibid. December, 1939. p.6. One Patrick Hamilton from Glasgow.

35. Report of the Special Conference of the 12th of December, 1939. p.1. Young Mss. NLS.

36. Neil M. Gunn to J.M. MacCormick, 4th of December, 1939. Gunn Mss. NLS.

37. Report of the Special Conference of the 12th of December, 1939. Young Mss. Box 44, NLS.

38. Ibid.

39. Ibid.

40. *Scots Independent*, December, 1939. p.7.

41. Ibid.

42. Ibid.

43. A.D. Gibb to R.R. Dewar, 19th of November, 1939. Gibb Mss. Box 4, NLS.

44. Minute Book of the National Council, 10th of January, 1940. p.373.

45. Ibid.

46. Ibid. 27th of April, 1940. p.383.

47. Ibid. 2nd of March, 1940. p.378. It was reported out of 75 branches only 29 were functioning normally.

48. Ibid. 10th of January, 1940. p.374.

49. Ibid. 2nd of March, 1940. pp. 377-378.

50. Ibid.

51. Ibid. 27th of April, 1940. pp. 383-384.

52. Emrys Hughes to R.E. Muirhead, 29th of March, 1940. Muirhead Mss. Box ll, NLS.

53. At this time Brown was still conducting peace campaigns with Muirhead's support. Muirhead to Brown, 24th of March, 1940. Muirhead Mss. Box 5, NLS.
54. See the campaign press cuttings in the Muirhead papers. Boxes 89-100. NLS.
55. The exact figures were Conservative 12,317 Nationalist 7,308 F.W.S. Craig, *British parliamentary by-election results.*
56. Press cuttings of the Campaign, Muirhead Mss. NLS.
57. Ibid. Also, Scots Independent, May, 1940. p.4.
58. Ibid. May, 1940. p.6.
59. Ibid.
60. Report of the Annual Conference of May, 1940. Young Mss. Box 44, NLS.
61. See the correspondence between the two men for details. Box 5. Muirhead Mss. NLS.
62. Private information given to the author by two members involved in anti-conscription activities.
63. Report of the Annual Conference of May, 1940. Young Mss. Box 44, NLS.
64. Ibid.
65. Ibid.
66. Minute Book of the National Council, 3rd of July, 1940. p.395.
67. Ibid. p.396.
68. Ibid. p.397.
69. These proposals were reprinted in the *Scots Independent*, September, 1940. p.3.
70. Ibid.
71. Gibb resigned at the National Council meeting of the 27th of April, 1940.
72. See the previous chapter.
73. Minute Book of the National Council, 2nd of November, 1940. p.415.
74. Ibid.
75. Ibid. 21st of December, 1940. p.417.
76. Ibid.
77. Ibid. 1st of February, 1941. p.432.
78. Ibid. 1st of March, 1941. pp. 433-434.
79. Among the most prominent were Annie S. Swan, the Duke of Montrose, Sir Daniel Stevenson, J.M. Bannerman and J.B. Webster.
80. See the previous chapter for MacCormick's Liberal tendencies.
81. Report of the joint talks given in the Minute Book of the National Council, 1st of March, 1941. pp. 435-436.
82. See M. Keating and D. Bleiman, *Labour and Scottish Nationalism,* (London,1979) pp. 128-130.
83. Minute Book of the National Council, 1st of February, 1941. p.430.
84. *Scots Independent*, February, 1941.
85. Minute Book of the National Council, 1st of February, 1941. p.430.
86. Ibid.
87. *Scots Independent*, March, 1941. p.1.
88. Ibid. p.2.
89. Ibid.

90. Based on evidence from the Minute Book of the National Council.

91. Ibid. Based on the Organising Secretary's monthly reports.

92. J.M. MacCormick to R.E. Muirhead, 12thof March, 1941. Box 6. Muirhead Mss. NLS.

93. See the previous chapter.

94. J.M. MacCormick to J.M. McNicol, 24th of April, 1941. Gunn Mss. NLS. Also *Flag in the Wind*, p.104.

95. See Keating and Bleiman op.cit. p.129. G. Walker, Thomas Johnston (Manchester 1988). pp. 151-178. Also, Christopher Harvie,'Labour and Scottish Government: The Age of Tom Johnston', *The Bulletin of Scottish Politics* (Spring 1981) pp. 1-20.

96. See chapter four for MacCormick's role in the formation of the SNP.

97. Evidence taken from the Minute Book of the National Council.

98. For example, *Scots Independent*, May, 1941. p.4.

99. This impression is firmly conveyed in the works of J. Brand, *The National Movement in Scotland* (London,1978) pp. 239-241, H.J.Hanham, *Scottish Nationalism (London 1969) pp166-172,* and MacCormick's own account of events in the *Flag in the Wind, (London 1955).*

100. *Glasgow Herald,* 14th of July, 1941.

101. Letter to the *Scottish Co-operator,* 25th of May, 1941.

102. *Scots Independent,* October, 1941. p.1.

103. Ibid.

104. Report on the Convention Committee in the Minute Book of the National Council, 8th of November, 1941. p.477.

105. Glasgow Herald, 16th of December, 1941.

106. Ibid.

107. *Scots Independent,* June, 1941. p.1.

108. Minute Book of the National Council, 4th of October, 1941. p.471.

109. *Scots Independent,* June, 1941. p.1.

110. Minute Book of the National Council, 7th of June, 1941. p.448.

111. R.E. Muirhead to T. Johnston, 6th of June, 1941. Box 3. Muirhead Mss. NLS.

112. R.E. Muirhead to A.W. Donaldson, 4th of May, 1941, Box 1. Donaldson Mss. NLS.

113. Amongst the most prominent of these were J.B. Brown, Angus Clark, R.D. McIntyre, Douglas Young and R.B. Wilke.

114. *Scots Independent,* May, 1942.

115. Ibid. February, 1941.

116. A.W. Donaldson to R.E. Muirhead, December, 1941. Box 5. Muirhead Mss. NLS.

117. Ibid.

118. Minute book of the National Council, 1st of March, 1941. p.436.

119. Ibid.

120. Based on the editorial comments of the *Scots Independent.*

121. Ibid.

122. Based on the monthly reports of the Organising Secretary in the Minute Book of the National Council.

123. Ibid.
124. Ibid.
125. Douglas Young to R.E. Muirhead, 18th of August, 1941. Box 42. Young Mss. NLS.
126. Minute book of the National Council, 4th of October, 1941. p.473.
127. Minute Book of the National Council, vol.II. 4th of December, 1941. Box 43. Young Mss. NLS.
128. Walker, op.cit. pp. 154-157.
129. Keating and Bleiman, op.cit. pp. 130-132.
130. *Scots Independent*, May, 1942. p.4.
131. Ibid.
132. Ibid.
133. The most notable was W.Douglas-Home standing as an Independent Progressive.
134. Press cuttings of the campaign. Box 100. Muirhead Mss. NLS.
135. The results were: F.Beathie Conservative 10,786 Hon W. Douglas Home Independent Progressive 3,807 J.Carmichael ILP 2,493 Whyte Independent 1,000 source F.W.S. Craig op.cit.
136. A.W. Donaldson to Douglas Young, 18th of April, 1942. Box 43. Young Mss. NLS.
137. Whyte blamed Young's trial for his poor result. Report of the Annual Conference of May, 1942. Box 44. Young Mss. NLS.
138. Brand, op.cit. pp. 240-241,
139. Hanham, op.cit. pp. 167-169.
140. Whyte had called for an expulsion of the anti-conscriptionists. Minute book of the National Council vol. II. 21st of April, 1942. Box 43. Young Mss. NLS.
141. Ibid.
142. Ibid.
143. Based on the evidence contained in the Minute Book of the National Council.
144. Hanham, op.cit. pp. 167-169. Brand, op.cit. pp. 240-241.
145. See chapter four.
146. From the evidence of the Report of the Annual Conference of 1942, they had little support in the branches.
147. This version of events tends to come across in both Brand and Hanham's accounts.
148. See the previous chapter.
149. This is the opinion of both Brand and Hanham. Young wrote to Neil.M. Gunn on the 8th of June, 1942 stating: "I hope MacCormick will succeed with his new venture which he had, if I recall correctly, proposed to the Council in February, 1940, with my support." Gunn Mss. Box 15, NLS.
150. Young was later to support the Convention after leaving the SNP in 1948.
151. Report of the Annual Conference of June, 1942. Young Mss. NLS.
152. A.W. Donaldson to R.D. McIntyre, 10th of May, 1942. McIntyre Mss. NLS.
153. For MacCormick's interpretation of events see *Flag in the Wind* pp. 103-106.
154. Douglas Young to Neil.M. Gunn, 8th of June, 1942. Gunn Mss. NLS.
155. Ibid.

156. *Scots Independent*, which was firmly pushing the new line, actually increased its sales to over 4,000 in the following year, also membership was to go up. Report of the Annual Conference of May, 1943. Young Mss. NLS.

157. Muirhead, McIntyre and other hard liners supported the Convention.

158. Throughout the Minute Book of the National Council there is no mention of MacCormick wanting to abandon the policy of contesting elections. Hanham and Brand have accepted the account in the Flag in the Wind too uncritically.

159. *Scots Independent*, July, 1942. p.7.

160. R.D. McIntyre to Neil M. Gunn, 8th of June, 1942. Gunn Mss. Box 15, NLS.

161. Douglas Young to Neil M. Gunn, 7th of June, 1942. Gunn Mss. NLS.

162. *Scots Independent*, August, 1942.

163. R.E. Muirhead to C.M. Grieve, (undated) Muirhead Mss. Box 4. NLS.

164. See the previous chapter.

165. Report of the Annual Conference of June, 1942. Young Mss. NLS.

166. *Scots Independent*, July, 1942.

167. Among whom were Walter Elliot and several prominent members of the STUC.

168. R.E. Muirhead to Oliver Brown, 25th of May, 1942. Box 4. Muirhead Mss. NLS.

169. R.E. Muirhead to Tom Johnston, 12th of August, 1942. Box 3. Muirhead Mss. NLS.

170. Walker, op.cit. p.153.

171. T. Johnston to R.E. Muirhead, 29th of August, 1942. Box 3. Muirhead Mss. NLS.

172. Walker fails to take account of the tight rope Johnston was walking in relation to the Home Rule issue, nor does he explain how and why his ideas on the subject shifted.

173. Robert McIntyre was Chairman of Edinburgh University Labour Club and a public health specialist.

174. R.D. McIntyre to A.W. Donaldson, 1st of July, 1943. Donaldson Mss. Box 1, NLS.

175. *Scots Independent*, January, 1943. p.6.

176. This information was gathered from the correspondence between McIntyre and Donaldson. Donaldson Mss. Box 1, NLS.

177. He spent 8 months of a twelve month sentence during the second half of 1943 and former part of 1944.

178. For example, *Scots Independent*, January, 1943, Colin Walkinshaw began a monthly series of articles on nationalist economic policy.

179. R.E. Muirhead to R.D. McIntyre. 21st of June, 1943. McIntyre Mss. NLS.

180. R.D. McIntyre to A.W. Donaldson. 15th of January, 1943. Donaldson Mss. NLS.

181. *Scots Independent*, July, 1943. p.2.

182. Ibid.

183. Ibid.

184. Ibid.

185. Ibid.

186. R.E. Muirhead to T.H. Gibson. 8th of March, 1943. Box 8. Muirhead Mss. NLS.

187. Douglas Young to A.W. Donaldson. 25th of April, 1943. Box 43. Young Mss. NLS.

188. R.D. McIntyre to A.W. Donaldson. 16th of June, 1943. McIntyre Mss. NLS.

189. *Scots Independent,* December, 1943.

190. This is also the view of Brand and Hanham. McIntyre in a letter to A.W.Donaldson described him as a "political playboy". 20th of August, 1944. McIntyre Mss. NLS.

191. *Scots Independent,* July, 1943. p.2.

192. Report of the campaign. Box 100. Muirhead Mss. NLS.

193. Ibid.

194. Young's manifesto. Box 100. Muirhead Mss. NLS.

195. *Hitlerism in the Highlands* (Glasgow, 1944) p.2.

196. Young's manifesto.

197. Ibid.

198. Iibid.

199. F.W.S. Craig, op.cit.

200. Press cuttings of the campaign. Box 100. Muirhead Mss. NLS.

201. *Scots Independent,* June, 1944. p.7.

202. R.D. McIntyre to A.W. Donaldson, 18th of May, 1944. NLS.

203. *Scots Independent,* June, 1944. p.7.

204. Ibid.

205. Ibid.

206. F.C. Yeaman, R.E. Muirhead and R.D. McIntyre, none of whom endorsed MacCormick's strategy.

207. It was reported in *Scots Independent,* February, 1945, that Douglas Young would contest Kirkcaldy, Austin Walker, North Aberdeen, Arthur Donaldson, Dundee, Robert Blair Wilkie, West Renfrewshire and Robert McIntyre, Motherwell.

208. Robert Hurd was the last remaining member of the old leadership and resigned in June, 1944.

209. See the previous chapter.

210. R.D. McIntyre, *Some Principles for Scottish Reconstruction,* (Glasgow, 1944).

211. See the previous chapter.

212. McIntyre, op.cit. p.1.

213. Ibid. p.3.

214. Ibid. p.10.

215. McIntyre published a whole series of letters on this theme in the *Motherwell Times* and *Wishaw Advertiser* throughout the latter half of 1944 and part of 1945.

216. McIntyre, op.cit. p.3.

217. *Scots Independent,* February, 1945.

218. Press cutting of the campaign. McIntyre Mss. NLS.

219. C.Harvie, ' The Recovery of Scottish Labour, 1939-1951', in Donnachie, Harvie, and Wood, (eds), *Forward: Labour Politics in Scotland 1888-1988* (Edinburgh, 1989) p.76.

220. McIntyre was not known as a conscientious objector as Harvie, op.cit. states.

221. 51.4% to be precise.
222. Press cutting in the McIntyre Mss. NLS. He was also the subject of a cartoon in Punch.
223. *Hansard,* 1st of May, 1945 and 12th of June, 1945.
224. The results were:

Aberdeen North	5.3%	
Dundee	4.6%	
Edinburgh East	6.3%	
Glasgow Kelvingrove		4.9%
Kirkcaldy		17.0%
Motherwell		26.7%
Perth	4.3%	
West Renfrewshire		6.3%

    The total percentage of the overall Scottish vote 1.2%.

    The percentage of the total seats contested by nationalists 9%.
225. This is reprinted in full in Hanham op.cit. pp. 213-231.

Conclusion

The most obvious and striking feature concerning the political development of the Scottish nationalist movement in the period 1919-1942 was its divisiveness and the difficulty it had in maintaining a united and cohesive front. There were two principal sources of contention and dispute. The first was over the definition of self-government and to what extent it should be taken. The second was over the means by which this objective would be achieved. Throughout this era, the Home Rule cause was torn between two factions which jostled for control of nationalist direction and strategy. Prior to the formation of the National Party of Scotland in 1928, these two elements existed in their purest forms as separate organisations. The Scots National League advocated complete independence from England and was prepared to fight elections in order to win the political authority necessary to achieve its objective. In complete contrast to this body was the Scottish Home Rule Association, which had the goal of administrative devolution and furthered its ends by attempting to utilise pressure group tactics on the established political parties. However, it was the latter group's failure which caused these two distinct and, in many ways, incompatible, organisations to merge to form the NPS.

The National Party of Scotland was created with many inbuilt contradictions on a foundation of uneasy compromise. The collapse of the SHRA had provided the 'radicals' with an opportunity, in the absence of any feasible alternative, to impose their direction on the new party. However, when it became apparent that the 'fundamentalist' position was not bearing fruit and indeed, might be frightening away potential support, the moderates imposed their numerical superiority by expelling the more extreme elements. The expulsions of 1933 marked a turning point in nationalist direction which, under the watchful eye of chief strategist John MacCormick, would now seek to make Home Rule attractive to the establishment. 'King John' was of the correct opinion that the present policy of the NPS would not attract sufficient support to make the attainment of self-government a realisable objective in the current political scenario. He argued that the nationalists would have to widen their appeal and remove all aspects which would threaten potential support. This new departure was successful and facilitated

the formation of the SNP which involved the fusion of his own
organisation with the right-wing Scottish Party. The newly created
Scottish National Party encompassed elements from all shades of
political opinion and it was believed that the existence of such a body
vindicated the idea that Home Rule could act as a cohesive force, relying
simply on its own momentum to achieve constitutional change.

However, it was the radical element which had provided the
underpinning philosophy of the nationalist parties. In essence, this
involved three key elements. The first concerned the definition of self-
government which, when the NPS was founded, meant as much
sovereignty as was enjoyed by the Dominion nations. The second
concerned the use of the electoral system to achieve their political
objective, while the third sought to isolate the nationalist movement
from other British parties by forbidding members from belonging to,
or become involved with, other organisations. In an attempt to widen
the appeal of the National Party, MacCormick altered the objective to
place greater emphasis on cooperation with England and maintaining
a Scottish role in the running of the British Empire. When the SNP
was created, it was likewise built with the same philosophical
underpinning and although the objective was subjected to further
modification, the most important fact was that the party still had an
aim which would act as the raison d'être for the existence of their own
political organisation. So long as the SNP maintained the three tenets
of having a political objective, contesting elections and remaining a
distinct and separate organisation, they would be able to preserve a
minimum of political identity which would act as a sufficient cohesive
force in binding them together.

In the quest for further modification and the need to appeal to a
wider audience, the party gradually let go of the props which were
essential in maintaining its existence as a distinct political entity. The
first to crumble was the principle that members of the SNP could not
belong to other parties. The Duke of Montrose's decision to join the
Liberal Party shattered any illusions of political exclusivity and rendered
redundant any attempts to strengthen nationalist political identity by
building up social and economic policies. The two other props which
held up the justification for the existence of a separate nationalist party
were likewise soon to disintegrate. The objective was shortened to 'self-
government for Scotland' which was so loose a definition as to be almost
meaningless. Also, the efficacy of contesting elections was called into
question after a series of humiliating defeats and instead attention
increasingly focused on the idea of a National Convention as the means

by which their aims could be achieved. In short, there was little to distinguish between members of the SNP and their ideological bed-fellows in the other respective British parties. By the outbreak of the Second World War the Scottish National Party had almost ceased to be a conventional political party.

It was the outbreak of war which provided the radicals with the opportunity to regain control of nationalist direction. Although they had been outnumbered by moderates, their depth of commitment was much greater and whereas the faint hearted were prone to leave when the going got tough, the radicals braved it out by maintaining a steady critical barrage on the leadership's lack of direction. The hierarchy's opportunism during the war and their failure to support the principle of the anti-conscriptionist resolution provided the hard line nationalists with valuable ammunition. Also, the fact that the organisation was allowed to fall into chaos while MacCormick attempted to form a 'united front' left the field open for the radicals to exploit the remaining rank and file's discontent. Whereas the moderate position contained fundamental weaknesses which inhibited normal party political development, the radicals were imbued with innate qualities which strengthened their cohesiveness. They were all to the left of centre, they believed in the formulation of specific economic and social policies, they advocated complete independence, they did not want links with other organisations and they were prepared to contest elections. In other words, they made up a coherent entity which was something that could not be said for the moderates.

In 1942 the radicals took control of the party and established a political character which would last up until the present day. MacCormick's experiment with moderation and latterly, with cross-party cooperation, had proved to be a failure. When the radicals took over the nationalist movement for the second time there were a number of vital differences from the first. In 1942, they established the SNP's political direction not through the exploitation of a vacuum, but as the deliberate choice of the membership. Also, they had acquired more experience and were determined that principle, and not expediency, would be their guiding light, come what may.

Bibliography

A.MANUSCRIPT SOURCES

1. PERSONAL PAPERS

   R.B.Cunninhame Graham, Dep.205, National Library of Scotland.
   A.W.Donaldson, Acc.6038, National Library of Scotland.
   G.Dott, Acc.5927, Acc.5542 and Acc.8371, National Library of Scotland.
   A.D.Gibb, Dep.217 and Acc.9188, National Library of Scotland.
   T.H.Gibson, Acc.6058, National library of Scotland.
   C.M.Grieve, Acc.7361, National Library of Scotland.
   N.M.Gunn, Dep.2O7, National Library of Scotland.
   T.Johnston, Acc.5862, National Library of Scotland.
   J.L.Kinloch, Mitchell Library, Glasgow.
   E.Linklater, Acc.5665, National Library of Scotland.
   A.A.MacEwen, Acc.6113, National Library of Scotland.
   R.D.McIntyre, (Recent acquisition), National Library of Scotland.
   J.Maclean, Acc.4334, National Library of Scotland.
   R.E.Muirhead, Acc. 3721, National Library of Scotland.
   R.E.Muirhead, Mitchell Library, Glasgow.
   L.Spence, Acc.5916, National Library of Scotland.
   W.Wood, Acc.7980, National Library of Scotland.

2. NATIONALIST RECORDS AND OTHER COLLECTIONS.

   Minute Book of the Scottish National Movement, Acc.5927, Box 1, National Library of Scotland.

   Minute Book of the National Executive Council of the National Party of Scotland, 1933-1934, and subsequently, the Minute Book of the National Executive of the Scottish National Party, 1934-1942, McIntyre Mss. National Library of Scotland.

   Minute Book of the National Executive Council of the Scottish National Party, 1942-1945, Acc.6419, Box 6. National Library of Scotland.

   Records of the NPS and SNP Annual Conferences 1928-1943, Acc.6419, Box 4, National Library of Scotland.

   Scottish National Party (Miscellaneous Collection), Acc.7295, National Library of Scotland.

B.PRINTED SOURCES.

1. IMPORTANT NATIONALIST PAMPHLETS.

Black, C.S.,'Scottish Nationalism: Its Aims and Inspirations' (Glasgow, 1933)

Burns, T., 'The Real Rulers of Scotland' (Glasgow, 1940)

Donaldson, A.W.,'Scotland's Tomorrow' (Glasgow, 1943)

McIntyre, R.D., 'Some Principles for Scottish Reconstruction' (Glasgow, 1944)

The Duke of Montrose, 'Scottish Self-Government' (Glasgow, 1933)

Torrence, J., 'Scotland's Dilemma: Province or Nation' (Edinburgh, 1939)

'Scottish National Convention 1939' (Glasgow, 1939)

'Self-Government in Practice: A report from a delegation of the Scottish National Party's visit to the Isle of Man, Northern Ireland and the Irish Free State' (Glasgow, 1935)

Young, D.C.C., 'An Appeal to Scots Honour by Douglas Young: A Vindication of the Right of the Scottish People to Freedom from Industrial Conscription and Bureaucratic Despotism under the Treaty of Union with England' (Glasgow, 1944)

Young, D.C.C., 'The Free Minded Scot: Trial of Douglas C.C. Young in the High Court, Edinburgh' (Glasgow, 1942)

Young, D.C.C. 'Hitlerism in the Highlands' (Glasgow, 1944)

2. OTHER PRIMARY WORKS

Barr, J., *Lang Syne* (Glasgow, 1949)

Bowie, J.A., *The Future of Scotland* (Edinburgh, 1939)

Gibb, A.D., *Scotland in Eclipse* (London, 1930)

Gibb, A.D., *Scotland Resurgent* (Stirling, 1950)

Gibb, A.D., *Scottish Empire* (London, 1937)

Grieve, C.M., *Albyn: Scotland and the Future* (London, n.d.)

Johnston, T., *Memories* (London, 1952)

MacCormick, J.M., *The Flag in the Wind* (London, 1955)

MacEwen, A.M., *The Thistle and the Rose* (Edinburgh, 1932)

MacKenzie, C., *My Life and Times: Octave Six* (London, 1967)

Power, W., *Should Auld Acquaintance...* (London, 1937)

Thomson, G.M., *Caledonia or the Future of the Scots* (London, n.d.)

Thomsom, G.M., *Scotland that Distressed Area* (Edinburgh, 1937)

Thomson, G.M., *The Re-Discovery of Scotland* (London, 1928)

Home Rule for Scotland: The Case in 90 Points; with a Foreword by the Rev.James Barr (Glasgow, 1922)

The Campaign Guide, National Unionist Association (London, 1922)

3. SECONDARY WORKS

Addison, P., *The Road to 1945* (London, 1977)

Blake, R., *The Conservative Party from Peel to Churchill* (London, 1972)

Bleiman, D., and Keating, M., *Labour and Scottish Nationalism* (London, 1979)

Brand, J., *The National Movement in Scotland* (London, 1979)

Cook, C. and Ramsden, J., *By-elections in British Politics* (London, 1973)

Cook, C. and Stevenson, J., *The Slump. Society and Politics during the Depression* (London, 1977)

Craig, F.W.S., *British Parliamentary Election Statistics, 1918-1970* (Chichester, 1971)

Craig, F.W.S., *British Parliamentary By-elections, 1833-1987* (Chichester, 1988)

Craig, F.W.S., *Minor Parties in British Elections* (Chichester, 1988)

Dickson, T. (ed.), *Capital and Class in Scotland* (Edinburgh, 1982)

Ferguson, W., *Scotland, 1689 to the Present* (Edinburgh, 1968)

Fry, M., *Patronage and Principle. A Political History of Modern Scotland* (Aberdeen, 1987)

Gallagher, T., *Glasgow, the Uneasy Peace* (Manchester, 1987)

Griffiths, R., *Fellow Travellers of the Right* (Oxford, 1983)

Hanham, H.J., *Scottish Nationalism* (London, 1969)

Harvie, C., *Scotland and Nationalism* (London, 1977)

Harvie, C., *No Gods and Precious Few Heroes* (London, 1981)

Harvie, C., 'Labour and Scottish Government, the age of Tom Johnston', *Bulletin of Scottish Politics*, vol. 1 (1981)

Harvie, C., 'The Recovery of Scottish Labour, 1939-1951' in Donnachie, I.,

Harvie,C. and Wood,I.S. (eds.), *Forward, Labour Politics in Scotland, 1888-1988* (Edinburgh, 1989)

Howell, D., *A Lost Left, Three Studies in Socialism and Nationalism* (Manchester, 1986)

Hunter, J., *The Gaelic Connection: The Highlands, Ireland, and Nationalism*,SHR 1975

Hutchison, I.G.C. *A Political History of Scotland, 1832-1924* (Edinburgh, 1986)

Kendall, W., *The Revolutionary Movement in Britain, 1900-1921* (London, 1969)

Knox, W., *Scottish Labour Leaders, 1918-1939* (Edinburgh, 1984)

Leventhal, F., *Arthur Henderson* (Manchester, 1989)

MacDougall, I. (ed.), *Essays in Scottish Labour History* (Edinburgh, 1987)

McKibbin, R., *The Evolution of the Labour Party 1906-1924* (Oxford, 1974)

McLean, I., *The Legend of Red Clydeside* (Edinburgh, 1983)

Marquand, D., *Ramsay MacDonald* (London, 1977)

Middlemas, R.E., *The Clydesiders* (London, 1965)

Milton, N., *John MacLean* (Bristol, 1973)

Skidelsky, R., *Politicians and the Slump* (London, 1967)

Smout, T.C., *A Century of the Scottish People* (London, 1986)

Walker, G., *Thomas Johnston* (Manchester, 1988)

Webb, K., *The Growth of Nationalism in Scotland* (Glasgow, 1977)

Wolfe, J.N., *Government and Nationalism in Scotland* (Edinburgh, 1969)

Young, J.D., *The Rousing of the Scottish Working Class* (London, 1979)

Index